As a practicing Catholic for over seventy years, I was interested, enlightened, and challenged by *Looking for God*. It certainly might anger some, especially those who profess to be leaders of their church, because it clearly points out how ineffectual many of their approaches are in properly [guiding] their followers to find God. It provides the process and practical applications that not only church leaders should learn, but more importantly, every Christian should learn so others find God in them. It deserves to be read.

—Richard Scholtes, retired major general

looking for

GOD

Alexys V. Wolf

looking for
GOD

Spiritual Intimacy
and a Personal Relationship with Christ

TATE PUBLISHING & *Enterprises*

Published by Tate Publishing & Enterprises, LLC
127 E. Trade Center Terrace | Mustang, Oklahoma 73064 USA
1.888.361.9473 | www.tatepublishing.com

Tate Publishing is committed to excellence in the publishing industry. The company reflects the philosophy established by the founders, based on Psalm 68:11,
"The Lord gave the word and great was the company of those who published it."

Book design copyright © 2009 by Tate Publishing, LLC. All rights reserved.
Cover design by Amber Gulilat
Interior design by Stephanie Woloszyn

Published in the United States of America

ISBN: 978-1-60799-854-9
1. Religion / Christian Life / Personal Growth
2. Religion / Christian Life / Spiritual Growth
09.07.08

Dedication

This book is dedicated to all the women at both Camille Griffin Graham and Goodman Correctional Institutions who have welcomed me into their hearts. You have constantly allowed me to grow in Christ with you by challenging me in the Word of God. Thank you!

Acknowledgments

I give a special thanks to my dear friend, Pamela Rogers, for your ongoing financial donations toward this growing ministry. More importantly, I thank you for your constant prayers and support that have flooded this ministry!

Always and forever, I would not be where I am with Christ without the continual guidance, prayers, accountability, and support of my mentor, prayer partner, teacher, and blessed friend, Ruby Huthmaker. Thank you for pushing me in the right direction.

Thank you, Laura Kirkland, for being my constant friend over these last eleven years. You are beautiful inside and out! You have been most patient and kind throughout my ever-evolving life. You are one of the most tenderhearted, loyal, and dedicated people I have ever known. Don't forget that.

Appreciation also goes to Jim and Jessica Huthmaker for their continual prayer and supplication spread over *The Fiery Sword* and my family. You guys are awesome! I know the Lord continues to abound effortlessly in your lives and growing ministry.

Helen Tanner, you are phenomenal! What would I do without you, my forever friend? Thank you for always being there when I need you and for your devout stand with God. You are an inspiration to me!

To my precious parents, I love you for everything that you have poured into me these forty-one years. Thank you for believing in *God,* that *he* would transform me when you could not. Thank you for all of your support, both financially and in prayer. You guys are awesome!

Michael, you are the kindest, most patient, loving, and amazing man I have ever known. Thank you for your steadfastness, love, and endurance. There is no one like you in all the world. If all women could have a husband like you, this world would be a marvelous place to dwell!

To Almighty God, the Great I AM, thank you for honoring me continually with your sovereignty, patience, power, guidance, humility, grace, mercy, compassion, and everlasting love. Thank you with all of my being for surrounding me and protecting me with the friends and family you have bestowed. May you richly bless each of them without measure. Each and every one of them reveals the glory of the Lord to me on a daily basis. Thank you especially for my enemies that push me closer to your heart! Through them, you perpetually teach me how to bless those who curse me and to truly love the unlovable. You remind me through them that everything and everyone has purpose and meaning.

Table of
CONTENTS

Foreword

Alexys Wolf's first book, *What Was God Thinking: Why Adam Had to Die,* opened my eyes to knowing who God is and what my place is in this life. I now talk about God like he is a real person because he is real in me. Being a Christian is not easy, but a lot of her topics help new Christians like me in our daily walk with God. *Looking for God* is not only for Christian people, but for people in general who may not have found him yet. I say this because when she gave me this book, it was a time when I had family members in a crisis. Her books have taught me patience and endurance, and what it is to have hope in God. I am learning to believe in myself as a child of God—to let go and let God handle all. She has taught me the real meaning of praise and worship and what it is to really have an intimate relationship with God. She gives Scripture to back everything she says.

—JLM inmate

Introduction

When a person is looking for God and cannot find him, the problem lays not so much in the one searching, but in the ones that should be properly representing him. The body of Christ as a whole has little idea of how to allow Christ to move *through* them. What we generally do is attempt with our flesh to *force* Christ onto others. It is what I refer to as *selling God,* just as one would sell a cheap perfume in a dollar store. If we would really become merged with his heart and understand how he operates, we wouldn't have to *sell* him at all. The Oxford Illustrated American dictionary defines the word merge as "lose or cause to lose character and identity in (something else)." We are to forfeit our own way of thinking. If you can visualize being swallowed up by God, this can give you an idea of the meaning of merging as one. Once consumed by him, you and Christ will move as one single entity—not two separate souls attempting with futility to get on the same page. With this, people would flock to us, desiring what and whom we have because they see only him in human form!

Congregations across the land meet regularly. They throw their hands in the air and shout with songs of praise to Almighty God. They fall on the floor, weep, shout amen and hallelujah, speak in tongues, laugh, run around, and do many things of the like. Or they bow quietly and never utter a sound in the attempt of being reverent. The Bible is full of worshipers just like all of this, so in itself I have no problem.

However, praise and worship to a God we do not sincerely know or understand is worthless! Praise and worship should always be an *outward* manifestation of the *inward* communion with the one whom we are praising. Too many times, there are external acts of worship without ever having intimacy with the Creator of heaven and earth. The result is that people in search for the one true God go home frustrated and aggravated. They are unable to find the one for whom they are seeking.

One of my most earnest desires in this life is to help instruct believers to walk in balance and become in sync with the Lord. What I often find in the church is that there is a lot of excitement and hype, not only in the initial act of the acceptance of Christ, but way too much in everyday services. Hype and excitement in worship certainly have their place. However, too much of it without meat to follow leads one to discouragement because they leave church without knowing *how* to properly apply the word of God in their personal lives. When this happens, those searching for relationship with God cannot seem to find him. All they see are the *people* instead of *Christ* through the people.

This book is set in place as a source of instruction to help God's people learn how to draw near unto his bosom, grow in true faith, and live a life of unity, balance, hope, peace, and love. When we the body begin a walk of intimacy with God through Christ Jesus by making his heart our own, the lost will be able to identify him *through* us and be drawn *to* him.

What Is True
WORSHIP?

There is a lot of hype in the more charismatic churches these days than what is relevant to a service. Understand that I myself love loud, "stand up" praise and worship, but I also see that, many times, where there is hype in the praise and worship there is an absence of food to proceed. What I mean is that people are standing, lifting hands, bodies, and voices; yet they are void of intimacy of the God they are supposed to be worshipping. As a friend of mine says, "I want gravy on meat, not gravy on a plate!" My desire in this book is to bring those within the body of Christ into perfect balance of both intimacy and praise: intimacy being first, and praise to follow as an offshoot of the intimacy.

Anyone can get hyped. Just look at the Olympics, football, and other sporting events, beauty pageants, or whatever. That hype is real; it just doesn't glorify our Father. The same can be said about worship in churches. Most of them are caught in a whirlwind of excitement and then go home having no idea what they are to do with the spoken word. And in the midst of it all, God still cannot be identified by those seeking him.

This can equally be said about the hushed hype in the laid-back, quiet churches. Everything is ritualistic and has so-called reverence. It is still hype of another form. All the people of those denominations have hyped that style of worship for centuries, saying that it is the *proper* and respectful way to worship. No matter how quietly and reverently you go through your motions, if your heart is not set fully on intimacy with him, it is just as worthless as that of your loud brothers and sisters.

> Jehoshaphat bowed his head with his face to the ground, and all Judah and the inhabitants of Jerusalem fell down before the Lord, worshiping the Lord. The Levites...stood up to praise the Lord God of Israel, with a very loud voice. They rose early in the morning and went out to the wilderness of Tekoa...Jehoshaphat stood and said, "Listen to me, O Judah and inhabitants of Jerusalem, put your trust in the Lord your God and you will be established. Put your trust in his prophets and succeed." When he had consulted with the people, he appointed those who sang to the Lord and those who praised him in holy attire, as they went out before the army and said, "Give thanks to the Lord, for his loving kindness is everlasting." When they began singing and praising, the Lord set ambushes against the sons of Ammon, Moab and Mount Seir, who had come against Judah; so they were routed. For the sons of Ammon and Moab rose up against the inhabitants of Mount Seir destroying them completely; and when they had finished with the inhabitants of Seir, they helped to destroy one another.
>
> 2 Chronicles 20:18–22 (NAS)

"And a voice came from the throne, saying, 'Give praise to our God, all you his bond-servants, you who fear him, the small and the great" (Revelation 19:5, NAS).

I would like to state the obvious. There are many, many ways to physically express worship to our Lord God and Savior. Here in 2 Chronicles, they bowed, fell down, stood up, were loud, rose early, went to the wilderness (isolation), proclaimed that trust was the way to be established successfully, consulted with God's people for wisdom, and sang songs. This is quite a variety! Most people, as groups of denominations and as individuals, tend to prefer one way or another, and they stick primarily with that one way. I fault no one in this; each must find their own way of expressing gratitude to Father. True intimacy is different from relationship to relationship. Just as I can't dictate to you how to be intimate with your spouse, it is the same with God. It is personal.

Many churches are always loud while some are always quiet. Unfortunately, they tend to come one against the other. The quiet ones say that the loud ones are irreverent, and the loud ones say that the quiet ones are spiritually dead. In my experience, I have seen where both comments can be true, and both can be false. Stereotyping is always a bad thing! This message, however, is not one of fault-finding of any one choice of *worship*. It is set for the purpose of each individual checking their heart within to find whether or not, whatever way they choose to outwardly express their worship, it is from a sincere, pure, and contrite heart before Almighty God.

I have listed below a myriad of Scriptures of how different people have displayed worship. I will not elaborate on them because they are self-explanatory. I listed them simply to look at the broad spectrum of how those before us have done. One is not to be exalted above the other. You can read for yourself and decide what is best for you and when. For me personally, I choose a variety. I look to Father to guide me in how I am to worship on different occasions. You want to be careful not to *follow the crowd,* as it so often happens. If most are loud around you, he may lead you to bow in quietude. He may be testing your level of obedience. Crowd following is a common thing among worshippers. If most are quiet around you, you may need to lift your hands in praise or shout. Of course the Lord always expects his people to be respectful, but he also wants you to follow *his* lead, not the lead of others. Be *balanced* in this as well as all areas of life.

I knew someone once who worshipped in a quieter church. She got fired up and began speaking in tongues when no one in the congregation did. She would cry out loudly and speak in tongues during service. The elders went to her several times and asked her to stop because it was a disruption. She refused, became offended, and left the church begrudgingly when they asked her to find another place of worship that was conducive to her style.

This is the *wrong* way to handle things! The Lord will never lead you in your spirit to be disruptive so that attention is drawn to *you*. Any *disruption of God* will draw attention to him and glorify him only! If you feel you need to find another place where they worship the way you currently worship, so be it. But do not act out because *you feel like it* and have the attitude in your heart that you will do as you please and call it *Holy Spirit leading.* That is rebellion because you are not obeying the authority set over you in that church. Also, God is a God of order.

What I am saying is simply to follow the Holy Spirit and not the crowd, all the while being respectful of the general worship. God never interrupts himself. When with the Jews, be like a Jew; the Greeks as the Greek, and so on. Use discernment in worship coupled with his leading. If it is in accordance to the type of worship at a particular congregation, and you are *truly* led (by God and not emotions) in a way different than the majority, go with what he is telling you. Otherwise, if you are like the person I just mentioned, you will draw attention to yourself, and that is *self-worship*, not *God* worship. Again, be balanced in all of your ways.

True worship in its purest form is an *outward* display of what is *inward.* To clarify, the act of worship, however you choose, should be the *reaction* of God having already transformed your inner man. Worship should never be an act of what *seems* right or acceptable in the eyes of man however that may be. Whether you are quiet and low or loud and up on your feet, both can honor God and both can honor man. What God always looks at is the condition of your heart, not the actions of your body!

No matter what outward way you prefer, your *heart* should praise him without end! Inward praise must be the root of all outward displays. You who love and fear him should never stop exalting his holiness and kindness toward mankind. He is perfect always, regardless of situation or circumstance! May praises toward our Lord and Savior never cease!

By you I have been sustained from my birth; you are he who took me from my mother's womb; my praise is continually of you... my mouth is filled with your praise and with your glory all day long... but as for me, I will hope continually, and will praise you yet more and more.

Psalm 71:6, 8, 14 (NAS)

"The twenty-four elders will fall down before him who sits on the throne, and will worship him who lives forever and ever, and will cast their crowns before the throne, saying, "Worthy are you, our Lord and our God, to receive glory and honor and power; for you created all things, and because of your will they existed, and were created" (Revelation 4:10–11, NAS)

To worship any other than the One True God is idolatry and his wrath will come upon you sooner or later. It is his law and it cannot be undone. Whether you worship a statue, nature, your flesh, or anyone or thing other than he, it is corrupt and must be stopped and repented immediately. Ask forgiveness and he will forgive. Turn from your wickedness and idolatry and he will turn from his wrath!

"For even though they knew God, they did not honor him as God or give thanks, but they became futile in their speculations, and their foolish heart was darkened" (Romans 1:21, NAS).

"The fool has said in his heart, "There is no God." They are corrupt, and have committed abominable injustice; there is no one who does good" (Psalm 53:1, NAS).

"Being darkened in their understanding, excluded from the life of God because of the ignorance that is in them, because of the hardness of their heart; and they, having become callous, have given themselves over to sensuality for the practice of every kind of impurity with greediness" (Ephesians 4:18, NAS).

"Now therefore, put away the foreign gods which are in your midst, and incline your hearts to the Lord, the God of Israel" (Joshua 24:23, NAS).

"Ascribe to the Lord the glory due to his name; worship the

Lord in holy array,"is the quote from Psalm 29:2. Holy array, in this day, should be your inner man set on purity and righteousness. A holy garment should be your heart set on all things holy, all things pleasing to God. Come before him desiring always and in everything to honor and glorify him and his majesty. Cleanse yourself daily of all unrighteousness. Do not allow pride, bitterness, hatred, malice, contempt, gossip, murder, etc. to remain in your life. If it begins, bring it down into the obedience of Christ the moment you recognize the sin (2 Corinthians 10:5). Bathe yourself in righteousness and clothe yourself in humility.

> ... even to celebrate and to thank and praise the Lord God of Israel ... ascribe to the Lord the glory due his name; bring an offering, and come before him; worship the Lord in holy array ... blessed be the Lord, the God of Israel, from everlasting even to everlasting. Then all the people said, "Amen," and praised the Lord.
>
> 1 Chronicles 16:4, 29, 36 (NAS)

"For all of you who were baptized into Christ have clothed yourselves with Christ" (Galatians 3:27, NAS).

"Worship the Lord in holy attire; tremble before him, all the earth" (Psalm 96:9, NAS).

Worshipping him in spirit and in truth is vital information to any and every believer. The only way to *truly* worship as the Father sees worship is to be anointed (baptized, covered, consumed) by the Holy Spirit. John states that a day is coming where *true worshipers* will do so in *spirit and in truth*. These are the people the Father seeks.

Let me attempt to break it down as simply as possible:

1. First John 5 reads that the Spirit of God testifies (proclaims) because his Spirit *is* the truth. He is three in one—Spirit, water, and blood. When one makes a profession of faith, in the spirit realm, this is what happens: the water that flowed from Jesus' side pours through you, making a clean living space for the Spirit, who is pure in every way. He cannot reside in an impure

space. Then, once clean, the Spirit moves in. After that, the blood—pure in every way—covers and seals the Spirit within. "For the Word of God is living and active and sharper than any two-edged sword, and piercing as far as the division of soul and spirit, of both joints and marrow, and able to judge the thoughts and intentions of the heart," (Hebrews 4:12, NAS).

2. John 3:5–6 (NAS) reads, "Jesus answered, 'Truly, truly, I say to you, unless one is born of water and the Spirit he cannot enter into the kingdom of God. That which is born of the flesh is flesh, and that which is born of the Spirit is spirit.'" Jesus himself said that one must be born of water and Spirit. Otherwise, he has no place in the kingdom of God.

3. Romans 2:5 (NAS) states, "But because of your stubbornness and unrepentant heart you are storing up wrath for yourself in the day of wrath and revelation of the righteous judgment of God...but he is a Jew who is one inwardly; and circumcision is that which is of the heart, by the Spirit, not by the letter; and his praise is not from men, but from God." A true Jew (believer of Christ) is one who circumcises (tears, rips, cuts) his heart by the Spirit of God, not by the Law. In this, his praise is not of men, but of God. I take that to mean that praise (worship) to God is as *he* leads, not as *man* leads because the praise *to* God comes from the Spirit of God *within* the believer *through* the believer.

4. Ephesians 5 makes clear one must be filled with the Spirit of God so that he may then (and only then) be capable of true praise. Again, it is the Spirit praising through the body of the child of God. Note specifically chapter 5 verses 18 and 19 (NAS), "and do not get drunk with wine, for that is dissipation, but be filled with the Spirit, speaking to one another in psalms and hymns and spiritual songs, singing and making melody with your *heart* to the Lord; always giving thanks for all things in the name of our Lord Jesus Christ to God, even the Father."

5. Romans 8:16 reads that the Spirit testifies with our spirit. This is why your spirit must be cut away from your soul, which is adjoined at birth. The soul (mind, will, emotions) leads a person into a fleshly life because it smothers the spirit. Once the sword of the Spirit which is the Word of God is activated in your life and allowed to sever the two, your spirit man is now available to receive communion with the Spirit of the Living God. This is, in essence, the baptism of the Holy Spirit. You can simply pray, "Father, please separate my soul from my spirit." This testimony (Jesus himself is *The Testimony*) is now allowed to move freely through your human body and commune with your spirit. Now your spirit, as it communes constantly with Holy Spirit, will be able to readily override your fleshly mind, will and emotions. Once your spirit is separated from your soul, and you choose life only through his testimony, worship becomes truth because He who is Truth in you is worshiping himself through your obedience.

Notice the words of the following Scripture references.

"Beware of the dogs, beware of the evil workers, beware of the false circumcision; for we are the true circumcision, who worship in the Spirit of God and glory in Christ Jesus and put no confidence in the flesh" (Philippians 3:2–3, NAS).

"Therefore if you have been raised up with Christ, keep seeking the things above, where Christ is, seated at the right hand of God. Set your mind on the things above, not on the things that are on earth" (Colossians 3:1–2, NAS).

"But an hour is coming, and now is, when the true worshipers will worship the Father in spirit and truth; for such people the Father seeks to be his worshipers. God is spirit, and those who worship him must worship in spirit and truth" (John 4:23–24, NAS).

"For God, whom I serve *in my spirit* in the preaching of the gospel of his Son..." (Romans 1:9, NAS).

■ ■ ■ ■ ■

As I just mentioned, the splitting of your spirit from your soul and allowing Holy Spirit to move *through* you leads to purity of heart. True worship is that of a clean, pure heart set on God. He looks upon nothing but the heart. Yes, people make mistakes, just as did David, Moses, Abraham and others gone before. In 1 Samuel 17, God told Samuel not to look upon the outward appearance because *he* does not. Oh that mankind could grasp and receive this concept!

Without understanding of this simple way of God's, Satan is allowed a foothold in mankind. A person who loves the Lord may make a mistake. The person confesses and repents, yet continues to beat themselves up for the mistake. That is condemnation (to pronounce incurable), and that is of the evil one, not God! It is of the flesh, not of the Spirit of God. Romans 8:1 (KJV) states clearly, "There is therefore now no condemnation to them which are in Christ Jesus, who walk not after the flesh, but after the Spirit." This is where knowledge comes. With knowledge and understanding of God looking upon the heart, we would all be better-equipped to stand guard over our hearts, not allowing Satan to condemn us.

The more quickly you confess, repent, and are made clean without condemnation, the quicker you can move on doing the Lord's business. The catch is not wallowing in self-pity after you have repented. Many beat themselves through condemnation, and begin to stagnate, not allowing God to continue to minister in, to, or through them. This condition of constantly deeming yourself unfit for God's service will eventually bring about spiritual death to the believer if allowed to continue.

You must learn how to put aside the idea that you can force something to happen with God through your flesh. We often fail in our efforts for Christ because we are doing it with our self-will, mind, and emotions rather than total submission to the will of God. We can only really be productive for the Kingdom of God by submitting all of our desires for the perfect will of God no matter what the cost.

Many a time, God's anointed failed him through acts of sin, such as David. Yet, after all that happened, God continually called David "a man after God's own heart." It is always, always the *heart* of a man that God sees and judges. There are countless people running around doing *good* acts in the name of Jesus in the church, yet they have no true heart for God. One day, their heart will be exposed, and He will have to say, "Truly, truly I say to you, I do not know you." This is from the words he spoke in the parable of the 10 virgins in Matthew 25:12. They all wanted to marry the groom, yet only five were completely committed to put everything of themselves aside in order to marry him.

I do not say this as a scare tactic but rather as a truth. Each person calling himself a *believer of Christ* must check their heart. His heart is a heart of pure love. His Spirit living within the believer, when allowed to flow, will burst forth fruit of love through you. Acts of kindness should be him flowing through you, not you forcing yourself to do kind things, thinking it will somehow get you brownie points with God. They can often look the same outwardly to the human eye, but he knows the difference and will one day soon reveal all that is in the heart of every man.

Make sure your heart is one set on Christ Jesus. Only you and he know the truth. If you find your heart is not completely set upon his, ask him to show you how to fall in love with him and to change your heart. In Ezekiel, it states that he will give you a new heart and a new spirit. Ask for that newness! He wants you to have it more than you!

Remember that the price of all sin is paid in full. There are none that are not covered by his death, burial, and resurrection. When you sin, and you are one who does have a heart set on God, the sin does not separate you from his love—it merely separates you from the blessings of his covenant.

This being said, don't allow an *act* of sin, once confessed, to keep you down! Too many of God's chosen allow the evil one to make us *feel* less than anointed because they made a mistake. Remember,

David committed adultery, lied, murdered, and then continued to allow it to go unconfessed for a long time. There were consequences to his actions because we all reap what we sow, but ultimately the Lord never ceased to call him a *man after his own heart.*

Sin is a tricky thing when you don't continue to seek understanding, wisdom, and knowledge of how God operates. I don't claim to fully understand, but as I seek daily, I continue to come into a greater understanding. Understanding and knowledge keep the enemy further and further away because it weakens his stronghold over you. Keep in mind that Satan is always a defeated foe. It is lack of knowledge that kills mankind. Hosea makes it clear. Knowledge, wisdom, and understanding of the Word of God (sword of the Spirit) are your greatest weapons against the enemy!

■ ■ ■ ■ ■

"You hypocrites, rightly did Isaiah prophesy of you: 'This people honors Me with their lips, but their heart is far away from Me. But in vain do they worship Me, teaching as doctrines the precepts of men'" (Mark 7:7, NAS).

"But the Lord said to Samuel, "Do not look at his appearance or at the height of his stature, because I have rejected him; for God sees not as man sees, for man looks at the outward appearance, but the Lord looks at the heart" (1 Samuel 16:7, NAS).

"Let us draw near with a sincere heart in full assurance of faith, having our hearts washed with pure water" (Hebrews 10:22, NAS).

"Let the words of my mouth and the meditation of my heart be acceptable in your sight, O Lord, my Rock and my Redeemer" (Psalm 19:14, NAS).

"Create in me a clean heart, O God, and renew a steadfast spirit within me. Do not cast me away from your presence and do not take your Holy Spirit from me … the sacrifices of God are a broken spirit; a broken and a contrite heart, O God, you will not despise" (Psalm 51:10, 17, NAS).

■ ■ ■ ■ ■

Prayer

Show me, Father, how to worship you in spirit and in truth. Teach me how to be transformed in my inner man so that my worship will simply be an outward display of inward change. I love you, O God. Amen.

Fear & Love Him with a Clean
HEART

To all God's people I say, "Fear Him and worship the Lord God Almighty with a heart of everlasting love toward Him!" Without reverent fear *of* Him, you can do nothing successfully *for* him. This goes back to dying to the flesh and living a Spirit-filled life. Though many people within the body of Christ can quote Scripture, their outer man has not been broken. Their inner man (spirit) is still united with and controlled by their soul (mind, will, emotions). When a person fears Almighty God simply for who he is, they will be a broken person just as Job was. At the end of his sufferings, he repented before the Almighty as "dust and ashes." When a person is broken, they will no longer depend upon their own physical or intellectual ability to accomplish anything for Christ. Again, they may preach and teach with their natural abilities, but the kingdom of heaven will not advance through them as God designed.

The fear of God is the beginning of wisdom. True success is pleasing the Father regardless of whether or not one receives any earthly accolades. Wisdom from above is a requirement for spiritual success. Read the following texts. They make it abundantly clear that this is a fact. Many try for years on end to *please* Him, to *do right* in His sight, yet they can't quite seem to stand or to continue in righteousness.

I have said many times before, and it bears repeating: The one who reverently fears the Lord God will run from iniquity! They will never want to displease this awesome, mighty, reverent, sovereign, holy, and magnificent God! Fear of God is where it begins and ends and nothing short of that will do!

To reverently fear is not the kind of fear one thinks when you are afraid of a snake, shark, darkness, whatever. That is a fleshly, natural-type fear. This, on the other hand, is a fear that is a fear of respect and absolute awe; knowing he could wipe you off the planet, yet through obedience to him, knowing he will not. It is an inner trembling in your spirit man due to his majesty, purity, and holiness.

This inner trembling is to be in complete and utter awe of one so splendid, majestic, and magnificent as the Lord God of heaven and earth! Every person in the Old and New Testament trembled in the presence of the angel of the Lord to near death! It is not an "I'm gonna getcha if your bad" kind of fear. By no means. He wants you to fear him to understand the complete worthlessness of your human condition. In this, you become humbled to the point that you would not even consider making a move on this earth without consultation with him first. Then, and only then, may he pour out blessings bountifully upon your head from his grace through your humble estate!

Notice the first few Scriptures on the following pages. They all speak of fear of God and *then* praise and worship. The fear of the Lord brings about holiness. Worship of God should come from a heart set on reverently fearing the One True God. All too often, there is so-called worship going on around the world by people who have never feared him. They may look good on the surface to many people, yet in their heart of hearts, they are inwardly rebellious. It happens all the time.

People who do not genuinely know or understand his holiness or his heart, who do not begin their walk with fear and trembling, are the ones who constantly get angry with the Lord, feeling like he wrongs them when things don't go their way. They (inwardly or outwardly) say, "But God, I did this, this, this, this, and this for you, and this is the thanks I get?!" It is a "How dare you, God" mentality. These are the ones who look godly for many, many years, and then one day, something goes terribly wrong in their life; tragedy strikes. All of a sudden they are screaming and cursing the very God they claimed to have loved for so long. This was once me.

The foundation of a true relationship with Christ must be one of a heart of *love, faith,* and *fear.* Though I had made an acceptance of Jesus through His blood at the age of six, it wasn't until my thirties that I began to understand the things of Holy Spirit; how to die to selfish desires and live only unto the Spirit of God. Until I began to develop this reverent fear of God and understand that all things (no matter how they look on the surface) work for good for those who love him, I was simply a Christian salesperson! We need to know his heart and how it operates so that we do not become embittered like the way I used to be. These three factors of love, faith, and fear keep the desire of obedience alive within the inner man. Without these, your walk is in vain, and the words may be heard by your ears, "I never knew you. Depart from Me." Take a look at the definitions of love, faith, and fear.

■ ■ ■ ■ ■

Love: This is where you become aware of how much he loves you and died specifically for you, and because of his love for you, you want to love him so much in return that you would never want to displease him. Love the Lord your God with all of your heart, soul, mind, and strength. *Know* the height, width, length, and depth of his love. The commandment of love is the one that all else of the word hangs. Without it, no gift, word, deed, or ability will be worth anything (1 Corinthians 13). All is useless without love.

Faith: Without faith, it is impossible to please him. You begin at ground zero but have enough faith to begin saying that you want his way over your own. Faith begins to grow into a deeper and deeper relationship of trust. Trust is that element of, no matter what you see with your natural eyes, you *know* that he will work it all for your good because you love him (Romans 8:28). And he always keeps his promises, because he is the Promise! Blessed is the man who trusts in the Lord, and whose trust is the Lord (Jeremiah 17:7)!

Fear: It is the beginning of understanding that he is the Triune God who created everything in existence. There is nothing living that he did not give the breath of life. Without fear of him, the heavenly door cannot be opened to you for understanding, knowledge, wisdom, confidence, blessings, life, or anything of him. That being said, you reverence this being because, without him, you perish eternally. That alone should make one tremble at his presence and name!

"The fear of the Lord is the beginning of knowledge; fools despise wisdom and instruction" (Proverbs 1:7, NAS).

> ... so that you and your son and your grandson might fear the Lord your God, to keep all his statutes and his commandments which I command you, all the days of your life, and that your days may be prolonged ... you shall fear only the Lord your God; and you shall worship him and swear by his name ... so the Lord commanded us to observe all these statutes, to fear the Lord our God for our good always and for our survival, as it is today.
>
> Deuteronomy 6:2, 13, 24 (NAS)

All words of correction/rebuke are for the *benefit* of the child of God; not for condemnation but for restoration and deliverance. As a whole, the body of Christ does not know or even desire to fear the Lord. *Fear the Lord* is a term grossly tossed about to many but few understand. When a person begins to truly, reverently fear him, transformation comes. He is stating in the text below that his people are foolish and senseless because of lack of fear. Please read it carefully.

"Now hear this, O foolish and senseless people, who have eyes but do not see; who have ears but do not hear. *Do you not fear Me?*" declares the Lord. "Do you not tremble in My presence? For I have placed the sand as a boundary for the sea, an eternal decree, so it cannot cross over it. Though the waves toss, yet they cannot prevail; though they roar, yet they cannot cross over it. But this people has a stubborn and rebellious heart; they have turned aside and departed. They do not say in their heart, 'Let us now fear the Lord our God, who gives rain in its season'...your iniquities have turned these away, and your sins have withheld good from you. For wicked men are found among my people, they watch like fowlers lying in wait; they set a trap, they catch men. Like a cage full of birds, so their houses are full of deceit; therefore they have become great and rich. They are fat, they are sleek, they also excel in deeds of wickedness; they do not plead the cause of the orphan, that they may prosper; and they do not defend the rights of the poor. Shall I not punish these people?" declares the Lord. "On a nation such as this shall I not avenge myself? An appalling and horrible thing has happened in the land; the prophets prophesy falsely. And the priests rule on their own authority; and my people love it so! But what will you do at the end of it?"

Jeremiah 5:21–31 (NAS) (italics added)

For many, your destruction (bad times) has come upon you because of your *lack of fear* of God. As you seek holiness and putting God first because he is your life, he wants you to know that it all starts with this reverent fear, not with doing *right* or *good* things. Without it, you will not understand how to love him as a bride to her husband; you only fear him as one who holds his proverbial thumb over you like a rigid disciplinarian.

Allow me to explain. Remember, as God has designed things in the natural, an earthly husband is supposed to be the protector to his wife. God is our heavenly Father to his children, but also our heavenly husband to his bride (Bride of Christ). A true husband loves his wife so much that he would do whatever is best for her. I am in love with my husband, Michael. I have a reverent fear of him out of respect for who he is as my covenant covering. This does not mean I am consciously going around thinking how afraid I am of him; on the contrary. I have an inner reverence for him so to not disrespect him. Because I know how in love he is with me and, I have this reverent fear of him, I do not come against him if he makes a decision that I do not initially understand. Also, I am more focused on the *love* rather than the *fear*. This is because perfect love casts out fear (I John 4:18–19)—love takes precedence over the fear. In other words, though the fear is ever present, the love is dominant.

In the passage in Jeremiah you just read, God continues to talk about a people with a stubborn and rebellious heart. Anyone who continually disobeys his commands is rebellious in the sight of God. Everyone knows on some level right from wrong, yet you do not seek him; you have sought only the things that bring you personal pleasure.

Again in Jeremiah, the Lord goes on to say that they *did not* say in their heart, "I fear you, Almighty God." When he said that, because of their sin, he *could not* bless them as he wished to do. God always desires to bless his people. He has always loved you so completely that he *wants* to bless you. Because of rebellion, we stop his hand of blessing upon our life. He states that these peoples' houses (their inner spirit man and heart) are full of deceit. This does not mean that we are just deceitful, but that we have allowed ourselves to be deceived. We have for a long time deceived ourselves into believing that what is actually sin is *good* or *right*. The world says, "Follow your heart." God says, "Never trust your heart, for it will lead you astray." You, I, and the body of Christ, are to be moved only by the Spirit of the Living God, not the emotions of our heart. Only a heart set on God will be trustworthy, because it has been consigned to him and not the desire of the fleshly man.

He continues by asking the question, which is rhetorical, "Should I not punish this wickedness?" One can sin for a long, long time as far as man's timeframe is concerned. However, God watches until the people (or person) nearly destroy themselves, and then he punishes. It is for his holy and pure name's sake, as well as for the well-being of the individual.

An excellent case in point is the lives of many of the women I minister to in the prisons. Many of them went about their daily lives, sinning by selling drugs and themselves. They had no concept of a holy God, or if they did, they paid no heed. But in each of their lives, a day came where they were captured and incarcerated—some after many years of disobedience. They were enraged that God put them in prison! Many have said that they were mad that God did not show them mercy in their situation. Nonetheless, for those who sought him, they came to realize that they had to be stopped for their own sake, as well as for those whom they were hurting. It was in prison that they came to a place of brokenness. This is the best place to be in the eyes of our Savior! He punished them because of the wicked acts and to get their attention. It was the only way to help them see the error in order to turn to repentance and newness of life.

Let us look at the latter part of the text in Jeremiah. We read, "The priests rule on their own authority; and my people love it so!" First of all, once you accept Christ through repentance, you are now of a royal priesthood. Since you are a priest, as each believer is, you must seek *his* authority instead of the authority you *think* you have over your own body. By conducting yourself in a manner unworthy of the gospel of Christ, you are actually overriding his authority. This too equals rebellion!

So many appear to succeed as the world considers success, but he asks, "What will come of it all in the end?" He is saying that you need to stop doing what pleases your fleshly man, turn your heart toward him, have it set on him at all times and in all seasons, and the desires of your heart will change. The sin in your life that currently pleases you for a moment does not please you at all; rather, it brings about destruction and curses upon your head.

The excellent news is that, as you turn your heart to be set on

him and his righteousness, the blessings will begin to abound endlessly in your life! It is a promise to the righteous seed of Abraham!
You just haven't lived a life that depicts it. All throughout the Word,
God scorns the wicked, but then says, "Turn from your wicked ways
and I will bless you!" All you have to do is make your flesh die, and
then make your body a slave to yourself. Paul writes this in 1 Corinthians 9:27, "but I discipline my body and make it my slave, so that,
after I have preached to others, I myself will not be disqualified."

You do not need to receive salvation over and over; you simply
need to pull your earthly shell back into obedience to the Master—your Owner, the One who paid the highest price in order that
you may live a life of freedom instead of bondage. The evil one,
who is death, oppresses you. The Righteous One, who is life, gives
freedom. The more obedient you are to the word of God, the more
the blessings will fall upon you and overtake you. There are times
of rededication after slipping out of obedience, but know that Holy
Spirit does not come in and out of a person like a yo-yo just because
we make an error. He is there; he just needs to, once again, be given
full reign from time to time.

The fear of God, as you come into this new place, will turn
your heart away from wickedness and toward holiness. You will care
more about pleasing him than yourself. It means that no matter
what your *flesh* desires, your desire to please him will override. This
is sacrifice. He sacrificed everything that you may live. What are
you willing to *sacrifice* that you may please such a holy God?

I say this to bring you into a higher place of freedom than you can
ever imagine! You will begin to surely have "eyes that see, ears that
hear, and a mind that truly understands and comprehends." Obedience will become, in time, a pleasure to you and not a burden.

Romans 16:17–18 reads, "Now I urge you, brethren, keep your
eye on those who cause dissensions and hindrances contrary to the
teaching which you learned, and turn away from them. For such
men are slaves, not of our Lord Christ but of their own appetites;
and by their smooth and flattering speech they deceive the hearts
of the unsuspecting."

1 John 3:19–21 quotes, "We will know by this that we are of the truth, and will assure our heart before him in whatever our heart condemns us; for God is greater than our heart and knows all things. Beloved, if our heart does not condemn us, we have confidence before God; and whatever we ask we receive from him, because we keep his commandments and do the things that are pleasing in his sight."

This passage in 1 John sums all said in this chapter. The condition of your heart is everything to God, so I can't mention it enough! The body of Christ is greatly lacking understanding in this area. God is greater than your heart and knows all things. If your heart does not condemn you, you have a pure heart before him. You can then be confident before him, and you can have whatever you want. Fleshliness always condemns. If you are condemned, know that your fleshly nature is at hand.

Remember, a pure heart before him will want *only* what *he* desires for you. This is not a Scripture for selfish hearts. A selfish heart is *not* set on the things of Christ. *Purity* of heart *is* the confidence in him. We all make mistakes; there is no one exempt because we live in this earthen vessel. That is why it is imperative for him to look only upon the heart, and for you to seek purity in it.

This text in 1 John 3 is one that I have read over many times, yet always knew I didn't quite understand its meaning. As I sought revelation, this is what he revealed. It reads, "If our heart does not condemn us, we have confidence before God." I find this has great substance, yet it is widely overlooked. God does not condemn. I refer back to Romans 8:1 which states that there is now *no* condemnation *in* Christ Jesus for those who live according to the Spirit and not the flesh. That being an indisputable fact, if your heart is condemned, it is not of God. *Good* (there is none good but God) on the surface is worthless lest it is Christ acting through you. When you are *in* him (consumed by him) your heart will not condemn you because your heart is one with God.

Paul says to keep your spiritual eye open. Eye is singular, representing the single vision of God. With two eyes, there is the chance of one going astray. One is singleness; one vision, one God, one way. I believe the reason he gave us two is to represent the spiritual and carnal man. Man sees whatever man wants, whether physical or spiritual. Everyone has a choice. To turn a blind eye to God is to have single vision focused only on self. To open your eye is to have unity with the one true God, saying in your heart and with your mouth, "Not my will, but your will in all things." You have one heart. When it is in unity with Christ, your physical eyes and ears, as well as your spiritual eye, will follow suit.

■ ■ ■ ■ ■

"Make your ear attentive to wisdom, incline your heart to understanding ... for wisdom will enter your heart and knowledge will be pleasant to your soul" (Proverbs 2:2, 10, NAS).

> Then he taught me and said to me, "Let your heart hold fast my words; keep my commandments and live ... do not let them depart from your sight; keep them in the midst of your heart, for they are life to those who find them and health to all their body. Watch over your heart with all diligence, for from it flow the springs of life.
>
> Proverbs 4:4, 21–23 (NAS)

Who with perversity in his heart continually devises evil, who spread strife. Therefore his calamity will come suddenly; instantly he will be broken and there will be no healing ... a heart that devises wicked plans, feet that run rapidly to evil ... my son, observe the commandment of your father and do not forsake the teaching of your mother; bind them continually on your heart; tie them around your neck. When you walk about, they will guide you; when you sleep, they will watch over you; and when you awake, they will talk to you. For the commandment is a lamp and the teaching is light; and reproofs for discipline are the way of life ...

Proverbs 6:14–15, 18, 20–23 (NAS)

My son, keep my words and treasure my commandments within you. Keep my commandment and live, and my teaching as the apple of your eye. Bind them on your fingers; write them on the tablet of your heart... and behold, a woman comes to meet him, dressed as a harlot and cunning of heart...

Proverbs 7:1–3, 10 (NAS)

"For where your treasure is, there your heart will be also" (Luke 12:34, NAS).

■ ■ ■ ■

Prayer

"O Jesus, circumcise my heart today. Place in me, O Father, a new heart, and a new spirit. I desire with all of my heart, soul, mind, and strength to be as you desire. To have a clean, pure, contrite heart before you, O God. Show me the way of righteousness. Show me how to have a heart set on you at all times and in all things. Give me a heart that hates what you hate, loves what you love, goes where you go, and stays where you stay. Teach me, Father, how to be still and quiet in your holy presence that I may know your voice better than my own. Instill within me reverent, holy fear of you, Almighty Sovereign God! Show me the error of my ways, that I may quickly and without hesitation confess, repent, and be made clean in your sight. Reveal every wicked and fruitless deed of darkness within your holy temple (me) that it may be purged from my body. I pray, O Father, to have a sound mind, pure heart, and steadfast spirit all the days of my life. Teach me your love and how to grow in faith that you become my trust. I love you, O God. Help me to love you with the pure love you pour upon my head. Separate my spirit from my soul that I may commune with your Spirit to worship in spirit and in truth. Thanks be to God in heaven and earth. I rejoice in you, Sovereign, for you are worthy to be praised!"

Royal Priesthood—
Your New
STATUS

You are a Successor of a Royal Priesthood. You possess the keys to the Kingdom of Heaven because the Predecessor lives forever through you! "I will give you the **keys of the kingdom** of heaven ... whatever you *bind* on earth will be bound in heaven and whatever you *loose* on earth will be loosed in heaven" (Matthew 16:19; 18:18–19, NAS).

Key = authority to act in the king's name—In ancient times, a key expressed the idea of authority, power, or privilege.

Knowledge = allow, be aware of, feel (have), know (ledge), perceive, be sure, understand the fullness of Christ in you! His authority and power are yours to utilize on this earth! Whatever authority and power he gave to his initial twelve disciples, he gave also to you. You are supposed to be his disciple. You are not to go this journey without it. You cannot succeed in this life making disciples of many nations if you do not take up all he has graciously given. You harm yourself and others to talk a good talk without Jesus' walk of power and authority! You must know what is yours so you will better honor God. His power in operation through his body (the believers) glorifies him!

■ ■ ■ ■ ■

"For in him *all the fullness of Deity dwells in bodily form,* and in him you have been made complete, and *he is the head over all rule and authority"* (Colossians 2:9–10, NAS). (italics added).

"Once, having been asked by the Pharisees when the kingdom of God would come, Jesus replied, "The kingdom of God does not come with your careful observation, nor will people say, 'Here it is,' or 'There it is,' because *the kingdom of God is within you"* (Luke 17:20–21, NAS).

■ ■ ■ ■ ■

"They were amazed at his teaching; for he was *teaching them as one having authority,* and not as the scribes ..."What is this? *A new teaching with authority! He commands even the unclean spirits, and they obey him"* (Mark 1:22, 27, (NAS).

"For the Son of man is as a man taking a far journey, who left his house, and *gave authority to his servants,* and to every man his work..." (Mark 13:34, NAS).

"And he called the twelve together, and *gave them power and authority over all the demons and to heal diseases"* (Luke 9:1, NAS).

■ ■ ■ ■ ■

Please recognize that the same mission statement of Christ is *your* mission statement; whether you know it or not, fulfill it or not. You do not have a choice. If Jesus Christ lives *in* you, his mission does likewise. Luke four verses 18 and 19 states the mission clearly.

John 1:12 says that if you believe in his name, you have the God-given right as his child and all the same rights as his first-born—Jesus. Jesus' rights are all power and authority to rule things on the earth, under the earth, and things of the air. Since he is the head and you are the body, you move *with* the head—not separately, not differently. As he moves, so do you. Since he moves in humility, power, strength, and authority, so should you. Otherwise, you are in dissension with and disobedience to the Father. It is a tragedy for the body of Christ *not* to conduct itself in the same way as he. Otherwise, you are no greater than the fallen angel and those led by him on earth.

The Word states that Jesus is God's *firstborn,* not his only or last (Revelation 1:5). You and I are also his sons, no less in the sight of God. This is because it is he in you whom the Father sees when he looks at you. *The Son* lives in the sons of God. The same Spirit that raised Christ from the dead is living in you! No greater power could you possibly possess!

All Things Are Yours:

Jesus is seated at the right hand of God (Colossians 3:1), and all things are yours (I Corinthians 3). This means that whatever God possess belongs to you, his child, as an inheritance just as if your earthly parents were billionaires; what's theirs is yours by default! You don't get it all at once but as he recognizes that you are ready to receive. In Matthew chapter twenty-two and verse twenty nine, Jesus is talking to the scribes and Pharisees. He tells them that they do not understand the power of God. They tried to process everything through their natural thinking. God says that it is your *spirit* that comprehends the Spirit (Romans 8:16). Only through him leading you from the inside (your spirit) out will you be able to comprehend spiritual things.

God makes it clear that all things are yours, you who allow Holy Spirit to indwell. If *all things* are yours, what are all things? All spiritual truth, power, and authority are Jesus,' so also they are yours. Begin to rise up and take on the ways of God. Jesus was humble but no wimp. He knew what was his and when and how to utilize it. He knew when to speak and when to be silent. A true ruler and priest of God discerns just as Christ would.

You are a King and Priest:

But you are a chosen generation *a royal priesthood, a holy nation, a peculiar people;* that you should show forth the praises of him who has called you out of darkness into his marvelous light (1 Peter 2:9, NAS)

You are a king and priest of the holy heritage; therefore you are no longer an old, dirty sinner! Since you are born of the heavenly realm, you are now born into royalty and need to begin to conduct yourself as such. He is the King of kings, and Lord of lords. Who are the other kings and lords? He is the High Priest. Who are the other priests below him? *You* and *I!* You are a royal holy priesthood that is set aside unto God. Jesus (understanding authority that was set in place by God) came in the order of a *priest* who is said in the word to be without mother or father, beginning or end. This was Melchizedek. If he had come in any other way, the law would have had to change. The Word also states that Jesus is the son of David. He came into the world in the lineage of a *king* after God's own heart. To summarize, he came legally through natural royalty and priesthood. He obeyed the law of the earth that he set in place. His obedience gave him full right to present himself as the King and Priest over all.

God expects you to obey authority because he set it in motion. Likewise, he abides by the same law. If Jesus had just *appeared,* he could not rule or give you and me rule over the earth. He abided by the law in setting up a pure lineage (a priest "like the Son of God"; a king, a "man after God's own heart") for Jesus to be born into. Mary was a descendent of both Melchizedek and David. Also, since death came through man, so life also came through man.

Being of the royal bloodline, you are to be holy and set apart to Christ. Only God is holy. You can only be holy when you allow Holy Spirit to move freely through your body. This is the "dying to the flesh" the Word speaks of repeatedly. This brings understanding of no longer being an *old, dirty sinner.* Don't ever refer to me as that.

I am a royal, holy, blood-bought child of God; king; priest; and heir to the perfect, unshakable kingdom of God! It does not mean I don't make mistakes from time to time, but I am quickly convicted by he who is within and I repent. I don't have to wallow around in self-pity because I erred. Since Jesus Christ is a "priest forever," so are you. The High Priest lives *in* you. The King lives *in* you.

■ ■ ■ ■ ■

This Melchizedek was king of Salem and priest of God Most High... his name means *"king of righteousness"*; then also, *"king of Salem"* means *"king of peace."* Without father or mother, without genealogy, without beginning of days or end of life, *like the Son of God he remains a priest forever*... If perfection could have been attained through the Levitical priesthood (for on the basis of it the law was given to the people), why was there still need for another priest to come—one in the order of Melchizedek, not in the order of Aaron? For when there is a change of the priesthood, there must also be a change of the law... For it is declared: *"You are a priest forever, in the order of Melchizedek."* The former regulation is set aside because it was weak and useless (for the law made nothing perfect), and a better hope is introduced, by which we draw near to God. And it was not without an oath! Others became priests without any oath, but he became a priest with an oath when God said to him: "The Lord has sworn and will not change his mind: *'You are a priest forever.'"* Because of this oath, Jesus has become the guarantee of a better covenant... but because Jesus lives forever, he has a permanent priesthood. Therefore, he is able to save completely those who come to God through him, because he always lives to intercede for them. Such a high priest meets our need—one who is *holy, blameless, pure, set apart from sinners, exalted above the heavens.*

Hebrews 7:1–3, 11–13, 17–26 (NIV)

■　■　■　■　■

The secrets of the kingdom are within you because Jesus is within! In knowing that Jesus is the head with all power and you are his body, you too have his power and authority. Knowing that God is Spirit and you are human, he must operate through your spirit within your mortal body. This is how he *saves your soul.* It is by teaching you how to stop allowing the soul to lead your body astray. With separation of the soul from the spirit, the spirit can clearly hear Holy Spirit, instruct the soul in righteousness, and the soul (under authority of Holy Spirit) then tells the body what to do.

He says in Hebrews 10:12–13, "Until I put your enemies under your feet." This is where binding and loosing come in. It is *you,* the body of Christ, who is to do the "putting under his feet." *You* are to command the enemy to flee, be bound, and gagged, and bind to and loose onto yourself and others the Word of God. I reiterate: this can only happen with the division of soul from spirit. When your soul is the one in control, it leads your outer man into perpetual sin. Therefore, though you are saved from hell, you cannot rule here on earth as ordained king and priest.

■　■　■　■　■

He told them, *"The secret of the kingdom of God has been given to you..."* (Mark 4:11, NAS).

■　■　■　■　■

Righteousness is your kingdom scepter (Hebrews 1:8 and 4:16). Your walk in righteousness will be your scepter (a symbol of sovereignty). When you walk a Holy Spirit-led life, you will absolutely conduct yourself in righteousness; in Deuteronomy chapter 28, the Lord said this is where the world will fear the obedient.

"Make every effort to live in peace with all men and to *be holy;* without holiness no one will see the Lord. See to it that no one misses the grace of God and that no bitter root grows up to cause trouble and defile many" (Hebrews 12:14–15, NAS).

> Don't you know that you yourselves are God's temple and that God's Spirit lives in you? If anyone destroys God's temple, God will destroy him; for God's temple is sacred, and you are that temple. Do not deceive yourselves. If any one of you thinks he is wise by the standards of this age, he should become a "fool" so that he may become wise. For the wisdom of this world is foolishness in God's sight...*All things are yours*, whether Paul or Apollos or Cephas or the world or life or death or the present or the future—*all are yours, and you are of Christ, and Christ is of God.*
>
> 1 Corinthians 3:16–21 (NAS)

"And he put all things in subjection under his feet, and gave him as head over all things to the church, which is his body, the fullness of him who fills all in all," Ephesians 1:22–23 (NAS). All of this *is for this age!* Ephesians 1:21 reads, "not only in this age ..." The power he has given to Jesus, the head, Jesus gave to the church, the body. We are to learn to properly utilize the authority and power that Jesus walked in while in human form. We are to rule this earth as Adam once did from the Garden of Eden! Only now we are to rule with the power of Holy Spirit as opposed to soul power.

Watchman Nee speaks in depth about this in *The Latent Power of the Soul.* He points out that God had given Adam the supernaturally natural ability of soul power to run the entire earth from the Garden. After the fall, God did not remove this power but made it dormant within mankind. Now we must choose one or the other. *Soul* power can be utilized outside intimacy with God. This is how witchcraft and all sorts of supernatural power can come through people absent of God. *Spirit* power can only be taped when intimate with our Creator. When a person chooses to live according to the Spirit instead of the soul, his power and authority will govern properly as it should through your mortal body.

Please note carefully that many Christians, unaware of the difference between the soul and the spirit, regularly tap soul power. It is very dangerous to be ignorant of the two. I highly recommend obtaining a copy of *The Latent Power of the Soul* by Watchman Nee.

■ ■ ■ ■ ■

Prayer:

"I pray, Almighty God, that I will begin to see myself as you see me. I bless you that when you look upon me, you see only the pure blood of your son, Jesus. Show me how to be led only by he who is within and not by my fleshly desires. Reveal to me your holiness that I too may be holy. Remind me that I am a stranger in this land because I am of heaven and not of earth; rather, I am of the royal priesthood of you, O God. I bless your name that my old self is dead to sin and destruction, and I am now alive to purity and life everlasting. I love you, Jesus, and I thank you for giving me the honor and privilege of being seated at the right hand of the Father with you. Give me heavenly insight so to live in peace, though the world around me is in chaos. Teach me your ways and to know how to utilize the tools of the kingdom to bring heaven down to earth. I love you, Lord and Savior. Amen."

Obedience without Understanding Is
BONDAGE

Make your ear attentive to wisdom, incline your heart to understanding; for if you cry for discernment, lift your voice for understanding; if you seek her as silver and search for her as for hidden treasures; then you will discern the fear of the Lord and discover the knowledge of God. For the Lord gives wisdom; from his mouth come knowledge and understanding. He stores up sound wisdom for the upright; he is a shield to those who walk in integrity, guarding the paths of justice, and he preserves the way of his godly ones. Then you will discern righteousness and justice and equity and every good course. For wisdom will enter your heart and knowledge will be pleasant to your soul; discretion will guard you, understanding will watch over you.

Proverbs 2:2–11 (NAS)

Look at this text above. Notice that it takes *silence* and *listening* to receive wisdom from God; you must be *quiet* in order to *hear*. Silent observance of a situation and fearing him develops wisdom. However, it takes *asking* to receive understanding. *Asking* paints a picture of someone in need who has knowledge that, whatever it is that they need, someone else has it. For example, if you *need* five hundred dollars and your neighbor across the street *has* that amount, you must remove whatever pride lies within you in order to go and ask to be given what they have. It is humiliating to be in need, and more so to ask for someone outside of yourself to supply it. Nonetheless, you have to first recognize your need. Then you must humble yourself to ask the person who has the money to give it to you. The awesome thing about God is that he already knows that you need understanding. He is simply waiting for you to acknowledge that you need it because he longs to give it to you! Once you admit your need, then you can humble yourself in his presence and ask to be given.

Only God possesses ownership of spiritual understanding. The human race can, in our flesh absent from God, get *information*. We can read every book, listen to every scholar, and memorize all of everything you read and hear. However, to get *understanding* of what we are informed, we must humble ourselves; acknowledge that we cannot attain comprehension without him giving it, and that we must first ask in order to receive. Understanding of the things of the spiritual realm is completely supernatural!

Ephesians 1, verses 17–18 (KJV) read as follows, "That the *God* of our Lord Jesus Christ… may *give* unto you the *spirit* of wisdom and revelation in the knowledge of him; the *eyes of your understanding be enlightened.*" Wisdom, revelation, and understanding are a *spirit,* which means it is nothing of the natural. It is to *accompany* the information you already have. Knowledge precedes understanding. Information without the gift of understanding is worse than useless—it is dangerous! Only God can do the giving! It is an anointing from the heavenly realm that must be poured out *from* him *to* you.

The *giving* comes through asking. Whatever amount of humility is in your heart will determine what and how much you will ask. Remember, whatever is in your heart comes out of your mouth. The text in Proverbs reads, "… incline your heart to understanding… lift your *voice*…" I have quoted endlessly Hosea 4:14, "… so the people without understanding are ruined," yet it bears repeating!

I was watching the old classic *The Miracle Worker* with Anne Bancroft playing the part of Anne Sullivan, the teacher, and Patty Duke portraying Helen Keller, a blind, deaf, mute girl. The story of Helen Keller is amazing in itself—how she overcame her obstacles no one could begin to imagine. However, I heard the words Anne spoke to Helen's father: "Obedience without understanding is blindness." She said this to him after a few weeks of training when Helen learned a few tasks of obedience. He was satisfied with this condition simply because it was better than how things had been. Helen had been unruly because of her impediments, kicking, screaming, slapping, eating with her hands, etc. She had been as a rabid dog. Anything was an improvement!

Anne's point was that *tasks of obedience* are worthless without *understanding why* they must be done. Anne taught Helen sign language. Helen did not understand the meaning of the sign words; she simply learned to mimic Anne. She was still unable to *communicate* with the learning because the learning had no meaning. Anne knew that, given more time with Helen, she could get through to her that the sign language actually had meaning, purpose, and would open doors of communication with those in her world. She had to build a relationship with Helen and teach her basic things before understanding could follow. Once the foundation was laid, then the real work came! That foundation had to be built upon through patience and time spent teaching the basics. The foundation is worthless without being built upon.

In the natural, you cannot live on a concrete foundation on a plot of land. You must lay it out first, but then you must build a structure on it. It is the *structure on the foundation* that gives you shelter from the storm, not the foundation itself. Think of understanding as the secure structure. The more tools you have, the better built the structure; the better prepared you are in the storm. The teachers are the tools (Holy Spirit, those led by Holy Spirit, the Word of God) and your willingness to learn determines how well-built the structure (you, the temple of God) will be. At first, Helen hated Anne with venom because the world she knew was being forced to change! But, once she began to realize that the change from the teachings would better her life, she loved Anne like she loved no other. Understanding gives purpose and meaning to the tasks laid before us from God.

So it is in the body of Christ. We have salvation (from hell) shoved down our throats. It comes with a long list of do's and don'ts; tasks that no one can abide in and of themselves. There is very little proper teaching; therefore, there is little learning of what it's all about. There is minimal comprehension of *why* there are rules; that they are out of the loving heart of the Father; that there are curses if we disobey, and blessings if we obey. We become like trained dogs, often becoming rabid through frustration of seeing no immediate results from our obedience.

Because human nature dictates hatred of bondage, rebellion is the result of the frustration because the obedience feels like a choker around our necks. In turn, we become more and more frustrated at God when simple understanding of him would usher relief from the chains of this world. So, in essence, we go from bondage to bondage instead of victory to victory.

We have become like Helen's father. He just wanted to see a small result rather than being patient with both Anne and Helen to allow her to go all the way to bountiful blessings through understanding and knowledge! We go around preaching and teaching salvation from hell damnation, lead people through some faint prayer of repentance, and then send them on their way as if all that was to be accomplished with that person is. We train people in the church like we train a dog. We bark orders at people with condemnation dripping from our lips. We become no more than trained animals waiting to be slapped by God when we disobey or to get a treat when we obey! We are naturally afraid of what we do not understand, kind of like standing in a foreign country where they speak another language. The native person may be welcoming you in their custom but, because of your lack of understanding, you interpret them as trying to insult or assault you, so you are afraid. God's people generally don't understand obedience, so we are afraid of it and run from it.

I will venture to guess that this is why the majority of people profess Christ for a season, get bored or discouraged, then fall away to the next exciting thing. It is monotonous to do, do, do without having a reason for the tireless doing! God gave us magnificent minds to understand. Therefore, when we don't, naturally we have to stop whatever *right* thing we have been doing for feeling foolish because we don't even understand patience to wait for the harvest of our labor. However, when we do understand that there is purpose behind the command, we can move past any and every obstacle that tries to stop the work at hand. Once Helen understood, she couldn't wait to learn more! She began to thrive on learning regardless of blindness or deafness because there was purpose!

Once understanding of the supernatural behind the natural becomes alive within you, you will begin to view God's rules of obedience, such as "don't have sex before marriage," as God's way of protecting you instead of some strange form of punishment or torture. AIDS and other sexual diseases are scarcely heard of in marriages where both were virgins going into holy matrimony. When he says, "honor your father and mother," it is because, among many reasons, you will be honored by your children when you are a parent because you reap what you sow. When he states, "forgive to be forgiven; do not judge and you will not be judged," it is because he understands the human nature. We must all be forgiven, and he wants each of us to allow ourselves to be in position to receive forgiveness. We receive forgiveness as we are willing to forgive others their transgressions.

God's rules, commands, and ordinances actually have meaning! We keep ourselves in bondage when we learn only the dos and don'ts, as opposed to the dos and don'ts *combined* with the reason *why*. I have heard all my life within the church that we should never question God. I think I understand why they say that, but it is not

true. I believe maybe they mean that our *reasoning* for questioning needs to come from a heart of purity and correct motives, not
from a heart wanting to blame God for his choices in our lives. Job
questioned God for his troubles, and God came against him with
reprimand in his tongue, saying, "Were you there when I laid the
foundation of the earth? Were you there when I parted the seas
from the land?" This is because Job *doubted* God's way of thinking.
It was not because he had, at that time, a heart set on real understanding. He was mad at God and wanted to point out to God that
he (God) had made a mistake!

We are not to grow weary in well-doing (2 Thessalonians 3:13).
What frequently happens is that we do grow faint because it all
begins to seem meaningless compared to the wickedness of the
hearts of men. We start to question the *why,* only we aren't *really*
asking God; rather, we are looking for an excuse to get out. Again,
there was either no understanding to begin with, or they got their
eyes on the obstacles instead of the remover of the obstacles, the
great I AM. We must be vigilant and sober constantly, and in every
new level he takes us, seeking his understanding so that we have
secure structure to our *solid foundation.*

You can see your *calling from God* as the foundation on which
you will build the kingdom of heaven. This calling will vary from
person to person and from season to season. Initially, your calling will be simply to call upon the name of the Lord to become
his child—a new creation. This is the first teaching that will come
before understanding, much like Helen's sign language. The next
call of God in anyone's life is to fall in love with our Creator, Husband, Father, and Redeemer. Seeking to *fall in love* with him will
continually bring new and beautiful understanding of whom and
how he is.

Here is another example of the *why* of obedience. We are each
called to be holy and pure as he is pure and holy and walk in faith
in Christ despite the circumstances around us. Of course there
are many facets of this, but I'll speak of them generally. It seems

extremely difficult, especially in this day and age, to *abstain* from all the lusts of the flesh. It seems even more difficult to have *faith* when all the things in the natural don't add up to victory! There are many forms of wickedness that we excuse in our lives. We justify our *exceptions* to God's rules by telling ourselves "we aren't hurting anyone," or "it's just this one thing," or "he'll forgive me every time I repent." We ask ourselves, "What will this one thing hurt? It's just this or that." We have anxiety attacks, buckets of tears, and nervousness, but proclaim faith in the one true God.

Though we choose to let all of this to be allowed to stay in an otherwise clean vessel of God, we wonder why our prayers don't get answered the way we think they should. We tell ourselves, and everyone around us, that we are a *good Christian*. We grumble and murmur about the slackness of God. We shake our fists at him in our hearts because, "After all I've done for him, this is the thanks I get?"

Take a look at James 5:15–16 (KJV): "And the prayer of faith shall save the sick, and the Lord shall raise him up; and if he has committed sins, they shall be forgiven him … the effectual fervent prayer of a righteous man availeth much." There are many other texts on these topics, but this one says so much! It states, in laymen terms that a person whose faith is grounded in Christ has the power! The person who earnestly seeks purity and holiness regardless of the lusts of their flesh has power!

In every life, saved or unsaved, suffering will come. That is part of the frailty of life which no one is exempt. It is obvious why the unbelieving suffer, so there's no need to cover that other than to say that they are out from under the protective *umbrella* covering of the blood of Christ. The believer, on the other hand, will also suffer. Without understanding of how the covenant covering works, we will become discouraged in our suffering and fall away in anger toward God.

Suffering can come to the believer for various reasons: generational or cultural curses that need to be dealt with by applying the blood, word curses from unholy vows (on purpose or through ignorance by self or others), satanic attacks upon the one in right standing with God, satanic attacks from moving out of the perfect will of God, testing of one's faith in God and his sovereignty, reaping what you sewn, and so on. There are many reasons one will suffer. Without understanding *what* you are dealing with by seeking him, you will become disheartened and fall away in the suffering. Some suffering must be endured for a season, where other suffering can simply be bound away and spirits loosed from their assignment over you (Matthew 18:18). It is the *understanding* that will usher peace in your structure in the midst of the storm. It is *faith* in who he is that will stabilize the structure before understanding comes.

God's people need understanding! You can be a born again believer and live a life of obedience in *bondage* or a life of obedience in *freedom!* Obedience from the mindset of, "I must obey the Law of God lest he punish me and condemn me," will keep one bound in a condition of being blind, deaf, and dumb. This person forgets to praise him when things go well, and are quick to condemn him when things go wrong. However, one who sets his heart on knowing intimately the one who created him for his good pleasure, to bless and commune, is the one whose acts of obedience set them free from this perverse generation! They will rejoice and be content no matter the circumstance, in suffering and in pleasure; poverty or abundance; emptiness and fullness (Philippians 4:11–13). This freedom of contentment in obedience can only come from knowing the very heart of God who calls them to such obedience. They are quick to bless him for the bounty and quicker to praise him in any storm. They may not care for the storm itself, but trust implicitly the one who controls the storm.

Let's talk a bit more about the very nature, the essence of God. I would like to expound upon just *who* he is and *how* he functions as the Supreme Being. Above all, God Almighty is the God of *unfailing love*. He created us to have someone with whom he could commune. He created us in his image. Bearing this in mind, know that as *you* want acceptance, love, mercy, compassion, tenderness, and freedom, he too desires these for and from us. We are created to love him with the love he pours out to us. He does not want *trained animals.* He desires a people who are obedient because we are in love with him and trust that his ways are higher than our own; more importantly, that he had to die for us to live. He is a *forgiving, merciful,* and *compassionate* God. He sent his son to die that we may live eternally with him, as well as live a fulfilled life of abundance while in this world of depravation and perversion. He forgave us our transgressions before we were ever born or committed our first offense. Even on the cross, he asked Father to forgive his murderers because he *understood* that they were ignorant of what they had done.

He is *patient* beyond all imagination. Not only is he patient, but he extends his patience that we may learn for ourselves how to be patient toward others. He is also joy, peace, kindness, goodness, faithfulness, gentleness, and self-control. All these things that he is, we are more than capable of being through his Holy Spirit planted within. He is majestic, the Lord of lords, King of kings, the pure, unblemished Lamb, the Comforter, Husband, Lover of your soul, Counselor, Alpha, Omega, Beginning and End, Redeemer, and Savior. It is his righteous right hand that saves and shelters those who seek refuge in him. The list is endless! He is everything good in this life!

If we would get even a glimpse of his purity, we would beg him to kill us due to our wickedness! Fortunately, he is such a magnificent God that he spares us in spite of ourselves. Knowing even a fragment of who he is should make one beg to understand obedience; to release unto him anything of the flesh that may separate us from him. How he has tolerated such a magnitude of iniquity is beyond me! I just bless his holy name for being so patient and kind toward me. He is life!

I was once a sinner, but now I am white as snow! I say again, you won't catch me referring to myself as an "old, dirty sinner"! No way! He died and rose again that I might live as an heir and child of God—I will not blaspheme this gift by calling myself something that is buried and passed away. I now live as Christ because of his splendid, gracious heart of love! Why wouldn't I, or you, O child of the King, want with all of our being to be obedient to the highest capability? *He is in you;* it is *his* power that allows this level of obedience. Begin to thank him for every commandment set before you because they are set in place to protect you!

■ ■ ■ ■ ■

Prayer:

"O merciful Savior, show me the simplicity of obedience with a heart completely given over to yours. I pray to know the freedom of obedience instead of the burden of it. Reveal to me in any way you desire what true obedience looks like that I may never cease to please you. I want to be as a poured out drink offering holy and acceptable to you. Burn me from the inside out so to be as a sweet, fragrant aroma to your nostrils. I pray that obedience will be a blessing to me instead of a curse."

> A wise man will hear and increase in learning, and a man of understanding will acquire wise counsel; to understand a proverb and a figure, the words of the wise and their riddles. The fear of the Lord is the beginning of knowledge; fools despise wisdom and instruction.
>
> Proverbs 1:3–7 (NAS)

Breaking
Through Invisible
BARRIERS

For he himself is our peace, who made both groups into one
and broke down the barrier of the dividing wall, by abolish-
ing in his flesh the enmity, which is the Law of commandments contained in ordinances, so that in himself he might
make the two into one new man, thus establishing peace.

Ephesians 2:14–17 (NAS)

Part of my most earnest desire is to teach people of every age, race,
gender, and denomination how to love and respect themselves so
they too can attain the high calling of Christ Jesus. As you know,
the greatest commandment is to love the Lord our God above all
else. The second is like it—love our neighbor as ourselves.

That is exactly what we do! The problem is not the command,
but rather the lack of understanding of *how* to love ourselves. Most
of us hate ourselves so we hate others. We, the human race, are
insecure and angry for a million different reasons, so we belittle and
degrade others to make ourselves feel better. When we learn from
the heavenly Father how to reverently love and fear *him*, we will
better understand how to love ourselves. Once we get that concept,
then we will begin to love our neighbors in the way the Lord God
intended. Our closest neighbors are in fact our families: husbands,

wives, children, parents, siblings. We traditionally are the worst to the ones we are to love the most. Even when we desperately try to change, there seems to be invisible barriers standing in our way. These invisible barriers are the generational cycles/patterns/ strongholds most people never can comprehend how to break from themselves.

This reading is designed to take you through the basic but necessary steps to get you to the place where you can *receive* love from him. Once you get to that place of reception, you will be able to move further into love so as to *give* love. No one is capable of giving what they have never known existed. With this teaching, you will begin to learn how to apply the love of Christ Jesus to the invisible walls that stand in your way and walk in freedom. He is the ultimate barrier breaker as noted in Ephesians 2 above!

Envision yourself as a jar. If the jar is filled with filthy, slimy water—there is no room for clean, pure water. Even if there were empty space, the present filth would contaminate the clean. Both Galatians 5:9 and 1 Corinthians 5:6 speak of a little leaven leavening the entire lump. In the Old Testament, repeatedly the Lord makes abundantly clear that the clean does not make the unclean clean, but the unclean makes the clean unclean. The jar must be emptied and cleaned before it can be refilled with anything good. Otherwise, whatever you try to put into yourself that is of God, will become contaminated and, consequently, useless.

To be *emptied,* you must have a willing desire to look at the filth within; to accept what he shows you without condemnation. The *cleansing* is repenting of and rebuking whatever God reveals in your heart that is not of him, whether it comes from generations before you, or something new you brought in yourself. The *filling* is receiving as absolute truth that his ways are indeed above your own, and accepting that his ways are exceedingly greater than anything of your flesh (the natural man).

God has given us tools to move mountains that have been building for centuries!

> Though we walk in the flesh, we do not war according to
> the flesh, for the weapons of our warfare are not of the flesh,
> but divinely powerful for the destruction of fortresses. We
> are destroying speculations and every lofty (high) thing
> raised up against the knowledge of God, and we are taking
> every thought captive to the obedience of Christ, and we are
> ready to punish all disobedience, whenever your obedience
> is complete.
>
> 2 Corinthians 10:4–6 (NAS)

You can utilize these spiritual weapons when you *make* yourself
teachable and willing to face things that are very ugly about yourself.
It is a progressive work, but the payoff is priceless! Notice the verses
above state that *we* are to take every thought captive (prisoner).
There are thought patterns that go back many generations. But, if
you are willing to say, "No more!" to the traditions that have held
you and your family in bondage, supernatural change will come. It
is altogether possible when anchored in the Word of God! Knowledge (and comprehension of it) is power, so set your mind and heart
to know the power and authority he gave with his life!

"…Yes, the perpetual mountains were shattered, the ancient
hills collapsed. His ways are everlasting" (Habakkuk 3:6, NAS).

As the body of Christ, we must be a people merged together
through his blood. As I mentioned in the introduction, this merging together as one is exactly what will usher and establish peace
in your life as an individual, a family, and as a collective people!
Jesus Christ is the quintessential barrier breaker! The anointing of
Almighty God breaks *all* yokes of bondage!

So many families and ministries today are being ripped apart by
open doors of destruction. I could list a million scenarios, but, for
sake of time, paper, and ink, I will get to the root of these problems.
All parents were once children. I am going to throw a blanket rule
upon an entire people, so please forgive me if you are the exception.
Generally speaking, if you were an abused child, you only know
abuse. Unless someone comes along to teach you differently, you

become a parent that abuses. Likewise, if you were neglected, you neglect; rejected, you reject; talked down to, you talk down to your children; if all you heard was negative talk, you exude the same; if you were told you would be nothing, you speak the same words, and so on.

The root of this process is the law from God which is the *law of increase*. I learned this from John and Paula Sanford years ago. God set it in motion in the Garden with Adam and Eve. They were to *multiply*. Through obedience to the Father, the multiplication was for blessing. Although after sin, the increase became that of curses. Like throwing a ball against a wall, the ball doesn't change. It merely comes back to you with greater force than which it was thrown. This understanding being established, you will begin to grasp how each generation gets worse and worse. The sin and negativity continue to become more intense and harder to break. Only the proper *application* of the blood of Jesus Christ can break such a generational stronghold, pattern, and mindset!

My strong desire as from the Lord is to teach people how to deal with their own issues so that they can live a life set apart unto our Holy God. You cannot tell a person how to live correctly if you don't know how yourself. This is where personal accountability comes in. Most want to blame their problems on everyone and everything around them. Yes, there are people and circumstances that make life difficult. They are set in place on purpose by Satan to discourage and destroy you.

However, when you begin to *choose to change your vantage point* from the earthy to the heavenly, you won't be able to stop yourself from seeing things completely differently! You will begin to understand that what Satan intends against you for evil, God in his sovereignty and wisdom purposes it for your good *if* you love him. Satan has no authority to do anything without consent from God (Romans 8:28; Job 1; Genesis 50:20).

For instance, when you look at the life of Joseph in Genesis and all of the bad encounters that came his way, by chapter fifty and verse twenty, he tells his brothers (who were afraid he would return evil to them after the death of their father), "As for you, you meant evil against me, but God meant it for good in order to bring about this present result, to preserve many people alive" (NAS). The bottom line in this message is that, though times can be tough and bring much travail, God always has something excellent and bountiful at the end of it.

As a person who has already made mistakes, know that you can do all things through Christ who gives you strength! The only irreversible things are the ones not surrendered to the hand of God, which cannot be shortened. The longer there has been a problem, the longer it will take to come out. There is a process to everything. It took time to get in the mess; therefore, it will take time to come out, which is why now is the best time to begin! The hope is *knowing* and *trusting through faith* that God is greater than the situation, so learn to become patient as he is patient. Don't seek God one day, and if it doesn't change overnight, throw your hands in the air in defeat and go back to what you are used to. *Impatience* is a key factor in Satan's success of your defeat!

With this foundation laid, let's look at some basics about God and his Word so you can better analyze whatever junk may be in you that stems all the way back to your birth and before. Unforgiveness and judgment against others are key elements that keep you forever bound. They are the opposite of love. They stand as barriers between you and the blessings of God, as well as you and undefiled relationships with those in your life. Note the next few texts:

■ ■ ■ ■ ■

"*You have no excuse,* you who pass judgment on someone else, for at whatever point you judge the other, you are condemning yourself, because you who pass judgment do the same things" (Romans 2:1, NAS).

"For if you forgive others for their transgressions, your heavenly Father will also forgive you. But if you do not forgive others, then your Father will not forgive your transgressions" (Matthew 6:14–15, NAS).

"There is no fear in love; but perfect love casts out fear, because fear involves punishment, and the one who fears is not perfected in love. We love, because he first loved us" (1 John 4:18–19, NAS).

■ ■ ■ ■ ■

As you can plainly see, *unforgiveness* and harbored *judgment* are a downfall. Hebrews 12:15 (NAS) reads *"See to it* that no one *misses the grace* of God and that no *bitter root* grows up to cause trouble and defile many. *Resentment,* as mentioned in Job 36:21, is the equivalent of godlessness. I challenge you to dig deeply into your past and inspect your heart. Only God can reveal to you the genuine condition of your heart. Seek him to expose all roots of bitterness, unforgiveness, and judgment that have been allowed to take hold and defile not only you but family and other relationships in your life. As hard as this may be, the outcome is far superior to your current condition.

Let's look at a hypothetical situation:

Say there is a young *boy* of four or five, and he has a mother that is an addict of some sort. Because she is either working odd jobs or high, the house stays a mess. His father is nowhere to be found. If he were found, he would be without a care for him, his siblings, or mother. He is heartless and gutless. Because of this situation, the boy is often left alone or with siblings, a babysitter, or revolving family members or acquaintances. His mother is absent both when physically present and when she is working to put food on the table.

Now look at the young *girl* he will eventually marry. Her mother is home because they have financial stability, even enough for a housekeeper. She is so busy playing tennis and shopping that she forgets to spend quality time helping the girl with her homework or simply listening to the concerns of her heart. The father is a well-respected businessman. Everyone thinks he is wonderful. Unfortunately, he is molesting her in the middle of the night and when the mother is out. He tells the girl that this is the way he shows *love*. She hates it, but she doesn't want him to stop *loving* her.

Even as small children, both this man and woman sense the rejection and fear deeply within. Throughout the years, they pack it into their hearts as they constantly long to hear, "I love you. Good job. Well-done. You are so sweet. What a good boy/girl you are." When they don't get these words or any other signs of love, they become more and more distant, shut down, repressed, depressed, and angry. When the girl's father keeps defiling her in acts of *love*, she begins to believe that there is something wrong with her. She never develops a pure concept of love and affection, authority or protection. She hates her father for his incest and her mother for not making it go away (along with everything else)! He hates both of his parents for their wrongs against him. Judgment against their parents builds in their little hearts.

Years go by and they somehow survive childhood—at least in the physical. They are able to do for themselves, make their own money, and move away from the cold madness they have always known. They each say to themselves, "I will never be like my mother and father! Never!" Eventually they meet one another and marry. All seems grand for a moment in time. Then the babies arrive, one right after the other. The bills start piling higher and higher. They begin to become stressed, agitated, and heavily burdened. They start seeing things in each other that weren't visible before. It isn't that they changed during their marriage; it is that their core person is being uncovered and unraveled. They begin to feel trapped in a cold and loveless marriage. The invisible barriers in their hearts that were built all those many years ago become more and more apparent, but no one understands *what* they are seeing or *why*.

The man begins to drink to push out the pain and stress, and the woman neglects the house and the children. He begins to look at his sons and daughters in an unholy manner. He is drawn to them as he used to be to his wife. He justifies his actions because the children are his own, and he feels he can do with them what he wants. Cycles they swore they would never repeat are being repeated, and they are spinning further and further out of control! The ball I mentioned earlier is coming out in them with greater intensity than with their parents. The *increase* is that of curses instead of blessings.

Let me explain what has happened here. There are bitter root *expectancies* and *judgments*. Bitter root expectancy is based on emotion, expecting that whatever happens to you at one point will always happen—it is psychological. As in the scenario above, because of her experiences with her dad, she *expects* men to molest children. Therefore, she was drawn to one who does.

Bitter root *judgment* is based on *law* and is stronger than expectancy. You will be judged as you judge because it is the *law of God* (Reference Romans 2:1). Again, this is from the teaching of John and Paula Sanford's study, in which I fully agree. I recommend getting some of their studies for more detailed information.

Both the man and woman in this scenario passed *judgment* against their parents early in life. They did not realize what they were doing, but it happened all the same. No one can blame them given the circumstances, but it is against the law of God nonetheless. As the two became one flesh in marriage, they merged all of their bitter roots. There was a multiplication (not addition) of garbage that had been packed in the basements of their hearts! When they became one in marriage, so did their judgments. At whatever points they judged their parents, they eventually turned to do the same things.

The words in Hebrews 12 read, "See to it…" That means *you* take care of it! It is *your* responsibility to keep yourself cleansed of bitterness (unforgiveness). Forgiveness is two-fold. Most realize on some level that they must forgive, but they generally don't realize that after you forgive someone you must then ask the Lord to *forgive you* for judgment. It is part of the filth that must be removed before purity can be put in. Most forgive begrudgingly out of obligation because it is the *right thing to do.*

Matthew 18:35 reads that you must forgive *from the heart.* That means idle words of forgiveness are useless. Unless you forgive with the boundless love of Christ, you have not been set free. A heart truly set on pleasing the Father is a heart ready at all times to forgive. This is the essence of true love. It is a *sacrificial forgiveness* just as God's forgiveness is 100 percent sacrificial. Until you *see to it* to cleanse your heart of hatred of any kind, unforgiveness, and judgment against your parents, grandparents, siblings, bosses, strangers, spouses (ex or current), or whomever, you will continue to conduct yourself in ways you do not want. You won't be able to stop being like those you hate! It is the law of God. Hence, those around you will also, on some level, hate you. The *generational patterns* of hatred can only be overridden by supernatural love *purposefully* brought in by you through Christ as you seek it from the heavenly realm.

If you want your children to stop being like you, *you* must stop being like you! You cannot do this on your own. Only a supernatural move of God can incite an otherwise impossible change of your character. A friend of mine called me some time ago asking advice on how to get her six-year-old to stop acting with ingratitude and haughtiness. I told her (with love) that the only way she could teach humility and gratefulness was to change her own conduct and ask the Lord to teach *her* gratitude and humility. She didn't like that at all! She told me of her difficulty to be humble and gracious. I insisted that her efforts were useless because children live what they see, not what they hear from lip service, as well as living according to unbroken, unrepented generational patterns.

You as the parent must *humble yourself* in a childlike manner before Almighty God. Ask him to show you every wicked way within *you* so *you* may confess, repent, and be made whole. Until you let *him* fix you, *you* cannot fix your child. No amount of yelling, belittling, restriction, beating, or insults will change them. No matter how many times you start a sentence with, "When I was your age..." or, "Don't be like me," or, "If you only knew what I know," or, "it was good enough for me," they will continue on the wrong path. Without repenting of *your* judgment and all bitterness, you continue to fuel the fire of rebellion in your children. You need to take the time to look within, allowing the Holy Spirit to do a work of love in *you,* and be patient upon the Lord to do a work in them. Your job is to change *yourself!*

Most importantly, your job is to learn to love your children (and the other people in your life) just as they are; something you probably never received yourself from people around you. Christ loved you before you changed! One is much more willing to bend when they know you love them regardless. Without love, there is nothing and you are nothing. Love is the perfect bond of unity. Begin to ask the Lord to show you how to love as he loves the church; to restore your broken, shattered heart that was broken by your parents, ex-spouse, or whomever.

Love is a rare thing in the world, and to my chagrin, within the body of Christ. Take a look at God's description of true love. We are to seek to know the height, width, length, and depth of his unfailing love. Just because you never knew love through a human, know that he wants to show you in another way. Whatever that way may be, you will be certain that it is from him supernaturally and nothing of human ability.

> If I speak with the tongues of men and of angels, but do not have love, I have become a noisy gong or a clanging cymbal. If I have the gift of prophecy, and know all mysteries and all knowledge; and if I have all faith, so as to remove mountains, but do not have love, I am nothing. And if I give all my possessions to feed the poor, and if I surrender my body to be burned, but do not have love, it profits me nothing. Love is patient, love is kind and is not jealous; love does not brag and is not arrogant, does not act unbecomingly; it does not seek its own, is not provoked, does not take into account a wrong suffered, does not rejoice in unrighteousness, but rejoices with the truth; bears all things, believes all things, hopes all things, endures all things. Love never fails... but

now faith, hope, love, abide these three; but the greatest of
these is love.

1 Corinthians 13:1–8, 13 (NAS)

I looked further in these texts, and verse 11 reads, "When I was a
child, I used to speak like a child, think like a child, reason like a
child; when I became a man, I did away with childish things." 1
Corinthians 3:3 states, "for you are still fleshly. For since there is
jealousy and strife among you, are you not fleshly, and are you not
walking like mere men?" This jumped out at me as though I had
never read it before! Parents who harbor hatred against someone
are still acting like a child because they still are children. Their
body grew older, but their inner man stayed in the mindset of the
neglected, hurt, abused child. If this is you, you are a child trying to
teach a physical child how to be something you are not.

■ ■ ■ ■ ■

"For many walk, of whom I often told you, and now tell you even
weeping, that they are enemies of the cross of Christ, whose end is
destruction, whose god is their appetite, and whose glory is in their
shame, who set their minds on earthly things" (Philippians 3:18–19,
NAS).

"Therefore, *if* you have been raised up with Christ, keep seeking the things above, where Christ is, seated at the right hand of
God. Set your mind on the things above, not on the things that are
on earth. For you have died and your life is hidden with Christ in
God" (Colossians 3:1–2, NAS).

■ ■ ■ ■ ■

We must each *choose* to come up and out of all old ways of thinking and into the heavenly mindset of Christ Jesus. It must be a
conscious act of your will. Many parents, especially those who have
children at a young age, become jealous of them. Their jealousy

is driven by their children's excelled intellect, abilities, abundance, opportunities, charm, looks, friends, whatever. This is not love, but another form of childish hatred. Jealousy is a murdering spirit and needs to be addressed as such.

Many parents are driven by fear: fear that their kids will turn out as worthless as they believe themselves to be. They are afraid that if their offspring ends up in the same condition as them, shame will be upon their heads. The flip side of that is the parent's inner fear that their child will exceed far beyond them, hence bringing that parent shame in another way. No parent wants to be shamed by their children. *Shame* seems to be the key, and shame is steeped in pride. Pride is always a blockade between us and peace, love, and joy. It must be torn down by the one operating in it!

Pride ushers fear of anything and everything. A spirit and mindset of pride dictates that you focus on how your children will make *you* look; either not good enough because they turn out just like you, not as well as you, or too good because they excel beyond you. This person seems to feel that if they are *stupid*, it reflects stupidity on them. If they excel and exceed expectations, it reflects stupidity on them because they never went that far! Please recognize that it is a mind of self-absorption, and that is not love.

Any form of fear other than holy fear of God is never of God! "Fear is to Satan as faith is to God," I heard Creflo Dollar say. Look at it this way, when you fear the Lord, you find yourself right in his midst. When you fear anything of this earth (like Job), the very thing you fear tends to be what you find yourself in the presence of. Job says in chapter three verse twenty-five (NAS), "What I feared has come upon me; what I dreaded has happened to me, I have no peace, no quietness; I have no rest, but only turmoil." Stop being afraid of your children and other people around you—both their failures and successes. If you are in constant fear of your child being a failure, you will somehow push them to the place of failure. Each generation should be greater than the last, not worse! I personally look at my girls, and I want them to be better at everything than I am. Of course, I want to give them a run for their money, but that is just striving for more greatness to honor the Father. At whatever level of greatness I achieve, it means even higher levels for them. We need as parents, bosses, co-workers, ministers, and teachers to set *heavenly* standards and goals instead of complacency, lethargy, indifference, and laziness. This world has enough of that already!

Once you start calling in the anointing of our great God, as it flows in and through you, changing you from the inside out, those around you will begin to take hold. These *children* can be physical or spiritual, young or old. We all nurture someone in our lives, whether we mean to or not. Freedom breeds freedom just as fear breeds fear; or anger, anger; or sadness, sadness, and so on. Everything repeats after its own kind.

It's time to start breaking through invisible blockades by the blood of the Lamb; through all the generational, cultural, and spoken curses, patterns, strongholds, and traditions from yourself and your lineage. Jesus Christ bore the curse on the cross of Calvary. Begin to seek how to properly *apply the blood* to the specific strongholds of your territory. It's a simple thing, really. Jesus laid out every supply for our needs. We just need wisdom, which comes from *fearing the Lord,* to operate in discernment as to where and when to anoint the specific wounds in our lives.

I will briefly explain how curses operate invisibly in our lives. The Old Testament reads that generational curses last for three to four generations. These are sins of the fathers (relatives) passed down. If a problem is generational, you will be able to look back and see a pattern of others having the same problems. Many say there are no more generational curses—that people act out of *learned behavior*—but I know many people who act like their parents or grandparents, yet never laid eyes on them! For instance, you may have a foul tempter you can't seem to shake, though you try. Look in your history to see if your mother, father, or grandparents had this problem. If so, and you are a child of God through the blood of Jesus, all you have to do is pray something like this: "Dear Jesus,

I plead the blood of Jesus Christ over myself and my offspring and ask you to break the curse of (blank) off of us for a thousand generations from both my mother and father's side of the family all the way back to Adam and Eve. I repent of this and ask you to replace it with (the opposite). Where there was a curse of anger, I now bind peace and love to myself in its place." Any time you take something out, put something of God in its place. You don't want to leave empty space for Satan to fill.

Everyone has some kind of generational baggage until it is confronted with the blood. Many people have a *curse of rejection* that dates back to being in their mother's womb. This tends to make a person be rejected as well as making them tend to reject others, especially their own children. Remember, as you pass your personal judgment against another person, one day you will likely turn and do the same thing that you are condemning. You hated your parents for rejecting you in some way; therefore, you turn and reject your children. This is in the simplest form, God's law of passing judgment in motion. It doesn't matter what *surface* issues bring about your problems; it is always the *root* that you need to seek, locate, and pull out!

To find out if this applies to you, ask yourself if your parents wanted you; be honest with yourself. Did they want you to be different in any way than what you are? Some parents wanted a boy but got a girl or vice versa. It is possible that they loved you but the timing seemed wrong because they weren't married. Maybe they wanted you, but their parents rejected you *and* them for whatever reason.

Maybe you have issues with hatred, lying, perversion, shame, guilt, depression, thievery, addiction, fear, abandonment, torment, rebellion, insanity, poverty, insecurity, fornication, adultery, imprisonment, unwed pregnancy, or even death. There are many more than these, but this gives you an idea of what you may be dealing with. If you see a line of suicide, premature death, or murder, there is probably a curse of death over you. These are things that will keep you from walking in freedom, not only with God, but with the people in your life.

If you strongly desire to live in peace, seek the Author of Peace. He offers so much more than a spot reserved for you in heaven! With knowledge and understanding of who he is, and how he operates, you can live a life abounding in peace and true love! It is not a fairy tale of old!

By seeking to get your inner man set free of excess weight, you can't help but become a better parent, spouse, boss, or leader of any kind. Your children and those who watch you for guidance need you to be a righteous man or woman of God. They need desperately to see you live a life that constantly seeks improvement of self so that they can emulate you. Even if they snub their nose at you on the surface, they secretly admire you for seeking change in your own life and will want it for themselves. We need to each choose to set our own bar of excellence higher than it has ever been. There are word curses that we speak over ourselves and others. Word curses are things we speak with our tongue. There are too many Scripture references to write, but the Bible makes it clear in the Old and New Testament that with the words of our mouths we bring either blessings or curses (Proverbs 18:20; 1 Peter 3:8–13; James 3; James 1:26; Matthew 15:11–19). When you constantly belittle people, you self-prophesy. Whatever negative things you have spoken over them or yourself, ask the Lord immediately to forgive you of those words and then take authority over them. Command them to be bound away and then loose the abundance of Christ into them/you as a necklace around their necks and a bracelet around their wrists (Matthew 18:16; Proverbs 3:3).

Begin this process with your immediate family. Ask the Lord to break every negative or derogatory word you (or anyone) have ever spoken over your children, spouse, or self with the blood. Then begin to speak what you desire to see that is pure and holy. Don't be afraid or prideful of apologizing to them either. They need to see humility displayed through you.

God already knows the problem, so you don't have to tell him in your prayers! Stop speaking the problem and start declaring the solution. If your child is rebellious, after you break that curse from them, command a spirit of rebellion (or any other kind) to be loosed from its assignment over them. Then decree, "I thank you, Almighty God, that my child no longer sits, stands, or walks in the way of the sinner, wicked, or mocker. I thank you that they delight in your Word, and on your Word they meditate day and night. I thank you, Father, that they are like a mighty oak planted by the streams of water, and in due season bear good fruit. Their leaf does not wither, and everything they touch prospers (Psalm 1)."

Get to know the Word of God intimately, and you'll begin to declare the written Word over others. The prayers of the righteous avail much (James 5:15–16). Leap into the process of change! The Lord God says through his Word that we are new *in* him; to put the past behind you, and press on toward the mark of holiness (Philippians 3:14)!

Again, above all else, begin to seek to know the height, width, length, and depth of his love. He loves you just as you are! He loved you before you were born. He died for you before you were born. He loves you in your hatred, and he will love you through it. He is the lover of your spirit, soul, and body. Just as you need the love of the Father, those people in your life need your love. Give them better than what you were given and better than what you currently think they deserve! Ask him to plow up the fallowed ground of your heart to expose the good, fresh soil (Jeremiah 4:3; Hosea 10:12). Arm yourself daily with the readiness of forgiveness.

> "My Father is glorified by this, that you bear much fruit, and so prove to be my disciples. Just as the Father has loved me, I have also loved you; abide in my love. *If* you keep my commandments, you will abide in my love; just as I have kept my Father's commandments and abide in his love … this is my *commandment,* that you *love one another,* just as I have loved you … you are my friends *if* you do what I command you … I *command you,* that you *love one another.*"
>
> John 15:8–10, 12–14, 17 (NAS)

■ ■ ■ ■ ■

Prayer:

"Oh gracious, heavenly please lay your heart in my body and consume me! Please let me be overtaken by your supernatural love. Pour out your love upon my head as the healing balm of Gilead. Let me open and expose myself to you completely. I desire to be a person of virtue, integrity, honor, love, peace, patience, and endless generosity. Teach me how to be unashamed of how you created me, fearfully and wonderfully. Show me how to not be prideful of how I look or what I possess on the outside; for I am saved by your grace like all those before and after me. Teach me how to be a gracious host for your Holy Spirit within. Father, give me the grace to see the evil I have allowed in my camp. I want my territory clean, unblemished, and spotless before you. Show me which relationships are ungodly and give me the supernatural strength to end them. Bring into my life relationships that are pure and holy. Give me, O gracious merciful God, clean hands and a pure heart before you, before man and before the demons of hell. I pray, O Sovereign Lord, that you, man, and demons will testify that I am a child of the King! Amen and amen. Selah."

Live Under Grace,
NOT LAW

"For sin shall not be master over you, for you are not under law but under grace" (Romans 6:14, NAS).

"But he gives greater grace (more and more continually). Therefore it says, 'God is opposed to the proud, but gives grace to the humble.' Submit therefore to God, resist the devil and he will flee from you. Draw near to God and he will draw near to you. Cleanse your hands, you sinners; and purify your hearts…" (James 4:6–8, NAS).

■ ■ ■ ■ ■

Made in Perfection

"Then God said, "Let Us make man in Our image, according to Our likeness; and let them rule over the fish of he sea and over the birds of the sky and over the cattle and over all the earth, and over every creeping thing that creeps on the earth." God created man in his own image, in the image of God he created him; male and female he created them" (Genesis 1:26–27, NAS).

■ ■ ■ ■ ■

Creep: 1. move with the body prone and close to the ground; 2. come, go, or move slowly and stealthily or timidly (fearfully); 3. enter slowly (into a person's affections, awareness, etc.) (a feeling crept over her); 5. (of the flesh) feel as if insects, etc., were creeping over it, as a result of fear, etc; 6. a feeling of revulsion or fear

Notice the words *us* and *our*. These refer to the Triune God: *Father, Son, and Holy Spirit*. He said that he created man (you and me) in *his* likeness. We are (supposed to be) a reflection of him. Unfortunately, we tend to imitate the image of Satan, a creation of God, more than God the Creator! He gave to mankind (the upright) authority over the things in the air, the sea, and every living thing that creeps on the earth.

Man should never *creep*. We are designed to walk upright, both physically and spiritually. Men are created to rule *together*—not one another! Things that creep are things that are fearful, timid, sneaky, and close to the ground. This is a description of Satan as a snake—creepy! He creeps deceitfully so to attack unawares. He had to be redesigned (from something upright originally) into the image of something slinky, without arms or legs, so he could not lift himself high. We, mankind, are created to be high and lifted up. In *his* image: Jesus has a humble (lowly) heart enabling *God* to lift him high above all in due season. The only thing low about you should be your heart that he may be able to lift you high in due season.

The Fall of Man

"Then the eyes of both of them were opened, and they knew that they were naked; and they sewed fig leaves together and made themselves loin coverings" (Genesis 3:7, NAS).

■ ■ ■ ■ ■

Adam and Eve's eyes were opened through sin after eating of the tree of knowledge of good and evil. Now they could *see* right and wrong with both their physical and spiritual eyes. Before the fall, their world was perfect. God graciously blinded them to protect them, but the blinders came off.

Afterwards, through shame of sin, they *crept* in the presence of the Lord. Shame is the *emotion* that makes you *feel* creepy and unworthy. Being led by your emotions (feelings) always leads you away from Holy Spirit. They covered their shame. Before sin, they were naked, *without* shame. They had nothing to hide. The *creepy* one had infiltrated their thinking with lies, shame, and fear. In the natural, we are ashamed of the way we look, walk, talk, and act. We are constantly covering something (spiritual, physical, mental, emotional, financial).

The only way to become upright again and able to stand unashamed and uncovered in the sight of an unblemished God is to humbly repent and give a sacrifice of atonement for sin. The atonement covers whatever is corrupt. This is why all sacrifices for sin had to be flawless.

The Curse

The Lord God said to the serpent, "Because you have done this, cursed are you more than all cattle … I will put enmity between you and the woman, and between your seed and her seed; he shall bruise you on the head, and you shall bruise him on the heel." Then to Adam he said, "Because you have listened to the voice of your wife, and have eaten from the tree about which I commanded you, saying, 'you shall not eat from it'; cursed is the ground because of you; in toil you will eat of it all the days of your life … so he drove the man out …"

Genesis 3:14, 17, 24 (NAS)

Adam gave the authority that God had originally given him (over the earth) to Satan. In giving this authority over to Satan, he brought a curse upon himself and all mankind: "Cursed is the ground." He cursed himself—he is *of the ground.* His place of origin, the ground, is cursed. This is a picture of each of us. Our *ground,* natural blood-line, is cursed. We come into the world at physical birth cursed. No one is exempt.

No Excuse, O Man of Sin!

"For the wrath of God is revealed from heaven against all ungodliness and unrighteousness of men who suppress the truth in unrighteousness, because that which is known about God is evident within them; for God made it evident to them. For since the creation of the world his invisible attributes, his eternal power and divine nature, have been clearly seen, being understood through what has been made, so that they are without excuse" (Romans 1:18–19, NAS).

> There will be tribulation and distress for every soul of man who does evil, of the Jew first and also of the Greek, but glory and honor and peace to everyone who does good, to the Jew first and also to the Greek. For there is no partiality with God. For all who have sinned without the Law will also perish without the Law, and all who have sinned under the Law will be judged by the Law; for it is not the hearers of the Law who are just before God, but the doers of the Law will be justified. For when Gentiles who do not have the Law do instinctively the things of the Law, these, not having the Law, are to themselves, in that they show the work of the Law written in their hearts, their conscience bearing witness and their thoughts alternately accusing or else defending them, on the day when, according to my gospel, God will judge the secrets of men through Christ Jesus.
>
> Romans 2:9–16 (NAS)

"Much more then, having now been justified by his blood, we shall be saved from the wrath of God through him" (Romans 5:9, NAS).

"For I consider that the sufferings of this present time are not worthy to be compared with the glory that is to be revealed to us" (Romans 8:18, NAS).

■ ■ ■ ■ ■

Law is evident in man even without having to be physically present. It is invisible before it is visible! Romans 1:18–19 states plainly that *no one* is without excuse. If a person who has never heard the Law knows instinctively to do what is right, how much more will a person be held accountable for their sins when they know the Law, yet break it? Because we are created "in his image," instinctively (whether acknowledged or not) the Law can be recognized when one chooses. In this, no one is *guiltless,* even if you are wrongly accused in a specific situation.

These verses read that the evidence of God is all around for those who will allow the eyes of their spirit man to be opened. Those who do evil simply suppress the truth of Christ by choice; it is not because God has not made himself known to them in their inner man. This being said, no person is without excuse when they choose evil on any level of any kind. God put his Law on the earth *with* mankind, and it has always been evident for those who seek to know. Everything created was breathed into being by his life breath. He cannot be denied, try though people may!

This is why justification had to come through his blood for all mankind; *before* a person is born and able to sin. *All* sin is covered before it is ever manifested. No matter how *good* a person thinks they are, they have no *good* lest Christ dwell *within* and *through* them. Whether a person has been born with or without the physical knowledge of laws, they are accountable *to* the Law. His invisible attributes have been "clearly seen."

Romans 2:9–16 makes this apparent. Those who keep the Law (through knowledge of it or instinctively) will be justified; those who do not, will not. Justification came through the fulfillment of the Law through the blood (death, burial, and resurrection) of Jesus Christ. The only way for a person to keep the Law is through receiving his blood atonement. Without reception, they break *all* of the Law by rejection of the Son of God and are accountable on the Day of Judgment. It is through his Spirit within that corrects and directs to help you keep the individual laws.

It is only through faith in Christ Jesus and his blood that you can attain the promise of God (eternal life) and individual promises while living on earth. Many are born *under* the Law naturally as Jewish people, being Abraham's natural descendants. However, through faith *in* Christ Jesus, anyone has opportunity to become an heir to the throne of God and all of his promises! Those who are *natural* descendants are not descendants *spiritually* if they reject the Son. Likewise, no matter what crime or sin you committed in the past, it is paid in full, giving you free access to peace, joy, and freedom within through repentance!

It is the knowledge and comprehension that we are no longer oppressed underneath the law that helps us attain freedom as well as intimacy with God. Once we become adopted into the kingdom of God through the blood of his son, we are no longer bound to the pressures of being perfect as the law demands. Yes, we are to obey the laws, but the entirety of the relationship with God becomes changed through this understanding. We are now under the blanket of grace instead of the weightiness of law. By getting this concept, we are able to become intimate with the God who is in love with us and does mean all for our good, as opposed to the idea that all the law is set over us to crush us.

Jesus Removed the Curse on the Cross

For as many as are of the works of the Law are under a curse;
for it is written, "Cursed is everyone who does not abide by
all things written in the book of the law, to perform them."

Now that no one is justified by the Law before God is evident; for, "The righteous man shall live by faith." However, the Law is not of faith; on the contrary, "he who practices them shall live by them." Christ redeemed us from the curse of the Law, having become a curse for us–for it is written, "cursed is everyone who hangs on a tree." In order that in Christ Jesus the blessing of Abraham might come to the Gentiles, so that we would receive the promise of the Spirit through faith.

Galatians 3:10–14 (NAS)

By law, the whole human race is cursed because, in sinful flesh, it is impossible to fulfill the law (verse 10). Jesus became our curse; therefore, you no longer have to bear it (verse 13).

Surely he took up our infirmities and carried our sorrows ... he was pierced for our transgressions, he was crushed for our iniquities; the punishment that brought us peace was upon him, and by his wounds (stripes) we are healed. By oppression and judgment he was taken away. And who can speak of his descendants? For he was cut off from the land of the living; for the transgression of my people he was stricken. He was assigned a grave with the wicked and with the rich is his death, though he had done no violence, nor was any deceit in his mouth.

Isaiah 53:4–5, 8–9 (NAS)

He bore your sorrows, transgressions, and iniquities. The punishment he bore (that belonged to you) brought *you* peace (freedom)! He was oppressed and judged so that you do not have to bear oppression and judgment. Look where it reads, "he had done no violence, nor was deceit in his mouth." This implies that those who justifiably hang are those who have done violence or were deceitful in some capacity. He paid for your violence and deceit! This is where you must allow your faith (that he instilled within you) to activate. It takes *faith* to forgive yourself as he has forgiven you; believing that he did in fact bear your sins, violence, and deceit.

Remember, as you forgive yourself of your past wrongs, allow him to wash away the sin and replace it with his attributes: love, joy, peace, patience, kindness, goodness, faithfulness, gentleness, self-control, compassion, mercy, humility, obedience. It is only when you can forgive yourself and let his grace *replace* the guilt that you can begin to forgive others.

You are to love others as you love yourself. Receive grace (God's unlimited favor), apply it in your everyday life, and you will begin to be able to freely give it to others!

> But some of the Pharisees said, 'Why do you do what is not lawful on the Sabbath?' And Jesus answering them said, "Have you not even read what David did when he was hungry, he and those who were with him, how he entered the house of God, and took and ate the consecrated bread which is not lawful for any to eat except the priests alone, and gave it to his companions?" And he was saying to them, "The Son of Man is Lord of the Sabbath." On another Sabbath he entered the synagogue and was teaching; and there was a man there whose right hand was withered. The scribes and the Pharisees were watching him closely to see if he healed on the Sabbath, so that they might find reason to accuse him. But he knew what they were thinking, and he said to the man with the withered hand, "Get up and come forward!" And he got up and came forward. And Jesus said to them, "I ask you, is it lawful to do good or to do harm on the Sabbath; to save a life or to destroy it?"
>
> Luke 6:2–9 (NAS)

"Jesus said to them, "The Sabbath was made for man, and not man for the Sabbath" (Mark 2:27, NAS).

"Do not think that I came to abolish the Law or the Prophets; I did not come to abolish but to fulfill. For truly I say to you, until heaven and earth pass away, not the smallest letter or stroke shall pass from the Law until all is accomplished. Whoever then annuls one of the least of these commandments, and teaches others to do the same, shall be called least in the kingdom of heaven; but whoever keeps and teaches them, he shall be called great in the kingdom of heaven" (Matthew 5:17–19, NAS).

■ ■ ■ ■ ■

The Law says not to work on the Sabbath, but Jesus said it is a law that brings bondage. The Sabbath was created for liberty, not a burden. The Sabbath was made for man, not man for the Sabbath! In the spiritual sense, he is the Sabbath (The Day of Rest). The Sabbath is the key (anointing) that unlocks the chains that have held you captive since natural birth.

God's Law is absolute. It cannot be changed and it is impossible to keep in the condition of sinful flesh. In being unable to keep the law, you are condemned by the Law that reveals your sin. Only a perfect man (Jesus Christ in human form) was able to accomplish and fulfill what you never could. Hence, you are released from the burden of the Law of bondage through his fulfillment!

■ ■ ■ ■ ■

"What I am saying is this: the Law, which came four hundred and thirty years later, does not invalidate a covenant previously ratified by God, so as to nullify the promise. For if the inheritance is based on law, it is no longer based on a promise; but God has granted it to Abraham by means of a promise. Why the Law then? It was added because of transgressions, having been ordained through angels by the agency of a mediator, until the seed would come to whom the promise had been made" (Galatians 3:19, NAS).

■ ■ ■ ■ ■

God's promises are intact and cannot be changed, no matter what. Inheritance to God is through promise, not law. Law came only to reveal sin so that you may realize your hopeless condition; therefore, the Law directs you to Jesus to know that, without him, you are doomed. Jesus is the mediator, your intercession for sin!

> But when the fullness of the time came, God sent forth his Son, born of a woman, born under the Law, so that he might redeem those who were under the Law, that we might receive the adoption as sons. Because you are sons, God has sent forth the Spirit of his Son into our hearts, crying, "Abba! Father!" Therefore you are no longer a slave, but a son; and if a son, then an heir through God.
>
> Galatians 4:4–7 (NAS)

He had to be born *into* bondage in order to break the cycle *of* bondage to be able to release you with authority through *chain of command* (verse four). This way, he could redeem you and have legal right to adopt you out of the *world of flesh* (sin nature, verse five)! Once you become a *son* through faith, you are deposited with the Son's spirit, the Holy Spirit, who now leads you instead of the old sin nature (verse seven). Holy Spirit anointing breaks all chains of bondage!

> Tell me, you who want to be under law, do you not listen to the law? For it is written that Abraham had two sons, one by the bondwoman and one by the free woman. But the son by the bondwoman was born according to the flesh, and the son by the free woman through the promise ... and your brothers, like Isaac, are children of promise. But at that time he who was born according to the flesh persecuted him who was born according to the Spirit, so it is now also. But what does the Scripture say? "Cast out the bondwoman and her son, for the son of the bondwoman shall not be an heir with the son of the free.
>
> Galatians 4:21–23, 28–31 (NAS)

Many choose to stay under the bondage of law (verse twenty-one). You are born either of the flesh, the law, or of the Spirit, through faith in Jesus (verse twenty-two). You are naturally born from your mother's womb *of the flesh.* Only through being born of the Spirit are you born of the free woman—the lineage of Christ. Eve became a bondwoman with the act of sin. In the natural, you are born *of Eve.* Mary is the free woman, the mother of Jesus. In the spiritual, you become born of Mary. This is neither to condemn Eve nor exalt Mary. It is simply the channel into the bloodline of Christ.

Slavery equals *no promise.* Freedom equals *covenant promise* (verse twenty-three). It was and is today; those of the flesh persecute those born of the Spirit. The world will never accept the Spirit or those he inhabits because the world, as a whole, is of the flesh (verse twenty-eight). That will soon end. Those born of the Spirit will rise because you are free through Christ (verse thirty)!

Bondwoman equals bondage under the law. Freewoman equals freedom through the promise which raised you above the law! If you are a blood-bought child of God, you are free, not a slave. Start living like it! You are a king among kings because your Daddy is the King of kings!

Grace Eternal: Put the Past Behind You!

"For sin shall not be master over you, for you are not under law but *under grace*" (Romans 6:14, NAS).

"Do not call to mind the former things, or ponder things of the past. Behold, I will do something new, now it will spring forth" (Isaiah 43:18–19, NAS).

"Brethren, I do not regard myself as having laid hold of it (perfection) yet; but one thing I do: *forgetting* what lies behind and reaching forward to what lies ahead, I press on toward the goal for the prize of the upward call of God in Christ Jesus" (Philippians 3:13–14, NAS).

"If we confess our sins, he is faithful and righteous to forgive us our sins and to cleanse us from *all* unrighteousness" (1 John 1:9, NAS).

■ ■ ■ ■ ■

Jesus Christ, because of his act on the cross, removed *all* condemnation that comes from the Law that reveals sin. He, taking your place, the last Adam in perfect form, took your sins to the cross. He, God Almighty in human form (who came as a descendant of Adam), fulfilled the requirement of law that you (also a descendant of Adam) could never fulfill. Before the cross, you were condemned to death. He did what you could not do because of sin nature. *He* fulfilled the perfection of the Law, and, through faith (applying the blood and righteousness of Jesus to your life), *you* are also considered having fulfilled the Law!

God's grace is enough for all eternity! It covers *all* sin—past, present, and future. Both in Isaiah and Philippians it states that each of us are to put our past behind us, remembering it no more. This is contrary to any concept of the world and the thinking of your natural man. I hear it said, "I'll forgive (self or others) but I'll never forget." That sounds good in theory, but it is completely against what God commands!

Paul afflicted, mocked, and murdered God's anointed. What if he sat around all day, every day condemning himself of his unworthy estate? He would have neglected and wasted the anointing God wanted to bring *in* and *through* him. To self-abase is to reject God's grace of forgiveness and throw it in the trash! The majority of the New Testament would not be what it is today had he not *forgotten* his past; meaning, he did not dwell on it. Every believer must view Paul as a *brother* in Christ who actually lived, not as some *feel-good* story of fiction. He was real. He lived, sinned, murdered, received grace, walked beyond his past, and allowed Holy Spirit from within to set the world ablaze with power and anointing!

There were always people who mocked, scorned, and doubted him. In the beginning, there were people afraid of him because of how he had conducted himself prior to his anointing. You, like Paul, will have to allow yourself time to be *established in righteousness* in the sight of others. You, though forgiven by God, will have to be patient with those around who are less forgiving. Remember, the best thing you can do is walk in patience and love toward those who oppose your newness of life. The more defensive you are, the more you will prove them right in their disbelief; the more loving, the more you prove Christ and his love! God is your defender. He will prove himself through you in your obedience and patience (with yourself and with others).

When you are a person who has lived an unrighteous lifestyle, received forgiveness, and chosen a life of dying to the flesh by taking up the cross of Christ, he is more highly exalted because he is able to display his supreme, infinite, sovereign love and never-ending patience. You *are not* to go to the other extreme and puff yourself up as though prideful of forgiveness, as if you have gotten away with something. Paul said he did not claim to be perfect, yet he did not wallow in self-pity; nor did he boast in anything of himself. He recognized his need for a Savior. Once he accepted Christ as his *all in all*, he moved closer toward Christ-like behavior until the day he died (physically). He kept no shame, he took no pride. He allowed the Lord to daily balance him in all his ways. Paul understood intimacy with the Lord.

God shed enough pure blood to cover your sins as far as the east is from the west to keep you from having to go back to those old places in your mind. Once you die to self, your past is buried *with* your old man. Your new start is without a past, just as a newborn baby. For me, when my past is brought up in conversation by others, I recall my past sins, but otherwise, I don't sit around pondering them, kicking myself, or abusing myself for things I can never change. That is self-abasement (self-destruction) and that is not of God. It is from the evil one, keeping you in a state of oppression and depression even after salvation. Once you have confessed your sins, repented of them, and allowed his grace to replace the condemnation, that should be the end of it in your heart.

> Owe nothing to anyone except to love one another; for he
> who loves his neighbor has fulfilled the law. For this, "you

shall not commit adultery, you shall not murder, you shall not steal, you shall not covet," and if there is any other commandment, it is summed up in this saying, "you shall love your neighbor as yourself." Love does no wrong to a neighbor; therefore love is the fulfillment of the law.

Romans 13:8–10 (NAS)

"Greater love has no one than this, that one lay down his life for his friends … this I command you, that you love one another" (John 15:13, NAS).

■ ■ ■ ■ ■

Adam could not fulfill the law of love, and neither can you! Jesus, in perfect love, laid down his life for yours and fulfilled the law, the law of perfect love. Through his perfect love covering you, you automatically are considered by God as having fulfilled the Law. It is his covenant promise to you. You are now to lay down your life (the life of the fleshly nature) for him, allowing him access to your mortal body through and through. Once you receive his death, burial, and life, you are free from the curse of the law! Grace has been granted and received, freeing you from the bondages of this condemned world and all its lusts!

You owe to one another only love. There are many ways to go with this text, but for this topic, I will discuss how you owe no one anything except to love them as Christ loves the church. You do not owe another person constant apologies for your past; nor do you owe anyone constant apologies for something you have not done but they are treating you like you have offended them. You do *owe them* love, regardless of *their* actions!

Creepers grovel. The upright humble themselves to ask forgiveness when necessary. Then they allow Holy Spirit to cover them in grace to allow them to move past the offense and to offend no longer. Once you arise from your past, you will choose to stop blatantly sinning; therefore, there will be less sin in your future to apologize for. Yes, you will make mistakes, but they will be ones committed unconsciously, not consciously. Holy Spirit within will reveal them to you, you will repent immediately, right your wrong, and move past it.

■ ■ ■ ■ ■

Prayer

Oh, Father, I pray in the holy name of Jesus Christ, that you will begin to show me how to forgive myself as you have forgiven me. Show me how to be obedient to the natural law, the law of man, and your holy ordinances. Please give me understanding of how to apply your grace in my life so to be free of the past of sin. I desire with all of my heart, soul, mind, and strength to please you completely. I praise you that peace that passes all understanding is bound to me as I line up my life with you. Give me a God conscience at all times and in all things so that the moment I begin to be disobedient, you are free to rebuke me, correct me, and allow me to confess, repent, and be made complete again in you. Bless you, O heavenly Father, for your everlasting love and patience for me. Amen.

Reaping What You
SOW

In this chapter, I am going to be very, very candid with you about my own life and how God continues to reveal how all this *sowing* and *reaping* works. Let me start with how it is in operation in my own life.

One day, I was sitting on the sofa with my daughter, wishing my husband of several years did not have such a grueling work schedule. I hated that he had to work six days a week, and many times twelve to fourteen hours a day. I had gotten off the phone with a friend of mine about a half hour prior. We had been talking in general about people we know and how frustrating it is that they cannot understand that what they sow now they will reap in their future. I expressed my dismay that I can't seem to get through to some people that the more they continue in their path of sin, the harder it will be for them once they get lined up in obedience to God.

Suddenly it occurred to me: "I am reaping what I sewn so long ago!" Although it was not a shock, it was. I have paid a large price in other ways for my sinful ways. But this was a new revelation. I know that part of my husband's work hours is because God is working on *him*. However, I realized in an instant that because *I* had spent so much time years ago with him when he was not my husband and while I was legally married to another, I am now reaping an unfinished harvest.

That was an unpleasant realization, yet without guilt or condemnation. I had long since repented; that was not the issue at hand. The issue was that I needed to understand that this situation would not change until the harvest of bad seed was complete. Frankly, I don't know God's timing on this matter. I do know that as I continue to sow good seed during the finishing of a bad harvest, the bad *will* end! I see our finances finally getting back on track from years of sowing bad financial seed. I also know that one day I will have to answer to my children concerning my past sin. That won't be pleasant, but God is already preparing our hearts for that day.

A family member is another part of my previously planted seed of sin. This person cannot get past the way they saw me live my life many years ago. This person is unrelenting in animosity toward me, no matter how I live my life today. This has bothered me for years. But once I began to understand all this planting and harvesting, peace and pure love began to take over. Although they will answer to God directly for their treatment against me, I am now better-equipped to love them regardless. I now understand that, though their attitude against me is unwarranted in the natural, in the spiritual, *I* planted poorly. Therefore, this is part of my reaping.

Now the accountability belongs to me! With accountability, I can continue to walk in peace instead of constant anger and unforgiveness, regardless of their bitterness. I can love them as *unto God* as opposed to *unto them*, which is impossible in the flesh. The only way to love the unlovely (those who hate and mistreat you) is to do it *unto God.* This way, *he* is responsible for rendering payment instead of the person. Though I do not like their conduct toward me, I can take responsibility in the situation and quickly be forgiving. Now the control over my own life belongs to me and not them. As I stated in chapter four, *understanding* brings greater ability and desire to do as God commands, which is to love your neighbor as yourself and bless those who curse you.

My reason for sharing this with you is to help you wake up and stop sinning now! Not because I condemn you, but because I want the best for your life, as does the Father. He set the law of sowing and reaping in motion, and it cannot be changed. This is why he can't just sweep in the moment you confess and repent to make all your problems go away. It is in no way a lack of love or power on his part. In fact, because of his immeasurable love, he repeatedly tells us in his Word to stop our sinful ways, confess, and repent that he may make us whole as soon as possible.

Please comprehend that *making you whole* is instantaneous in his sight. The wholeness is his Son infilling you. Only he is the perfection of wholeness. Unfortunately, there is still a mess you have made for yourself that takes time to clean in the natural. The longer you go on sinning in full conscience, the bigger your bad harvest and the longer your time spent reaping will be. Repenting is totally for your benefit! When you get a picture of that in your mind, I pray you will not spend a moment hanging on to sin!

Look at David and Moses. They both were men after God's own heart. They were chosen by God and set in authority to glorify Father. They both sinned against Almighty God. They both repented. But, both of them forever reaped what they sewn. David was a negligent father to his children. The throne was taken away from David by a son. His daughter was raped by one of his sons, two of his sons were murdered, and others were murderers. He brought this on himself. Moses did not get to go into the Promised Land because of sin. I repeat, it had nothing to do with God no longer loving them! It did have everything to do with what they sewn in the spiritual and physical realm. Both are forever highly revered by God as men after his heart and friends of his, but they, like everyone, reap whatever they sow.

Elijah is another one. He is the greatest prophet ever. When he sinned by rising up in pride in front of Jezebel and put on a big show, he not only turned and ran for his life, begging God to kill him, he also did not get to complete his time on earth. He was told by God to train Elisha to take his place. Forever blessed by God and highly exalted, he still reaped what he had sewn. There is always a price to pay for sin, though forgiven.

Ultimately, God is still blessing these men today. They simply missed out on much of what God had for them here on earth. You likewise will miss out on what God has for you here because of blatant disobedience, no matter what excuse you may have. As a child of God, you too will ultimately be blessed in heaven, but why would you purpose to miss out on what he has for you here? It really doesn't make sense.

Now we come to Paul. Everyone uses him to cop out when tribulations come their way. They say that Paul was the greatest of the apostles, yet he suffered the most. He had a *thorn in his side* and asked God three times to remove it. That thorn many times was people who tormented and mocked him in his ministry. They kept him humble! But that is not so much where I am going with this. Paul suffered greatly during his ministry. This is not because of the good seed he sewn along the way, but the bad! God did not remove all of the repercussions of his past wickedness the moment the anointing of God fell upon him! Paul, though forgiven and greatly anointed, never stopped reaping the massive field of wickedness. Of course, he was still blessed and highly favored because of the good seed he began to sow (and continued to until death), but he just could not completely get away from the past seed.

■ ■ ■ ■ ■

"For I am the least of the apostles, and not fit to be called an apostle, because I persecuted the church of God. But by the grace of God I am what I am, and his grace toward me did not prove vain; but I labored even more than all of them, yet not I, but the grace of God with me" (1 Corinthians 15:9–10, NAS).

"As to zeal, a persecutor of the church; as to the righteousness which is in the Law, found blameless" (Philippians 3:6, 13, NAS).

This is not to discourage you, but to encourage you to stop the road of wickedness you are traveling. Turn and be separated completely unto God! The longer you go in rebellion, the longer the harvest of unpleasantness. If you are a person *of the Law* like

Paul, you will be judged by the same Law. No one can fulfill the Law except Christ, and he has. The Law will always condemn; faith through grace brings life. Paul said he was blameless *in* the Law, meaning absent of faith *in* God. You must walk a walk of faith, not religiosity. It is the religious that Jesus said were without relationship; they rejected the Son of God. Don't fool yourself and think you are something when you are not. That in itself is rebellion. You don't have to be a drunkard or drug addict to be a rebel!

Many seem to have the *in the sweet by and by* mentality. So many of God's own are looking only at the end result, yet totally missing the here and now. Multitudes make their own *hell on earth* because of disobedience and then question God as if he has wronged them in some way. He is the Almighty, Supreme, Sovereign, Righteous, Holy, Majestic God. You need to respectfully treat him as such and stop blaming him for the things you don't approve of in your life. He is the Perfect One. Check yourself!

And yes, forgiveness is ever present, but the Word is crystal clear that if you come into knowledge and you go back to sin, there is no more sacrifice for your sin. What then? You are doomed by your own hand. There is nothing more God can sacrifice to pay for your continued blatant disobedience.

Let's look at this from a different angle. Say you are someone who lived a sold out life to Christ. You sewn a good seed in Christ Jesus. Then you turned from him and went back to your vomit (so to speak). You, while you now sow bad seed, will continue to reap a good harvest until that harvest runs out. It would be like living on borrowed time, much like Satan is doing today. He seems to get away with much, yet he is still doomed to eternal fire.

■ ■ ■ ■ ■

"Now this I say, he who sows sparingly will also reap sparingly, and he who sows bountifully will also reap bountifully" (2 Corinthians 9:6, NAS).

"Do not be deceived, God is not mocked; for whatever a man

sows, this he will also reap. For the one who sows to his own flesh will from the flesh reap corruption, but the one who sows to the Spirit will from the Spirit reap eternal life" (Galatians 6:7–8, NAS).

You can look at this verse in 2 Corinthians and see several things. Of course the obvious is that whatever good in Christ you sow, however much you sow, you will reap its harvest.

Galatians chapter six is clear. This all goes back to dying to the flesh instead of attempting to *deal with* the flesh. Whatever you sow into the flesh, even if it is seemingly *good works for Christ,* you will reap only fleshly harvests, which are corrupt. I see it largely in ministry where a person starts off desiring God but ends up doing his/her own thing because they attain a level of *stardom.* They *work* in their flesh and eventually their ministry fails. I even hear of ministers supposedly strong in the Lord who commit suicide, adultery, and fornications including homosexuality. It is a great devastation to the kingdom of God. That is exactly what Satan wants! If he can convince people that they are holy when they barely genuinely know the Father, they fall because of lack of intimacy with him.

Every human being is created in the image of God: in that fact, every human represents God—either for the positive or negative. Example: if a person murders another and the family of the murder victim is unsaved, they generally question what kind of god would allow such a tragedy. If there was a chance of them coming in, it is lessened because of the one led by Satan. Also, if a minister has a large following, and their lives are impacted for Christ by that person, they trust him/her. Then that minister strays from God and sins openly. The majority of his/her followers fall away because the one whom they trusted was a liar to them. Most likely that minister taught truth but did not know how to walk in it. Therefore, ultimately, they were a worse example for Christ than if they had never made a public testimony of Christ.

It is imperative for you, and every believer, to seek his holy face, know the Trinity with all of your being, and then allow him to lead you into whatever ministry he desires. Otherwise, you are just doing something that someone told you was *good* but is not your calling at all. When you step outside of your spiritual gifts, you will fail! God does not intend for all to be apostles, or all to be prophets, or all to be healers, teachers, pastors, or administrators. To know his heart is the first step toward true ministry. Your calling and mine, first and foremost, is to *fall in love with him!* In loving him intimately, he will begin (as previously mentioned) to flow freely through you instead of you trying to force out of you something godly.

To truly sow good seed is to be led of, by, and through him. He is *good* and no one else. Nothing you put your hands to is good, unless he is doing the doing! Allow him to move and direct. Let him give you the seed to sow and direction to the proper field so that your harvest will always be a blessing and not a curse; an asset and not a liability.

■ ■ ■ ■ ■

"You shall not sow your vineyard with two kinds of seed, or all the produce of the seed which you have sown and the increase of the vineyard will become defiled" (Deuteronomy 22:9, NAS).

> The kingdom of heaven may be compared to a man who sewn good seed in his field. But while his men were sleeping, his enemy came and sewn tares among the wheat, and went away. But when the wheat sprouted and bore grain, then the tares became evident also. The slaves of the landowner came and said to him 'Sir, did you not sow good seed in your field? How then does it have tares?' And he said to them, 'An enemy has done this?' The slaves said to him, 'Do you want us, then, to go and gather them up?' But he said, 'No, for while you are gathering up the tares, you may uproot the wheat with them.
>
> Matthew 13:24–30 (NAS)

■ ■ ■ ■ ■

Matthew reiterates this point. God's workers sewn only good seed. While they were sleeping, the enemy came and sewn corrupt seed. This is why it is crucial to be vigil, sober-minded, awake, and alert at all times, spiritually speaking. If you slack off even for a moment in your walk with God, the enemy will take full advantage of you. When that happens, the bad seed is sown and you have to allow all things to grow together until you can tell the difference and pull out the wickedness.

"According to what I have seen, those who plow iniquity and those who sow trouble harvest it. By the breath of God they perish, and by the blast of his anger they come to an end" (Job 4:8–9, NAS).

"The wicked earns deceptive wages, but he who sows righteousness gets a true reward" (Proverbs 11:18, (NAS).

"He who sows iniquity will reap vanity, and the rod of his fury will fail" (Proverbs 22:8, NAS).

"Those who sow in tears shall reap with joyful shouting. He who goes to and fro weeping, carrying his bag of seed, shall indeed come again with a shout of joy, bringing his sheaves with him" (Psalm 126:5–6, NAS).

"And the seed whose fruit is righteousness is sown in peace by those who make peace" (James 3:18, NAS).

■ ■ ■ ■ ■

These four men are speaking about the same scenario. Job and Solomon refer to iniquity; David, James and Solomon to righteousness. If you live a life planting iniquity and trouble, you will be blown out by God eventually. You may think you are getting away with something, but surely you are not. Your time of wicked harvest will surely bring you to the grave!

David, on the other hand, though the message is the same, speaks of the one who puts in all of himself in sacrifice to the call of God. There is suffering for the cause of Christ, but, when the harvest arises, joy comes in the morning! When you are diligent in the field of God bearing his cross, your harvest is shouts of joy!

"Light is sown like seed for the righteous and gladness for the upright in heart. Be glad in the Lord, you righteous ones, and give thanks to his holy name," states Psalm 97:11–12. The Lord is likened unto the sower who sows the seed of light into the lives of his righteous holy ones. He is the True Sower and he plants his holy seed in those who seek him diligently!

"See, I have appointed you this day over the nations and over the kingdoms, to pluck up and to break down, to destroy and to overthrow, to build and to plant" (Jeremiah 1:10, NAS).

"Break up your fallow ground, and do not sow among thorns. Circumcise yourselves to the Lord and remove the foreskins of your heart" (Jeremiah 4:3–4, NAS).

"Sow with a view to righteousness, reap in accordance with kindness; *break up your fallow ground,* for it is time to seek the Lord until he comes to rain righteousness on you" (Hosea 10:12, NAS).

"They sow the wind and they reap the whirlwind. The standing grain has no heads; it yields no grain. Should it yield, strangers would swallow it up" (Hosea 8:7, NAS).

■ ■ ■ ■ ■

Both Hosea and Jeremiah talk about "plowing up fallowed ground." Remember that back in those days farming was their only source of food other than hunting. There were no grocery stores to buy fruit and veggies. If the ground was hard, they could not plant anything until it was tilled. They had to dig down to the tender soil. This, flipped to the spiritual, means to remove the hardness of your heart and allow God to plant his seed of light. It is the time of *preparation* of the field where the seed is to be planted. That is the meaning of "plucking up, breaking down, destroying, and overthrowing." Fields must have the nasty weeds of life removed in order for the good seed to take effect.

Unless and until you do, he cannot penetrate to show you how to sow good seed. Allow your heart to be tender like a child's, ready to receive all he has to do in you, through you, and for you!

> Behold, the sower went out to sow; and as he sewn, some seeds fell beside the road and the birds came and ate them up. Others fell on the rocky places, where they did not have much soil; and immediately they sprang up, because they had no depth of soil. But when the sun had risen, they were scorched; and because they had no root, they withered away. Others fell among the thorns, and the thorns came up and choked them out. And others fell on the good soil and yielded a crop, some a hundredfold, some sixty, and some thirty. He who has ears, let him hear."
>
> Matthew 13:3–9 (NAS)

This is a different sowing and reaping. This is of course God's Word being planted within your heart:

Some never receive (by the road)—they hear but quickly dismiss the Word.

Some receive quickly (rocky places), seemingly grow quickly, but it is a shallow growth, and they soon become bored and move on to the next "exciting" thing.

Some receive but are immediately turned back because the demons and circumstances of life devour the Word (among the thorns).

Then there are those few who receive the Word and then grow in the Word (good soil with yielded crop)—these are the ones who are excited, but also allow themselves time to gradually grow. They are not "overnight sensations." I am always concerned about those who jump in too quickly; they usually fall away just as quickly!

> So also is the resurrection of the dead. It is sown a perishable body, it is raised an imperishable body; it is sown in dishonor, it is raised in glory; it is sown in weakness, it is raised in power; it is sown a natural body, it is raised a spiritual body.

There is a natural body; there is also a spiritual body. So also it is written, "The first man, Adam, became a living soul." The last Adam became a life-giving spirit. However, the spiritual is not first, but the natural; then the spiritual. The first man is from the earth, earthly; the second man is from heaven. As is the earthy, so also are those who are earthy; and as is the heavenly, so also are those who are heavenly. Just as we have born the image of the earthy, we will also bear the image of the heavenly.

1 Corinthians 15:42–49 (NAS)

Here Paul so beautifully and eloquently depicts the glorious, majestic, and all-powerful God you and I have the privilege of calling Father, Friend, and Husband! These verses reveal not only what will happen at the rapture, but what happens during salvation!

You are born of Adam. When you choose to die to the flesh, he breathes his perfect breath of life into your *dead* body (spiritually speaking), giving you true life! Now you can walk this earth imperishable, full of his glory, full of his power, and wholly of the heavenly realm! How marvelous is this one called I AM!

It reads that the natural is first then the spiritual. You come into the world condemned in the earthly body. He resurrects you with his Spirit—allowing you to look human—but you are completely spiritual! Hallelujah to his holy, righteous name!

In summation, if you have sewn good seed but are currently sowing bad, don't think that your good harvest will last forever. *No harvest lasts forever!* This fact (law of God) will either be to your advantage or disadvantage!

If you are seeking the Lord with all of your heart, soul, mind, and strength and you are still reaping a bad harvest, the fact still remains that all harvests must end. The only ones that can last forever are the ones you continue to plant repeatedly. Even with Paul, his suffering ended when he transitioned from earth to heaven. He suffered long for the Lord because he suffered God's people so greatly and for so long.

If you stop planting corn and start planting beans, you will soon switch from a corn crop to beans. If you continue to plant corn, you will always get corn. The *type* of corn can't even change unless you change from yellow to white. There will be a time of overlap where you harvest both wheat and tares; the good and the bad. Endure through it. God will bless your perseverance and endurance.

You change the harvest when you change the seeds you plant! You and your choices of righteousness or unrighteousness determine your life of blessings or curses. Choose to stop sowing into the flesh and start sowing into the Spirit of God. Pray that the grace of Almighty God will bless you that you may humbly finish whatever you started while currently planting seed from heaven!

I want to share a personal story of sowing and reaping as I close this chapter. I used to be unforgiving: not so much on the surface for all to see, but in my heart where only God could see. As the Lord changed my perspective, I eventually repented, relented, and became forgiving as God himself is. As I mentioned before, there are those few who refuse to forgive my past. I *choose* to forgive those who will not forgive me. I say this to segue into my point of reaping.

My first marriage was one of great abuse and lies formed against me. In my despair, I married a nice man on the rebound. I, within two years of marriage, left him, got back together with him, and left him again; both times right around Christmas! For good reason, neither he nor his family had anything good to think or say about me. Many years passed. The Lord completely transformed me into a new creation, and I eventually remarried. Nonetheless, they still had their old perception of me.

Just in the past few days, I received a phone call from my mother-in-law from my second marriage. She lives many states away. She was here visiting and said she wanted to see *family and friends.* I couldn't have been more surprised that I fit either of those categories! I agreed to go and see her. Oh, and also with her was her son's (my ex) mother-in-law! I asked her if that would be awkward, but she insisted it would not.

Oddly enough, we visited for about two and a half hours. It was beautiful! She had forgiven me completely and without measure! She even wanted me to still refer to her and her husband as "Mom and Dad." I had the grand opportunity to apologize for my poor behavior toward the whole family and her son. She said she recognized that I had been a mess, and she understood. She even went so far as to say that she believes that, after all was said and done, I am supposed to be married to my current husband. What an intense blessing from God to give me that relief of guilt and anguish!

Here is the moral of the story. As I began over many years to sow good seeds of unconditional forgiveness and love toward those who are not so toward me, *he* rendered payment (for lack of a better term) to me when I least expected it, and in a way I could not have even imagined or requested! It far exceeds any *payment* from those who still hate me. When you sow righteousness (but don't see immediate results in the natural), his payment of your steadfastness in well-doing is exceedingly superior to that which we as mere men could think or imagine. This harvest was most sweet to my tongue and satisfying for my belly!

I am a firm believer in not living in guilt and shame. However, this opportunity took me into a deeper level of freedom from guilt and shame. When the Lord says to not grow weary in well-doing, know that there is payoff yet to come! God is the Promise Keeper. He will fulfill every promise he has made. He will not fail you. Stay the course of planting righteousness and purity when those around you mock and ridicule you, even when it seems futile.

■ ■ ■ ■ ■

Prayer

I pray, O heavenly Father, that you will show me the error of my ways, that I may see clearly how I came into the life I am currently living. Give me the grace to accept what you reveal to my spirit, that I not allow condemnation to come in. Show me, Jesus, how to finish this bad harvest with all humility. Show me, gracious Lord, how to sow seed from heaven so that the harvest will come up supernatural instead of natural. Make it clear to me what is of the flesh, and what is of the Spirit of Almighty God. I praise you, Father, that I will begin to see, hear, and think just as you. Place your mind in mine that I never again be deceived by the world and its lusts! I declare victory now over the rest of my life that all crooked paths are right now being made straight! I praise you that everything Satan means against me for evil is being turned around for good because I love you! Bless your holy name! Amen.

The
WILDERNESS

I would like to take some time to study three different mighty men of God that encountered *wilderness time*. Joseph, David, and Job all endured hardships. Each of them handled it differently. They all came out victoriously, but I want you to look at how each of them dealt with their wilderness, and why God allowed it in the first place.

First, you need to understand the *why* of the wilderness. The Israelites were not purposed to stay in the wilderness. They were supposed to *learn to lean on God* and to grow in *self-discipline.* Unfortunately, all they did was moan and grumble about what God provided and how it was insufficient. Then they desired to go back from whence they came. They hated where they were and forgot what it was like where they came from. They shook their fists at God with ungrateful hearts and stiff necks to the point that God had to kill off that entire generation before the next generation could enter the Promised Land!

It is the hard times that bring a person to humility, and it is humility that leads a person right into the blessings of God. Most, however, want to bypass the wilderness and skip right to the mountaintop, the place of authority and abundance. You ask God to remove something when you need to endure and overcome. You can never appreciate the abundance if you do not experience lack. In actuality, you cannot even handle the abundance unless you have learned self-discipline. You have to earn and learn your place of authority, so to speak. God's love and salvation do not have to be earned. A place of position in the kingdom, on the other hand, does.

The Word says that when you are faithful over the little, it will be increased. Increase comes when you prove yourself responsible with the little he does give. You say, "Your will, Lord," then get annoyed when his will is to teach you perseverance! Jesus wanted the *cup of the cross* to pass from him. However, God's will was not to remove the cup. Jesus was in total agreement with God, *no matter what!* This is because Jesus' focus was *kingdom-minded* instead of *self-minded.*

Joseph

Let's look at Joseph, as we will each of these three men. Joseph's brothers hated him due to their jealousy. When he was seventeen years of age, his eleven brothers gave him over to the enemy and told his father he was dead. Then God poured out favor upon him, and he became the right-hand man to Potiphar, who was the captain of the bodyguard of Pharaoh. After being exalted to a high place, adversity came against Joseph again. Potiphar's wife accused him of trying to rape her because he refused to lay with her though she had great beauty. He was exceedingly faithful to his master. He refused time and again. He was thrown into prison for several years when falsely accused. Was this fair treatment? What does *fair* have to do with God's *sovereignty?* I heard T.D. Jakes comment that God is not fair, he is just.

At least we know that David had the sin of fear that had to be exposed and purged from him. I don't see an account of any known sin in Joseph, yet he still had to endure great adversity. None of us are sinless, but whatever was in Joseph was obviously nothing worth God mentioning in the Word. He was indeed a man after God's own heart. It stands to reason that whenever sin tried to enter, he did not allow it. He was strong in the Lord and in the power of *God's* might. He did not give in to temptation with a beautiful woman seducing him time and time again; it does not appear that he defended himself in any way to Potiphar when falsely accused.

You do not once hear of Joseph allowing self-pity or depression to come in on him.

Every place he went, he was anointed of God. He was always favored. He interpreted dreams in prison and was the right-hand man to the head guard. Don't you know that Joseph had to learn great self-discipline and endurance through these rough times? This does not mean that depression, self-pity, or even suicidal tendencies did not *try* to come in. It means he overcame through Holy Spirit. He kept his eye (single vision like Christ) on God and did not allow himself to be drawn away from God by mere circumstances. He trusted God implicitly no matter what circumstance he was in!

He was mocked and scorned by his own flesh and blood. The ones who should have loved and protected him gave him over to the enemy and wanted to kill him (Genesis 37:3–19). His brothers threw him into a pit without water with the soul purpose of cold-blooded murder. Then, without conscience, they sat and ate; no remorse, no grief, no guilt (Genesis 37:23–25). This shows the very nature within these eleven men.

Joseph had been sold into slavery and purchased by the enemy, the Egyptians (Genesis 37:28). Understand that his master, an enemy, was reverenced by Joseph to such a degree that Potiphar appointed him to a position just underneath himself (Genesis 39:1). What an intense honor for a man who he and his people (Israelites) were considered as dogs! Joseph must have understood early on how we are all to respect and honor *all* authority. If he had been indignant and rebellious (prideful), there is no way God could have poured out his favor upon Joseph.

You must always respect authority. This way, when you become authority yourself, you will receive the same respect that you gave when you were a slave. When you respect the authority of your enemy, God will give them into your hands at his appointed time. A soft word turns away wrath.

> It came about after these events that his master's wife looked with desire at Joseph, and she said, "Lie with me." But he

refused and said to his master's wife, "Behold, with me here, my master does not concern himself with anything in the house, and he has put all that he owns in my charge. There is not one greater in this house than I, and he has withheld nothing from me except you, because you are his wife. How then could I do this great evil and sin against God?"

Genesis 39:7–10 (NAS)

Again, notice how Joseph understood authority. He did not say to her that he could not sin against *Potiphar,* but that he could not sin against *God.* All authority over you is of God. God is the only One who sets authority in place. Therefore, God is always the head authority. If you sin against authority, you sin directly against God. You need to keep that in mind whenever you desire or consider coming against any authority over you. Pride says, "Don't they know who I am? How dare they treat me like this! They'll pay for this!" God cannot exalt or come to the aid of someone who exalts or defends themselves.

Do you see how much like Jesus Joseph was? Jesus never defended himself. Jesus, like Joseph, was so confident in his placement in God's eye, he felt no need to convince anyone. This is how Joseph conducted himself in every situation, and God blessed him everywhere he went (Genesis 39:2–3).

■ ■ ■ ■ ■

She caught him by his garment, saying, "Lie with me!" And he left his garment in her hand and fled, and went outside…then she spoke to him (Potiphar) these words, "The Hebrew slave, whom you brought to us, came in to me to make sport of me…so Joseph's master took him and put him into the jail, the place where the king's prisoners were confined; and he was there in the jail.

Genesis 39:12, 17, 20 (NAS)

Here it is again. There is no mention of Joseph defending himself to Potiphar. I would suppose that, if he had, Potiphar would have let him go. But, if that had happened, the God-ordained events that followed would not have come about. Joseph would have settled for his position with Potiphar (which was good) instead of allowing God to take him all the way to greatness! How many times have you spoiled God's perfect will for yourself by interceding and stopping God's greatness to come to fruition? If you, we, could only truly comprehend humility, life would be blessed without measure! I pray this for my own life, since I know how many times I have missed the sovereign plan of God. I wonder how many times I have done this unawares!

■　■　■　■　■

"But the Lord was with Joseph and extended kindness to him, and gave him favor in the sight of the chief jailer ... the chief jailer did not supervise anything under Joseph's charge because the Lord was with him; and whatever he did, the Lord made to prosper" (Genesis 39:21, 23 NAS).

"Now it happened at the end of two full years that Pharaoh had a dream" (Genesis 41:1, NAS).

■　■　■　■　■

Here you see the continued grace and favor of God, even in prison. This is two years from the time that Joseph correctly interpreted the dreams of two of Pharaoh's servants who were in jail with him. He had asked them to remember him. They did. It just took two years! Joseph could have gotten bent out of shape and bitter that these two men who promised to remember forgot him. Joseph must have clearly understood God's perfect timing. Because of his wisdom, he obviously did not sit around waiting for someone to release him from prison. No, he continued going about his business and left it all to God to take care.

Then Pharaoh sent and called for Joseph, and they hurriedly brought him out of the dungeon; and when he had shaved himself and changed his clothes, he came to Pharaoh … Pharaoh said to Joseph, "Since God has informed you of all this, there is no one so discerning and wise as you. You shall be over my house, and according to your command all my people shall do homage; only in the throne I will be greater than you. Pharaoh said to Joseph, "See, I have set you over all the land of Egypt." Then Pharaoh took off his signet ring from his hand and put it on Joseph's hand … moreover, Pharaoh said to Joseph, "Though I am Pharaoh, yet without your permission no one shall raise his hand or foot in all the land of Egypt.

Genesis 41:14, 39–44 (NAS)

■ ■ ■ ■ ■

He was seventeen when he was thrown into a pit by his brothers. He was thirty by the time he stood before Pharaoh (Genesis 41:46). Thirteen years lapsed before Joseph arrived at his destination foretold in his dreams. God gave him two dreams, prophesying that his brothers and his parents would bow down before him. Has God ever spoken something to you, and if it did not happen instantly, you gave up on God? You need to recognize that there is always a process to get where God is taking you. You must go *through* (not around) each step and not allow yourself to become impatient and take matters into your own hands. When you do, you birth your own enemy! Satan is the god of quick fixes. God is the God of patience and endurance. Observe what happened when Joseph *did not* come against authority. Joseph respected the authority in enemy territory and ended up ruling all the land of the enemy territory! He was not ruler in his own land, but foreign soil. That is the hand of a mighty and all-powerful God! What can't God accomplish when you just get lined up in obedience and humility in him?

■ ■ ■ ■ ■

These very people (his own flesh and blood who had mocked him, hated him, put him into a pit with the intention of murder, then turned and broke bread without care) are comforted and cared for by Joseph (Genesis 50:15–21). Joseph even spoke kindly to them without sarcasm or guilt laid upon them. This is the epitome of walking in humility. He blessed those who cursed him because he *understood* and recognized the hand of God in everything all along the path.

The Word says that integrity will protect you. It certainly protected Joseph. Do you conduct yourself with the integrity and faithfulness of Joseph, no matter what chaos surrounds you? Do you *trust* that God is *in love* with you and will allow all for *your* good and comfort? If so, there is nothing to fear and nothing worthy of anger because you have a heart set on Christ (James 1:20). Satan will try to provoke you to anger. Don't allow his tactics to affect you. When you sense it coming, remind yourself of the faithfulness of God, and that he *will* contend with those who contend with you!

David

"Then Samuel took the horn of oil and anointed him in the midst of his brothers; and the Spirit of the Lord came mightily upon David from that day forward" (1 Samuel 16:13, NAS).

"Then David spoke to the men who were standing by him, saying, '… For who is this uncircumcised Philistine, that he should taunt the armies of the living God" (1 Samuel 17:26, NAS).

"Now Eliab his oldest brother heard when he spoke to the men; and Eliab's anger burned against David and he said, "Why have you come down? And with whom have you left those few sheep in the wilderness? I know your insolence and the wickedness of your heart; for you have come down in order to see the battle." But David said, "What have I done now? Was it not just a question" (1 Samuel 17:28–29, NAS).

■ ■ ■ ■ ■

As a refresher, God looks only at the condition of the heart (I Samuel 16:7). Don't you know this caused great jealousy to arise in David's brothers against him?

Saul had an evil spirit which tormented him after the Holy Spirit left and fell upon David. He brought David in to play the harp to soothe him (I Samuel 16:21), so he thought. When David played the harp, the evil spirit left. It was not the music that made the spirit leave, but the power of Holy Spirit, who was in David.

What intense boldness came from David (1 Samuel 17:26, NAS). He was a man led by Holy Spirit, and therefore had no fear of any man! Anointed of God, it was God who called Goliath an "uncircumcised Philistine" through David. This Philistine came against God's anointed people, and this was unacceptable! David was obviously undermined and mocked by his elder brothers regularly.

> Then David said to the Philistine, "You come to me with a sword, a spear, and a javelin, but I come to you in the name of the Lord of hosts, the God of the armies of Israel, whom you have taunted ... and that all this assembly may know that he Lord does not deliver by sword or by spear; for the battle is the Lord's and he will give you into our hands ... Thus David prevailed over the Philistine with a sling and a stone, and he struck the Philistine and killed him; but there was no sword in David's hand.
>
> 1 Samuel 17:45, 47, 50 (NAS)

Why did the powerful Philistine come with the shield-bearer if there was nothing to fear? Don't you know that he had to know to some degree that God's anointed was standing before him? When you are led by Holy Spirit, the enemy always knows it and is fearful of you, even if they do not understand (Deuteronomy 28; I Samuel 18:14–15, NAS). Again, David knew from whence his power came and had no fear. God always works through weaknesses of man.

Why? It shows that only God Almighty could have won the battle and he receives the glory as he rightly deserves.

■ ■ ■ ■ ■

"An evil spirit from God came mightily upon Saul, and he raved in the midst of the house, while David was playing the harp with his hand, as usual; and a spear was in Saul's hand. Saul hurled the spear for he thought, "I will pin David to the wall." But David escaped from his presence twice" (1 Samuel 18:10–11, NAS).

Here is about the time that Saul realizes and recognizes the anointing of Holy Spirit on David. Jealousy overtakes him. Jealousy is a murdering spirit! Look again at Joseph's brothers: jealousy equals murder.

Now the God-anointed king had to flee his kingdom that God had promised (I Samuel 19:18 and 22:1–2). David could have crumbled and called God a liar. By all human standards, that is what he should have done. God *looked* like a liar on the surface. However, David knew God intimately. David had the Holy Spirit's anointing, even in the wilderness, running for his life. When you know God in the good times, you will not doubt him in the bad.

■ ■ ■ ■ ■

"The cords of death encompassed me, and the torrents of ungodliness terrified me. The cords of Sheol surrounded me; the snares of death confronted me. In my distress I called upon the Lord, and cried to my God for help; he heard my voice out of his temple, and my cry for help before him came into his ears" (Psalm 18:4–6, NAS).

"When I am afraid, I will put my trust in you. In God, whose Word I praise, in God I have put my trust; I shall not be afraid. What can mere man do to me" (Psalm 56:3–4, NAS).

■ ■ ■ ■ ■

He continues to praise and declare the goodness and majesty of God. He refused to give in to the terror surrounding him. He magnified the name of the Lord God. He praised his way *through* the wilderness all the way *to* victory!

"O Lord, do not rebuke me in your anger, nor chasten me in your wrath" (Psalm 6:1, NAS).

"O Lord, rebuke me not in your wrath, and chasten me not in your burning anger" (Psalm 38:1, NAS).

"With reproofs you chasten a man for iniquity" (Psalm 39:11, NAS).

Here we see a bit of self-pity. This is where David really begins to come into a place of discipline and self-discipline. First, he cries out to God for mercy. He asks God *not* to chasten him. But then we begin to see the breaking of David's outer man, the flesh. He begins to understand that everything is about God.

Then he gets to the place where he can say things like this in Psalm 94:12–14:

"Blessed is the man whom you discipline, O Lord, the man you teach from your law; you grant him relief from days of trouble, till a pit is dug for the wicked. For the Lord will not reject his people; he will never forsake his inheritance."

> I will give you thanks with all my heart; I will sing praises to you before the gods. I will bow down toward your holy temple and give thanks to your name for your loving kindness and your truth; for you have magnified your Word according to all your name. On the day I called, you answered me; you made me hold with strength in my soul. All the kings of the earth will give thanks to you, O Lord, when they have heard the words of your mouth. And they will sing of the ways of the Lord, for great is the glory of the Lord. For though the Lord is exalted, yet he regards the lowly, but the haughty he knows from afar. Though I walk in the midst of trouble, you will revive me; you will stretch forth your hand against

the wrath of my enemies, and your right hand will save me. The Lord will accomplish what concerns me; your loving kindness, O Lord, is everlasting; do not forsake the works of your hands.

Psalm 138:1–8 (NAS)

In this, David calls chastisement *blessed.* He had come to realize that rebuke from God is for his own benefit–not for condemnation, but refinement! You have to know what is in you that is *not* of God before it can be purged. This is a broken man before God! Though David loved him and knew him before the wilderness, now there is an even deeper, more precious, more concrete, and firm relationship with God.

The wilderness is a training ground, not a place to live and die! Allow God to show you what he wants you to see. If it is sin, deal with it. If a process to get you to the high ground he desires, let it come; stand strong in the face of adversity. Do not be focused on, "How can I get out?" but "How am I to conduct myself while here, and what do I need to learn?" It is your endurance and perseverance through trials that raises hope. When you overcome, you become the hope to others. Jesus, the Hope, is developed deeply within you, and therefore able to shine through you, the broken vessel.

Job

What about Job? His situation is quite different than that of Joseph and David. As far as I can tell in reading the book of Job, he never knew adversity or hard times until the situation you read. When Satan and God were discussing Job, Satan said that Job was only a righteous man because God had always made it so easy for him. God did call Job a *perfect man,* but that does not mean sinless. When God called him *perfect* (Job 1:1), there are two reasons: 1. Because he did not know adversity, his outward conduct was *right* in the natural. 2. God was speaking of the *future* Job, the man he would become when all was completed through the trials. God always deals with his chosen people looking at who they are *after* transformation, not before. God calls you to be perfect in the New Testament. The only way you are considered perfect is when the Holy Spirit, who is perfection, is in control *through* you. The *perfect man* is the man who is dead to the fleshly nature and alive through his Spirit. In the end, Job becomes such a man and is honored by God eternally. But what a journey he had to endure go get to that place!

Job had sins of stubbornness, pride, rebellion, and fear. Job himself did not know what was in him. It took unimaginable tragedy to bring to light the hidden sin. He could not see it in himself because of all the *good things* he did. Adversity does not change a person; it only brings to light the truth of the heart in a person. Anyone can hide things in a season of blessing; from others and themselves. But, when the hard times hit, sin will be exposed. Jesus says that everything hidden *will* be revealed.

Job is a story grossly misinterpreted! Job loved and served God. He was a *good* man. People often use Job as well as Paul as an excuse when they endure hardship. Instead of looking inward to see what God is trying to show that is wrong within, they say, "Well, Job was a righteous man, and he went through great suffering." They use him as an excuse to keep from looking at what God really wants them to see in themselves as if that is all there is to the story.

The real story begins with Satan going to God. He had come from roaming the earth, seeking whom he could devour. God asked Satan where he had come from, though God certainly already knew the answer. God suggested his servant Job. Satan insisted that Job was only faithful because of the protective covering God had faithfully given him. Not only did God suggest that Satan *try* Job, but God gave Satan permission to do his worst, only not to touch him (Job 1:8, 10). What was God thinking here? Is he just a mean God who wants to torment those who are faithful to him just because he has the power? If so, that would make him tyrannical and unloving; therefore, a liar. If you don't know the truth in this story, it would certainly be a natural assumption. Let's see what God was really doing here by sending Job into the wilderness.

After Satan took everything away from him, Job did not rebuke God. Satan went back to God. God suggested Job again (Job 2:3). God then allowed Satan to touch him, but he could not take his life. Job was stricken with great illness and pain. His three friends (Eliphaz, Bildad and Zophar) went to Job. Job cursed his own life and the day he was born, but not God.

Job 3:25 reads, "What I feared has come upon me; what I dreaded has happened to me, I have no peace, no quietness; I have no rest, but only turmoil." There's that dreaded word—*fear*. It is a pitfall for every Christian who gives in to it, and it is sin. This indicates that Job's faith was not fully in the Lord. Fear had been hidden, even from Job. God already knew what was in Job's heart, but Job did not. It had to be brought to the surface. No one operates in fear when it seems there is nothing to fear. It was only in the face of adversity that it was brought to light. It was already rooted deeply within him.

You need to continually seek God to reveal everything that is hidden *from* you so that you know what needs to be dealt with. This will certainly help you avoid more of the wilderness than God wants you to go through! If there is a sin you do not realize you have, once he uncovers it, you can repent and be cleansed. Job had to go through this *wilderness* for the hidden things to be revealed so to become perfected.

Now his friends came along and accused him of having secret sin. Job vehemently denied it, insisting that he had nothing hidden. Denial, defensiveness, and stubbornness are common manifestations stemming from deep-seeded pride. As they accused Job, he turned and accused them (Job 6:14–15).

Notice in this verse that Job seemed to seek flattery; kind words to stroke his ego and make him feel better about himself. You should never be dependent on flattering words of others to make you *feel good* about yourself. If you are confident in yourself instead of your identity in Christ, you will surely crumble and perish. This banter goes back and forth for many chapters. Job goes on, endlessly defending himself.

"What you know, I also know; I am not inferior to you. But I desire to speak to the Almighty and to argue my case with God. You, however, smear me with lies; you are worthless physicians, all of you" (Job 13:2–3, NAS).

By chapter 29, Job begins to speak of all the wonderful things *he* had done. He begins to absolutely exude pride. Pride is a powerful sin and enemy of God. Pride is the very sin that caused Lucifer to be cast from heaven. This is the second sin that had to be revealed that Job did not realize he had. Here is an example of his nauseating pride:

> Whoever heard me spoke well of me, and those who saw me commended me, because I rescued the poor who cried for help, and the fatherless who had no one to assist him. The man who was dying blessed me; I made the widow's heart sing. I put on righteousness as my clothing; justice was my robe and my turban. They waited for me as for showers and drank in my words as the spring rain. When I smiled at them, they scarcely believed it; the light of my face was precious to them.
>
> Job 29:11–14, 23–24 (NAS)

"So these three men stopped answering Job, because he was righteous in his own eyes" (Job 32:1, NAS).

"For he adds rebellion to his sin; he claps his hands among us, and multiplies his words against God" (Job 34:37, NAS).

"For rebellion is as the sin of divination (witchcraft), and stubbornness (arrogance) is as iniquity and idolatry" (1 Samuel 15:23, NAS).

■ ■ ■ ■ ■

God gives grace to the humble. I heard Kenneth Copeland say that God deals with us better in judgment than in blessings because that is what people best respond to. Too often, when blessed abundantly, you do not hear God, and you do not look inward to see the wickedness of your flesh. Job had to go through this terribly tragic wilderness for his inward sin to be exposed. Because of his stubborn pride, he had to go through this torment longer than he should have. It was not until he finally humbled himself and repented that God was able to restore him. Job acted as though God owed him something because of what a *good person* he was. You need to realize and accept the harsh truth that God Almighty owes you nothing! We are all unworthy and unacceptable to God. A jealous spirit will sever your communication from God. Jealousy tells you that you want something someone else has, whether it is a spouse, child, health, or riches. Every good thing, including our every breath, comes from God. When you are totally humble before him, dead to your selfish desires, he can come in and lift you up. Until then, you will wallow around in your sorrow, your wilderness, until you learn that you are blessed just to be privileged to call his holy name!

Once you seek God for purification, repentance is a part of the process. You are purified when you repent of whatever he reveals. If you are in a desert place, God is wooing you from the jaws of distress. He is trying to show you something that you could not see otherwise. You need to keenly discern his voice, listen, and then obey.

If you are standing strong in the good times, be warned. Trials are a sure way to find out where you really are with Christ. Job obviously had a mercy gift. God is the one who gave it. But, the mercy gift belonged to God, and Job took away all the credit that belonged to God. Look back at Job 29:11–14, 23–24. It is clear that Job thought so much of himself that he said of himself, "the light of my face was precious to them … they drank in my words as the spring rain … those who saw me commended me."

A human being is incapable of receiving and retaining complements, no matter how genuine. You are never, never to hold onto glory when you are serving Christ. How many times have I acted out in pride because others complimented something God did through me? Woe unto me or anyone who thinks more highly of themselves than they ought! You are to graciously say, "Thank you," when you are complimented on a job well done. Then, as soon as you are in quiet time with Father, pour it all out to him. Otherwise, you will fall quickly into the pit of destruction due to pride, just like Job. When that happens, you become ineffective for the body of Christ and the kingdom expansion.

Desert places are not supposed to be permanent. All three of these men had to go through a wilderness. They all came from different points of view, but the outcome was the same: they humbled themselves and God accomplished his will of blessing them and exalted them to the high place, and *God* was glorified. Everything is always for the glory of God. If God is not being exalted by you in your life, through every circumstance, there needs to be a change. The wilderness is set up for a person to go through to learn to trust in him and to develop a close, intimate relationship with Almighty God.

■ ■ ■ ■ ■

"You shall remember all the ways which the Lord your God has led you in the wilderness these forty years, that he might humble you, testing you, to know what was in your heart, whether you would keep his commandment or not. He humbled you and let you be hungry, and fed you with manna which you did not know, nor did your fathers know, that he might make you understand that man does not live by bread alone, but man lives by everything that proceeds out of the mouth of the Lord" (Deuteronomy 8:2–3, NAS).

■ ■ ■ ■ ■

"Blessed is the man who perseveres under trial; for once he has been approved, he will receive the crown of life which the Lord has promised to those who love him" (James 1:12, NAS).

It is in the *pit* where the seeds of righteousness are planted and developed! Generally speaking, physical seeds have to be planted deeply within the ground for them to be stable and secure so that the storms will not quickly uproot them. It is the "buried" part that makes them strong. You often feel *buried* in the ground, but this is where spiritual character and faith are developed. No one comes into this world physically or spiritually strong. Though you are not to revel in or stay in the wilderness, you are to rejoice in every circumstance, knowing that our Lord and Savior is faithful.

■ ■ ■ ■ ■

Prayer:

In the name of Jesus, I pray that you, Father, will see me through the storms of life by teaching me humility, faith, tenderness of heart, and obedience. Show me how to lean and depend completely upon you. I desire to be more pure than I have ever been. Take me to the next mantle in you, O God of heaven and earth. Teach me your sovereign ways that I may walk, talk, and look like Christ. Reveal to me how to be before you as dust and ashes. May there be no life breath in me except the breath of Almighty God.

Necessity of
WISDOM

"Say to wisdom, "you are my sister," and call understanding your intimate friend; that they may keep you from an adulteress, from the foreigner who flatters with her words" (Proverbs 7:4, NAS).

■ ■ ■ ■ ■

The dictionary describes wisdom as follows: 1. the state of being wise, 2. experience and knowledge together with the power of applying them, 3. prudence; common sense. I say that to be wise does not mean that you never make a mistake. It is, however, having the humility to recognize your mistakes and then allow them to be used to your advantage in Christ and not for your undoing.

True wisdom from above is in effect when one is humble enough to be wronged (as was Jesus) without retaliation. She dictates silence when your flesh wants to speak out against your offender. Wisdom in operation is a state of self-control and gentleness at all times in all things. Wisdom comes through (as mentioned in chapter four) experience. Experience cannot be bought! It should be prayed into one's life, yet it is not something that comes overnight. It is learned over time as you go through storms and trials of life through the quietude of watching and waiting.

Who among you is wise and understanding? Let him show
by his good behavior his deeds in the gentleness of wisdom.
But if you have bitter jealousy and selfish ambition in your
heart, do not be arrogant and so lie against the truth. This
wisdom is not that which comes down from above, but is
earthly, natural, demonic. For where jealousy and selfish
ambition exist, there is disorder and every evil thing. But the
wisdom from above is first pure, then peaceable, gentle, reasonable, full of mercy and good fruits, unwavering, without
hypocrisy. And the seed whose fruit is righteousness is sown
in peace by those who make peace.

James 3:13–18 (NAS)

Wisdom comes through adversity. Without trials and issues of life,
how would one develop such a God-like characteristic to know how
to conduct themselves? Wisdom does not mean that you never have
a foolish thought. It means that you have enough God-sense to know
the difference between the foolish and the righteous thoughts, and
then choose with purity to remove all that is not of God. It is like
purity. Purity does not mean you never have an impure thought, but
rather you *recognize* them as impure and remove them immediately
before they take root.

Wisdom protects you from the adulterer. Think of the adulterer
in the spiritual realm. The adulterer is actually Satan, the one who
perverts truth in anyway he can. He is the *foreigner* to anyone *of*
God. He flatters through any means possible, even other Christians, to entice you into pride which makes you fall. Wisdom allows
you to *recognize* the enemy in any form he may appear. Wisdom
allows you to *turn away* from the very thing your flesh wants that
is not of God. Wisdom allows you to say no when your fleshly man
wants to say yes, and yes when you want to say no.

A person who boasts in himself is not wise. That person has
wisdom that is of the earth, and it is a lie against God! A person
walking in wisdom from God is gentle, selfless, and peaceable; they
are not a hypocrite and they bear fruit of righteousness. A wise

person in the sight of God is one who understands the frailty of the flesh and acknowledges that, beyond his strength, there is none. A wise person does not allow himself to be deceived by flesh, giving into such thoughts as, "I can handle it (temptation). I don't have to remove myself; I'll be okay." That person will quickly find themselves in the pit of destruction! They are easily lured into the trap through pride.

A person wise in their own eyes is one who will surely fall! They are offended when corrected, and they boast in their own greatness in how *humble* they are. Their wisdom is but foolishness, and it will be their destruction. They do not know when to be quiet. They are a loose cannon quick to speak and slow to listen. They always defend their *rights* when they feel they have been misjudged or mismanaged. They will not die to pride, so pride will turn and kill them!

A genuinely wise person realizes that, compared to God, they will never fully achieve wisdom. It is a constant seeking the Lord in all things and circumstances. When the door is opened to pride, it is a foothold that will be used by the enemy to tell that person that they are always the teacher and never the student. We must be consummate students, even while teaching. A foolish person takes a morsel of information and tosses it about as though they have knowledge when it is really just enough to destroy them and others around them. This person lacks understanding. A person wise in their own estimation will perish by their own hand of ignorance!

"The fear of the Lord is the beginning of wisdom; a good understanding have all those who do his commandments; his praise endures forever" (Psalm 111:10, NAS).

Nothing short of the reverent fear of the Lord will allow you access to attaining wisdom. Without holy fear simply for his name's sake, you have no foundation for wisdom and understanding to take root. Once this foundation is in place, you will earnestly desire purity before such a holy, righteous God. The desire for purity will dictate a life of obedience to his commands. Obedience will usher understanding of his word.

Fear of the Most High God will command an attitude of cleanliness. You will begin to see yourself (before the washing from his holy water that ran from his side) as worthless; one who was conceived in unrighteousness. David plainly writes in Psalm 51 that he came into this world impure. Everyone comes into the world full of sin. It is the sinful nature of Adam. Only upon such realization can you allow him access to your spirit man. It is total humbling that gives him freedom to instill the spirit of wisdom and revelation.

> Then a shoot will spring from the stem of Jesse, and a branch from his roots will bear fruit. The Spirit of the Lord will rest on him, the spirit of wisdom and understanding, the spirit of counsel and strength, the spirit of knowledge and the fear of the Lord. And he will delight in the fear of the Lord, and he will not judge by what his eyes see, nor make a decision by what his ears hear.
>
> Isaiah 11:1–3 (NAS)

"So that the manifold wisdom of God might now be made known through the church to the rulers and the authorities in the heavenly places" (Ephesians 3:10, NAS).

God's desire *is* for everyone in his body to have wisdom and put it to good use. His Spirit *is* wisdom, and he *is* understanding. Everyone who accepts him as Savior receives his precious Holy Spirit. This means that every believer has been given in full the spirit of wisdom and revelation. If only they would tap into him! We each have such knowledge instilled deeply within. It's just that most people receive salvation from hell but never from the bondage of the carnal thinking. They never seek wisdom based on fear of the Lord. They just pack themselves full of Scripture memorization without wisdom or understanding to bring it to life. He is perceived as some being that created hell and then gave us a way out. From an earthly standpoint, it all seems ridiculous and cruel.

Wisdom is love. God *is* wisdom, and he *is* love. They cannot be separated. True love is wise (discerning), not emotional. A heart of man set on the heart of God will guarantee life eternal in heaven, as well as here on earth. Love removes fear that comes from the liar. Love covers a multitude of sin and reveals the possibility and hope of change. You will be wise, realizing that life on earth is not the end. In this understanding, you will not fear the threats of the enemy and will no longer be moved by them. You will no longer make decisions based on fear of loss because, through love, you have already surrendered all to him. There is nothing *of the earth* to lose. You have already *gained* the kingdom of heaven because Christ is *within* you before you physically get to heaven.

"Your heart was lifted up because of your beauty; you corrupted your wisdom by reason of your splendor, I cast you to the ground; I put you before *kings,* that they may *see* you" (Ezekiel 28:17, NAS).

The verse in Ezekiel is what the Lord God said referencing Lucifer, the highest and greatest, most beautiful angel. He is the one that stood right in front of God. He was given wisdom, yet he corrupted it by believing that he was greater than his Creator. He allowed a lie to take hold and ruin all that was pure within. Pride is always a lie!

Then it gets interesting. The Lord said he tossed him to the ground (to earth from heaven), and he put him before kings (mankind) that they (you and I) may *see* him. How utterly humiliating for such a magnificent creature! Eve could not *see* him for what he was—a liar, thief and murderer. He *appeared* wise and beautiful. He wants no one to see (truly see with the eye of God) what and who he really is. So, he spends all of his borrowed time on earth attempting to deceive kings. As long as you and I *believe* the lie, we become ensnared by him, and in turn, the lie robs us of our authority and position as kings!

Look back at Isaiah 11. Given that the Spirit of the Lord *is* wisdom, understanding, counsel, strength, fear of the Lord, it is also *vision* into the heavenly realm of Almighty God. Unless you humble yourself and daily die to your flesh, the Holy Spirit cannot rule. If he who is the King of kings is not given permission *by* you to rule *through* you, you cannot rule as a king among kings. You forfeit your kingship.

However, when the anointing of Holy Spirit is stirred within, you are allowed to rule because the Ruler of all rules through your mortal body. In this, you will have his *holy vision* allowing you to stop judging situations and people based on the lie of the natural; to stop making decisions based on the lie whispered in your mortal ear, hallelujah! Of course you know that what you see (i.e. television, media, addiction, lusts of the flesh, etc.) is not generally what is true. Falsehoods must *appear* true so that you will believe. If they *looked* false, you would not so easily be ensnared! Falsehoods are false balance. They only *seem* balanced and right.

"A false balance is an abomination to the Lord, but a just weight is his delight. When pride comes, then comes dishonor, but with the humble is wisdom. The integrity of the upright will guide them, but the crookedness of the treacherous will destroy them … he who despises his neighbor lacks sense (wisdom), but a man of understanding keeps silent" (Proverbs 11:2, 12, NAS).

"Through insolence (pride) comes nothing but strife, but wisdom is with those who receive counsel" (Proverbs 13:10, NAS).

God is the Great Counselor! Yes, receive counsel from people led by Holy Spirit, but in order to receive from those, *you* must be led by the same Spirit within them. This is unity within *one* body in Christ (the head of the body). Your spirit-man must be awakened to hear truth instead of the lie. earth is Satan's playground for a short season. Unless you ask the Lord to separate your soul from your spirit, your soul will rule. Pride keeps wisdom far away. Humility ushers her into your gates (your inner man).

"Death and life are in the power of the tongue, and those who love it will eat its fruit" (Proverbs 18:21, NAS).

"Keep your tongue from evil and your lips from speaking deceit" (Psalm 34:13, NAS).

"If anyone thinks himself to be religious, and yet does not bridle his tongue but deceives his own heart, this man's religion is worthless" (James 1:26, NAS).

On the lips of the discerning, wisdom is found, but a rod is for the back of him who lacks understanding. Wise men store up knowledge, but with the mouth of the foolish, ruin is at hand … the wages of the righteous is life, the income of the wicked, punishment. He is on the path of life who heeds instruction, but he who ignores reproof goes astray. He who conceals hatred has lying lips, and he who spreads slander is a fool. When there are many words, transgression is unavoidable, but he who restrains his lips is wise. The tongue of the righteous is a choice silver, the heart of the wicked is worth little … the mouth of the righteous flows with wisdom, but the perverted tongue will be cut out.

Proverbs 10:13–20, 31 (NAS)

Without question, a person who does not practice self-control in their speech will be destroyed by their own words. Death and life are in the power of the words that you speak on a daily basis. With the absence of wisdom and understanding of the ways of God, you will inadvertently speak your own death! For example, "I'm an addict and always will be … I'm an adulterer and I am forever scarred … I can't resist … I have no choice … I was born this way." Saved or unsaved, this is a law of God. You welcome into your life whatever you *speak* over it. A person speaks what they *think* they know. They think they know truth based on what they see in the natural. This is why it is imperative to *know* the Word of God in your innermost being so that your words will be in line with his.

An evil tongue (gossip, flattery, slander, malice, hatred, etc.) will reap the harvest of whatever you allow it to sow. In James chapter one, we are right back to the deception of Satan. If you do not allow Holy Spirit to control the thoughts before they become words, you have allowed the deception of him into your heart and spirit. You will speak the lies you see with your natural eyes and hear with your human ears—destruction will rule! You are to be led, not by your circumstances that surround you, but by the holy promises of God. Speak what you do not yet see (Romans 4)! Trust that he will do what he has promised. Jump into truth that you may then by faith, grow wings, and fly! The leap of faith comes before the manifestation of the promise!

The tongue of too many words and perversion will be cut out! These believe that their tongue belongs to themselves and not the One who created them! Only a fool would reject rebuke. With a person who refuses to restrain his tongue, sin is inevitable. Even if one is talking about God all the time and has to constantly get in the last word is without wisdom or balance. The wise *know* not to cast their pearls before swine and the dogs; that the swine and dogs will turn and destroy them for too much chatter. God's Word is precious and should not be spoken to just anyone anytime. Wisdom should be heeded when a mocker of the Word tries to entice you to speak out of turn about him. Mockers and scoffers will trap you. Jesus *grew* in wisdom. He knew exactly whom to answer and when. Look closely in the gospels and see how many times it reads that *he did not answer.*

The Lord states repeatedly that rebuke is for the righteous, not the unrighteous. A person who rejects discipline hates himself. They are set against themselves. The one who only wants their own way and get it are undisciplined and pave a road to hell! Discipline of the Lord and learning self-discipline is for the good of every believer desiring to be like him.

Remember when David said to the Lord to turn from his discipline? The more he *grew* in wisdom, the more he began to realize that discipline was for his advantage in life and begged God for it. The wise welcome correction. The wise grow even wiser with the receiving of correction. Even if you are wrongly corrected, humble yourself to receive it, go home (your prayer closet), discern it with your spirit, take what you can learn from it (if nothing more than deeper humility), and throw the rest away. You don't need to go to that person and tell them how wrong they were. That will only prove their correctness due to your display of pride.

Note Proverbs chapter eighteen, verse one. A person who separates himself seeks only his own desires. This is foolishness! No one is an island unto himself. Many think they are the only righteous one left so they remove themselves from *sinners*. This is against sound wisdom! You cannot succeed alone (Colossians 3). We are here *together* to be *united* and strengthened as one in him. When you remove yourself from the fold, it is pride. You already know where that leads. We all must learn to be patient one with another, growing up each other together. Where you are strong, strengthen the weak. Where you are weak, let those who are strong strengthen you. A critical spirit is a prideful one.

Many false accusations were hurled at Christ (Matthew 11:19). He did not have to speak to defend himself. His wisdom was vindicated by her constant display of integrity. It spoke louder than any amount of words of defense. Wisdom demands that you (more often than not) be silent and let he who is wisdom display himself by grace.

> "Nation will rise against nation and kingdom against kingdom, and there will be great earthquakes, and in various places plagues and famines; and there will be terrors and great signs from heaven. But before all these things, they will lay their hands on you and will persecute you, delivering you to the synagogues and prisons, bringing you before kings and governors for my name's sake. It will lead to an opportunity for your testimony. So make up your minds not to prepare beforehand to defend yourselves; for I will give you utterance and wisdom which none of your opponents will be able to resist or refute. But you will be betrayed even by parents and brothers and relatives and friends, and they will put some of you to death, and you will be hated by all because of my name. Yet not a hair of your head will perish. By your endurance you will gain your lives."

> Luke 21:10–19 (NAS)

You must get your words aligned with God's way of thinking! The one who understands the wisdom from above will move all authority because they know how to speak life, power, authority, and humility. This person's steps will be protected and will be healed. A soothing tongue is life and it breaks down barriers that have held them back from their blessings (Proverbs 12:18–19).

Your tongue should be a *ready writer* (Psalm 45:1). This means your heart is always set on God. Your heart dictates what your mouth speaks. A heart set on the Word of God will always be prepared to speak. He will put his words in your mouth.

> For the word of the cross is foolishness to those who are perishing, but to us who are being saved it is the power of God. For it is written, "I will destroy the wisdom of the wise, and the cleverness of the clever I will set aside." Where is the wise man? Where is the scribe? Where is the debater of this age? Has not God made foolish the wisdom of the world? For since in the wisdom of God the world through its wisdom did not come to know God, God was well-pleased through the foolishness of the message preached to save those who believe. For indeed Jews ask for signs and Greeks search for wisdom; but we preach Christ crucified, to Jews a stumbling block and to Gentiles foolishness, but to those who are the called, both Jews and Greeks, Christ the power of God and the wisdom of God. Because the foolishness of God is wiser than men, and the weakness of God is stronger than men. For consider your calling, brethren, that there were not many wise according to the flesh, not many mighty, not many noble; but God has chosen the foolish things of the world to shame the wise, and God has chosen the weak things of the world to shame the things which are strong, and the base things of the world and the despised God has chosen, the things that are not, so that he may nullify the things that are, so that no man may boast before God.
>
> 1 Corinthians 1:18–29 (NAS)

Don't allow the liar to fool you into believing that there is no hope for you! Whatever you've done, wherever you've gone, whatever you've spoken—it has no strength against our perfect Son of God! He will, if you allow him, open your eyes to a world you have not yet seen, hear the voice few have heard, and know what few have known! Allow him to restore you so that through you, those who think themselves wise will be humbled by *his* power and repent of *their* unrighteousness! I will go so far to say that the worse you have been, the greater his power will be revealed when the world sees the change *he* manifests in and through your mortal body!

The wise seek after wisdom until the day they leave this earth. You can never have enough! All perfect wisdom is *within* the believer, but it requires humbling yourself to ask him to allow it to manifest through your situations. You must stir Holy Spirit by recognizing before him and the world that only he can perform such greatness through you. Seek and you shall find. Ask and it will be given unto you. The Christ child himself had to *grow* in wisdom. He set the stage for us all. If *he* had to grow, so do *you and I* so much more!

He desires that you and I have *full confidence* of understanding so that, when the evil one comes knocking at your door, you are not persuaded (ignorantly) away from truth. Ground yourself in him. Wisdom will pull you out from beneath the death spirit! Wisdom and understanding bring life to the lifeless; hope to the hopeless; rest to the weary!

All who proclaim the blood of the resurrected Son of God are a part of his *wife*. Terms such as *son, king, wife,* and *bride* have no gender. Again, you must see as God sees to understand this concept that is far beyond the thinking of the natural man. Males and females *are* the *bride* of Christ, his *wife*. They declare the endless love he has for his people. Males and females are *kings, priests,* and *sons* of God. These terms from God decree authority of the highest degree.

With this understanding, Proverbs 31 applies to *all* of God's bride, wife, sons, and kings. We are to be good stewards of all he puts in our physical and spiritual territory. *She* (her) represents his bride. *He* (Husband) represents God, the Husband of his bride.

Ask the Lord to open your eye to all the written word so that you *see* it as *he* means it, not as humanly misrepresented. Your thinking must be raised to the *heaven* and away from the *ground.* The ground is cursed. Anything attached to it is also. If your thinking is *of the ground*—earthly—it is useless to your walk in Christ.

■ ■ ■ ■ ■

Prayer

O, most gracious heavenly Father, bestow me thy wisdom! Give me the spirit of wisdom and revelation that I may know you better. Pour into me your holiness, purity, humility, and reverent fear. I confess that, without you, I am nothing. I am everything with you, in you, and through you! My hope rests in you, not in myself. My confidence of change lays in your perfect Son, Jesus Christ. Please separate my spirit from my soul that I may fully commune with Holy Spirit within. Show me how to be like you in all my ways. Bridle my tongue from sin and iniquity. Tame my tongue as only you can. Put a watch over my mouth that I not sin against you. I praise you that, as I seek your wisdom, she will be my sister, and understanding will be my intimate friend for the rest of my life. I will not pull away from you. Deal with me ever so severely if I sin against you. Do not let me fall. Chastise me through your loving kindness. Teach me self-discipline and how to say no to the flesh! I declare and decree my everlasting love for you as you have already declared over me.

Patience:
Imperative for Spiritual
SUCCESS

When pride comes, then comes dishonor, but with the humble is wisdom … with his mouth the godless man destroys his neighbor, but through knowledge the righteous will be delivered … he who despises his neighbor lacks sense, but a man of understanding keeps silent.

Proverbs 11:2, 9, 12 (NAS)

The very nature and essence of God is quiet, gentle, humble, meek, and pure. Jesus Christ was not argumentative with people. Even in the face of adversity, he was neither defensive nor pushy. He was not timid, but humble. There is a fine line between the two, yet they are worlds apart. He had an answer when he needed to answer, and he remained silent when there was no need to speak. He was never out to defend his reputation, but in all circumstances remained humble so that God had leeway to come in later and exalt him.

His Word was an expression of his power. Therefore, he did not have to fight with people. People either received him or they did not. He did not badger people into believing. He is power, and when he speaks, it exudes. When we allow him to speak through us, it comes forth. Speaking the very name of Jesus is power without loudness or aggression! "He is upholding all things by the word of his power," states Hebrews 1:3.

"Take My yoke upon you and learn from Me, for I am gentle and humble in heart, and you will find rest for your souls" (Matthew 11:29, NAS).

"The fruit of the Spirit is love, joy, peace, patience, kindness, goodness, faithfulness, gentleness and self-control; against such things there is no law" (Galatians 5:22–23, NAS).

You must always conduct yourself in a manner worthy of the gospel of Christ with a gentle and quiet spirit (Ephesians 4:1–2). You can be bold and courageous at the same time of being humble, gentle, and meek. You being quiet and still in a chaotic situation can actually speak volumes over a loud, abrupt word. When Jesus was sought after in the garden, they did not know for whom they were seeking. He did not resist, but gave himself over humbly. His humility made *them* fall back. He did not yell and scream, demanding that they recognize who he is. His humility had more power than any loud speech he could have exerted toward them.

As a representative of Christ, neither should you be loud or argumentative with others. Jesus said to the disciples to "kick the dust off of your feet" when they were not received by others. Do not try to badger people into obedience to Christ. It is always non- productive. Let those who will listen and receive do so. Those who will not, let them go. *Do not* use the precious and sacred Word of God to annihilate those who are still in any kind of disobedience. If you do, you are also wrong. You are to be patient and kind with everyone. This means if you elevate yourself above others in your walk, your walk is not what it should be or what you perceive it to be. Be careful to simply separate yourself from whom God reveals you should and leave them alone. Do not speak unkindly of them, do not speak of them at all unless you are interceding for them in prayer.

"But we proved to be gentle among you, as a nursing mother tenderly cares for her own children" (1 Thessalonians 2:7, NAS).

"To malign (slander, speak evil of, abuse) no one, to be peaceable, gentle, showing every consideration for all men" (Titus 3:2, NAS).

You are to be patient with people at all times—saved or unsaved—just as God himself is patient with *you!* There are times that God will separate you from someone or something that is a constant hindrance to you. He has promised to contend with those who contend with his own. However, that is for God to decide the timing. Until that happens, stand strong in he who is within you, and do not allow the enemy (in whatever form he may come) to remove you from patience or any other attribute of Holy Spirit. Annoying people and things are tools of Satan to make you falter. God, on the other hand, intends them to be a sharpening tool to teach you how to stand in him. If you are never tested in the area of patience, how can you know how to stand in it?

Losing your patience allows room for anger; it allows all sorts of sin to enter, such as a lack of love, joy, peace, gentleness. The fruit of the Spirit is ONE. Like an apple tree, there are many from one tree but they are all of the same source and kind. You do not see stems hanging alone, or cores, skins, and inners. They all grow altogether. So it is with the fruit of the Spirit of God. He is love, joy, peace, patience, kindness, goodness, faithfulness, gentleness, and self-control. Take one away, and they all leave together! In addition, these are some attributes, but not limited to these alone. Others are compassion, mercy, and humility.

Recently I was in a position to teach the word to those who had merely made a profession of faith. Afterwards, they were still dead spiritually though they had been *saved* and had been in church many, many years. I expected more from them. When they did not grow as I thought they should, I became impatient—*very* impatient! I became arrogant in my demeanor, which led to unkindness, harshness, loveless-ness, and lack of joy. That in turn made me unfaithful because the very thing the Lord had called me to do, I no longer could do because I showed nothing of the love of Christ; I displayed anger and disapproval. James 1:20 proclaims, "The anger of man does not achieve the righteousness of God." This says to me that anger in humans is utterly useless in God's perspective! If we looking for god

could all get to the place where we understand this concept, there would be much less anger floating around killing people, and there would be much more patience through love drawing all men unto himself.

When I read that Scripture for the first time with anointing, I realized just how foolish anger is. It accomplishes nothing. This word is for the body of Christ; especially for the one who tries to yell, scream, and brow-beat someone into a relationship with God; for the one who quickly loses patience and temper with those not walking in a manner *that person* deems worthy. It is certainly for all in any situation, but those are just two specific examples. The point is that anger brings nothing of righteousness, and no one can make sound decisions in a state of anger. We are not to sin in our anger; a concept few achieve!

My anger toward that group of people only made God's Word seem harsh and unforgiving. That was not the intent of my heart, yet that is what I projected. My anger came from a lack of patience. When you are patient, you do not lose focus on the goal.

It is patience from a heart of pure love that wins others to Christ. His love is the minister *through* you, not you yourself. In that, it is not you doing the winning, but rather the display of the endless love of the Father. Paul in Philippians chapter three said it was not a problem to repeat the word. Most don't like to repeat themselves once, much less many times over. But Paul was patient as God is patient, because he understood his own frailty of the flesh and the frailty of all of mankind.

"We urge you, brothers, admonish the unruly, encourage the fainthearted, help the weak, be patient with everyone (toward all men)" (1 Thessalonians 5:14, NAS).

"The testing of your faith produces patience (endurance). Let endurance have its perfect result, so that you may be perfect and complete, lacking in nothing" (James 1:3–4, NAS).

Trials can be large, like being imprisoned, or they can be small, like a person that bugs you that will not go away. If you are distressed in any capacity, let your faith be proven that you may be refined by God. You are to *endure* hardships to develop patience. You either allow the trials to push you away from God or toward him. Trials merely prove your level of faith. He is the Holy Fire, and he desires to burn out of you all that is wicked. You need to allow the development of patience in all situations so that you can stand in the evil day. Most become impatient, not just with people, but circumstances surrounding them. Know that he is God, seek to grow in relationship with him, to be like him, so that you will be unstained by the world (James 1:27).

Will You Bear an Isaac or an Ishmael?

When you operate in impatience long enough, you birth into your life (spiritually speaking) an *Ishmael*. This means that you conceive and give birth to your own enemy! Ishmael was the illegitimate son of Abraham. He was the product of the anger and impatience toward God from Sarai. Abraham held out in faith for ten years. Then he caved to impatience and took his wife's handmaiden to *make* (force) God's promise of an heir into being.

He then wanted the Lord to bless that child and make covenant with him! We, more often than not, sin through lack of patience with God. Then we have the audacity to ask the Lord to bless the product of that sin! He was upset when the Lord said the covenant was with *Isaac* rather than Ishmael. He loved the product of the sin, as any natural human being would. As he saw things, Ishmael was his flesh and blood. His perspective was skewed by emotional attachment. That is always a big mistake! *Emotions* should never be what lead God's people into a decision. We are to be moved only by Holy Spirit. Let's back up and look at the texts to see how things came about.

"Then behold, the Word of the Lord came to him, saying, 'This man will not be your heir; but one who will come forth from your own body, he shall be your heir.' And he took him outside and said, 'now look toward the heavens, and count the stars, if you are able to count them." And he said to him, "So shall your descendants be.' Then he believed in the Lord; and he reckoned it to him as righteousness" (Genesis 15:4–6, NAS).

In this text above, they assumed that the son of a servant would become his heir.

> Now Sarai, Abram's wife had borne him no children, and she had an *Egyptian* maid whose name was Hagar. So Sarai said to Abram, "Now behold, *the Lord has prevented me* from bearing children. Please go in to my maid; perhaps I will obtain children through her." And Abram listened to the voice of Sarai. After Abram had lived ten years in the land of Canaan, Abram's wife Sarai took Hagar the Egyptian, her maid, and gave her to her husband Abram as his wife ... the angel of the Lord said to her further, "Behold, you are with child, and you will bear a son; and you shall call his name Ishmael because the Lord has given heed to your affliction. He will be a wild donkey of a man, his hand will be against everyone, and everyone's hand will be against him; and he will live to the east of all his brothers."
>
> Genesis 16:1–3, 11–12 (NAS)

Evidently, ten years was Abram's timeframe for God to fulfill his promise! Once Hagar conceived, an angel of the Lord told them that Ishmael would be a *wild donkey of a man;* he would be rebellious; he would fight all of his days. He will live east of all his brothers. This is the people of the Arab nations. We see this word intact today.

Sarai's anger toward God is revealed in verse two. She blames the Lord as though he forgot to give them what he promised. Her disdain for the Lord is evident as she offers her maid to Abram. It reads that Abram listened to the voice of Sarai. Big mistake. This means he was no longer listening to the voice of the Lord (so much like Adam and Eve!).

It is interesting that, though Ishmael came from him, because he did not come from Sarai (his wife) also, God translated that as *not of his own blood*. In other words, only that of his *wife* is considered *his* since they are one flesh. This solidifies the importance of marriage, faithfulness, and the sanctity of marriage. Anything less than that which comes from purity is tainted.

We, children of God, are God's wife. Anything conceived outside of relationship with him is illegitimate and is not accepted by God. You may have a prophecy spoken into your life that you are going to be something, have something, or go somewhere. If you *force* that prophecy into being of your flesh, though the word *appears* fulfilled, it is not. Only that which comes from the supernatural hand of God is fulfillment. Many ministries and good deeds fail because they were birthed into being out of season and from the flesh of man.

> Now when Abram was ninety-nine years old, the Lord appeared to Abram and said to him, "*I am God Almighty; walk before Me, and be blameless. I will establish My covenant between Me and you,* and I will multiply you exceedingly." "I will bless her, and indeed I will give you a son by her. Then I will bless her, and she shall be a mother of nations; kings of peoples will come from her." Then Abraham fell on his face and laughed, and said in his heart, "Will a child be born to a man one hundred years old? And will Sarah, who is ninety years old, bear a child?" And Abraham said, "Oh that Ishmael might live before you!" But God said, "No, but Sarah your wife will bear you a son, and you shall call his name *Isaac:* and I will establish my covenant with him for an everlasting covenant for his descendants after him. As for Ishamael, I have heard you; behold, I will bless him, and will make him fruitful and will multiply him exceedingly. He shall become the father of twelve princes, and I will make him a great nation. But My covenant I will establish with Isaac, whom Sarah will bear to you at this season next year."
>
> Genesis 17:1, 16–21 (NAS)

Notice the Lord starts his conversation by boldly reminding Abram that he *is* God Almighty! I take that as a chastisement for his actions. He commands him to walk upright and blameless. His action with Hagar was not upright or blameless. He goes on to make covenant with Abram and his descendants. Then he tells him that the covenant will be with seed from his wife, not the illegitimate child.

Abram found this statement from the Lord outrageous. This is when he asked the Lord to bless Ishmael, the seed of sin! Because Abraham loved his illegitimate son, he cried to God to bless him. The Lord had compassion for his plight and blessed Ishmael. By this act, Abraham asked the Lord to bless and multiply the very people who would rise against God's anointed people—Isaac's descendants!

> Then the Lord took note of Sarah as he had said, and the Lord did for Sarah as he had promised. 2. So Sarah conceived and bore a son to Abraham in his old age, at the *appointed time* of which God had spoken to him…3. Isaac…4. He was 100 years old. 10. Sarah said to Abraham, "Drive out this maid and her son, for the son of this maid shall not be an heir with my son Isaac." 12. But God said to Abraham, "Do not be distressed because of the lad and your maid; whatever Sarah tells you, listen to her, for through Isaac your descendants shall be named. 13. And of the son of the maid I will make a nation also, because he is your descendant."
>
> Genesis 21:1–4, 10, 12–13 (NAS)

Verse one of chapter twenty-one, twice makes it clear that what God said he would do, he will do! Verse 2 reads, "at the appointed time of which God had spoken to him." The timing of God and the timing of what Sarah and Abraham interpreted in their human minds as God's timing were entirely different. We must, when we receive a prophecy, not push to make it happen! Impatience is of the enemy every time! There are no exceptions. Patience is an attribute of God. Without it in operation in our lives, we will fail! Prophecy that has been spoken correctly will not come to pass as God intended without patience in operation.

When it doesn't, we turn and blame God, the Prophet, and everyone else involved except ourselves. Then we turn and toss aside faith in God. Then the real prophecy has to be shelved for a time until the righteous and patient of another generation come along, pick it up, and wait on God to bring it to fruition.

> Without becoming weak in faith he contemplated his own body, now as good as dead since he was about a hundred years old, and the deadness of Sarah's womb; *yet, with respect to the promise of God, he did not waver in unbelief but grew strong in faith, giving glory to God* and being fully assured that what God had promised, he was able also to perform.
>
> Romans 4:17:19–21 (NAS)

Fortunately, the second time around (after the Lord corrected him) Abraham refused to waver in his faith. It was completely grounded in God, no matter what he saw with his natural eyes. He basically said, "I see with my natural eyes that there is no way possible for us to conceive. However, I see only with the single vision of Almighty God, therefore, I believe the promise over what seems to be an absolute in the flesh. I trust the vision of God over the impossibility of the natural." He recognized that what God promises, God can and will perform!

> Tell me, you who want to be under law, do you not listen to the law? For it is written that Abraham had two sons, one by the bondwoman and one by the free woman. But the son by the bondwoman was born according to the flesh, and the son by the free woman through the promise ... and your brothers, like Isaac, are children of promise. But as at that time he who was born according to the flesh persecuted him who was born according to the Spirit, so it is now also. But what does the Scripture say? "Cast out the bondwoman and her son, for the son of the bondwoman shall not be an heir with the son of the free.
>
> Galatians 4:21–23, 28–31 (NAS)

"For where a covenant is, there must of necessity be the death of the one who made it. For a covenant is valid only when men are dead, for it is never in force while the one who made it lives" (Hebrews 9:16–17, NAS).

God promises to faithfully bless abundantly those who humble themselves. Patience and gentleness come from humility. He promises to come in and exalt you in due season, just as he did with Jesus, when you humble yourself before him and man. When you try to minister in his name with a prideful spirit, though his name may draw someone despite your attitude, you are the one who cannot be exalted by him.

"Let your gentle spirit be known to all men. *The Lord is near* ... the things you have learned and received and heard and seen in me, practice these things and the God of peace will be with you" (Philippians 4:5, 9, NAS).

"A soft answer turns away wrath" (Proverbs 15:1, NAS).

"The meek also shall increase their joy in the Lord, and the poor among men shall rejoice in the Holy One of Israel" (Isaiah 29:19, NAS).

Taming the Tongue of Correction

Any time you are correcting a brother or sister in Christ, it must be done in love and gentleness! It does not mean that the correction is not direct, but it must always be presented with the love of God with the purpose of turning that person to Christ and not for condemnation the Word speaks so much of. You are not to be combative as to engage in an argument of any kind with someone who does not agree. Let God deal with that person; you are not their judge, and you are not God. Only God can bring conviction. Your only job is to present the Word as Holy Spirit leads and leave that Word with them to do the work. God's Word will not return to him void. Present the Word, but let the Word itself do the work in the person.

"If I speak with the tongues of men and of angels, but do not have love, I have become a noisy gong or a clanging cymbal" (1 Corinthians 13:1, NAS).

"Brothers, even if anyone is caught in any trespass, you who are spiritual, restore such a one in a spirit of gentleness; each one looking to yourself, so that you too will not be tempted" (Galatians 6:1, NAS).

"What do you desire? Shall I come to you with a rod, or with love and a spirit of gentleness" (1 Corinthians 4:21, NAS).

> The Lord's bondservant must not be quarrelsome, but be kind to all, able to teach, patient when wronged, with gentleness correcting those who are in opposition, if perhaps God may grant them repentance leading to the knowledge of the truth, and they may come to their senses and escape from the snare of the devil, having been held captive by him to do his will.
>
> 2 Timothy 2:24–26 (NAS)

Only the Holy Spirit through you can tame the human tongue. A human being in himself cannot. The Word states that it is impossible. This is why you must know when to speak and when to be silent. Knowing God's timing is everything. God may give you a Word to speak, but you need to know *when* to speak it. A wise person waits upon the Lord to instruct as to when to give what he gives. Something of God can become evil if spoken out of his timing and will. We are the ones who corrupt his Word. His Word alone is pure, and you must be a good steward over it. A Word out of season can be too harsh for a person to receive. But a Word spoken in season (even if it is a correction) will be a blessing and even a confirmation to a person who is prepared by God to receive.

Stop wasting your time and God's by attempting to force someone to listen to you. Unless God instructs the reprimand, you are casting your pearls before swine and the dogs; they will take the Word and use it to kill you. You would better spend your time beating your head against a brick wall! Matthew says not to cast your pearls (the priceless Word of God) before dogs or swine. Leave alone those who will not receive. Ask God to develop discernment within you to know who is who. No more should there be a running around trying to *get everyone saved,* but rather allow Holy Spirit to work through you as he leads. You will have much less anxiety and aggravation in your daily life.

> And the tongue is a fire, the very world of iniquity; the tongue is set among our members as that which defiles the entire body, and sets on fire the course of our life, and is set on fire by hell. For every species of beasts and birds, of reptiles and creatures of the sea, is tamed and has been tamed by the human race. But no one can tame the tongue; it is a restless evil and full of deadly poison. With it we bless our Lord and Father, and with it we curse men, who have been made in the likeness of God; from the same mouth come both blessing and cursing. My brothers, these things ought not to be this way.
>
> James 3:6–10 (NAS)

■ ■ ■ ■ ■

Prayer

Lay in me, O God, your ways that I may conform to you. Pour into me your very Spirit that is gentle, patient, and humble that I may speak on your behalf as an ambassador in chains. Let your mighty voice be heard through me in all the territory you have given me. Teach me your immeasurable patience so that I, like Jesus, will be patient with all mankind. Bless you, O King of kings and Lord of lords! Bridle my tongue that I not defile my whole body, but in everything have knowledge and understanding of your perfect timing. May I never use your Word as a tool to tear others down, but rather as the tool for life. Allow me to endure whatever needs to be endured so that patience, gentleness, and humility will be able to freely flow from me in all love.

Self-Control: Key to
PROSPERITY

"But I discipline my body and make it my slave, so that, after I have preached to others, I myself will not be judged" (1 Corinthians 9:27, NAS).

Paul states that he disciplined his own body, making it his slave. You are to take control over your body in full. If it wants anything outside the boundaries of God's holiness, command it into obedience. Take control over yourself to the degree that it no longer controls you. Controlling your body is the first area of authority you are to walk. If you don't control the temple you reside, you cannot have legitimate authority in any other area of life. If you don't take control, you may be preaching and growing up others in Christ, yet you will fail in your own walk and be judged for the things you teach but do not walk yourself, which is the meaning of the latter part of this verse.

Obedience is a choice. God calls you to *self*-control, not *forced* control. He forces you to do nothing. There is a place in the life of every believer where you have to decide for yourself to know the Word, believe the Word, put faith in the Word, seek understanding of the Word, and choose to walk by the Word.

The Father calls you to self-control as Jesus himself was self-controlled. He *chose* not to sin though he was tempted on every side. There is no temptation befallen man that he did not *choose* to deny himself. He was the perfect example of *letting* or *allowing* himself not to give in to sin. He could have and very easily. His flesh was like yours and mine. His flesh desired the things of the world, the lusts thereof. He displayed in every circumstance the *dying to self,* which equals self-control. The *self* means that he did not pray, "Oh, God, because I am your Son, make this go away. *Make* me say no." He had to *choose* just like you and I.

As soon as you decide that you will be self-disciplined, prepare for tests! Don't get mad at God, assuming he allowed it to happen just to make you fall. He allows temptation to strengthen you. It is to develop self-control. You don't just choose self-discipline and then never have opportunity to walk in it. What good is it if you never have to use it? Living in Satan's territory (earth) either kills you spiritually and/or physically, or you train yourself to walk strongly in the Word by becoming disciplined in all your ways. The world is full of temptation without God or Satan having to put it in your face. It is already out there awaiting your destruction!

Food, perversion, pornography, lies, fear, shame, indulgence, greed, gluttony, debt, covetousness, drunkenness, prejudice, slander, rage, murder, gossip—you name it, it's there for the taking. You have to begin to *let* yourself be obedient to the Holy Spirit to be able to control your fleshly desire. This is the killing of the flesh. The more you *practice*, the stronger you will be spiritually. When someone goes to college to become a doctor, they are thoroughly tested before being given a degree (of authority). Even after graduation, it's called practice! Learning is continual so to continually grow.

First, you need to know what God says about the matter. You need to understand that *abstinence* from any sin is still an act of the flesh. Whatever you deny yourself just for the sake of denial will lead you right back to the thing you are trying to avoid. This is where it is imperative to be in *relationship* with the Father. You need to *eat* his word as God instructed Ezekiel. You need to become *one with the Word,* which is the same as becoming one with Father, Son, and Holy Spirit. It is a matter of being so in love with them that you never want to displease them as opposed to cold, lifeless religiosity. He is everyone's *first love* because he loved you first.

It sounds way more complicated than it is. It is really quite elementary. It's the *sacrifice* of obedience that opens the door to his power, authority, and bountiful, immeasurable blessings. Obedience is loving God more than you love the earthly lust. This is sacrifice. So many pray, "O Lord, remove my desire for (fill in the blank)." Rather, you should pray, "Father, who art in heaven, have your way with me. I surrender the desires of the flesh that I may please you. Show me how to love you more than the sin." James 1:21 states, "Put aside all filthiness and all that remains of wickedness." The *you* (as we were taught in middle school English) is understood. You can place it in front of the Scripture; therefore, it becomes a direct and personal command from God. So now this verse reads, "*You* put aside..." From this perspective, God is saying that he does not remove the wickedness, but rather you are to choose to dispose of it out of love for him. This is you choosing righteousness despite your carnal lust. This honors God.

With this approach, eventually the carnal desire will subside to the point of having no power over you. There may always be some draw by that particular thing. However, you are now stronger in Christ than the temptation is in you. This is the *fleeing* from temptation. If God took away all lustful desires there would be no sacrifice. Without sacrifice, there is no display of true love for him. His sacrifice was his heart; his Son, his *self.* Your true sacrifice is your earthly pleasures that go against his sovereign, holy Word.

Greater love has no man than he who lays down his life for his friends. Most associate this with God giving his life for yours. That is true, but it likewise is *you giving your life for him.* As Jesus constantly commands his followers to take up your cross and die to the flesh, he hates (and wants you to equally hate) conduct of self-indulgence. Self is the operative word. Anything that is *self*-led is not led of *Holy Spirit.* Jesus lumps self-indulgence in the same category as robbery. This is because when you are self-absorbed you are not glorifying Christ. Therefore, you are *robbing* Christ of what belongs to him. What should belong to him is all of your spirit, soul, body, and their functions. This includes all of your time and how it is spent!

"Woe to you, scribes and Pharisees, hypocrites! For you clean the outside of the cup and of the dish, but inside they are full of robbery and self-indulgence" (Matthew 23:25, NAS).

"You have lived luxuriously on the earth and led a life of wanton pleasure; you have fattened your hearts in a day of slaughter" (James 5:5, NAS).

"To those who by perseverance in doing good seek for glory and honor and immortality, eternal life; but to those who are selfishly ambitious and do not obey the truth, but obey unrighteousness, wrath and indignation" (Romans 2:7–8, NAS).

God calls you to a life of pure and holy love. Pure love is one that can love even the worst offender. Any love or action that seeks after the fulfillment of pleasing self is not love. Any act not led by the love of the Father is an act of the enemy. It is clear-cut and simple. Your actions are either *of God* or *of Satan*. There is no middle ground.

God calls you to a life of humility which takes exceeding self-discipline. You are called to a life of strength, courage, power, authority, love, and humility. Filled with the Spirit of God, you are filled with all authority and power because he is authority and power. Only a person of humility (led by the Holy Spirit) can operate in such. It is the love factor that makes one humble and strong at the same time. Jesus was the epitome of this. No one had greater authority and power than he. No one had more humility, strength, and courage than he. It took incredible strength of self-discipline not to call down his angels to remove him from the cross; to strike everyone dead that came against him and called him *of Satan;* to not say, "Don't you fools know I am the Son of the Living God? Let Me display my power!"; to not badmouth the authority set in place, such as Pilate and Caesar. No more extravagant display of love, strength, and humility has there ever been before or since Jesus!

It takes incredible self-control and humility to be in a position of authority. It also takes strength and courage. It is humbling to be in this position where many look to you for guidance and instruction. Only a meek person in Christ can truly succeed in a place of authority, because that person knows that they can accomplish the task only through the High Priest. An insecure person is the one who boasts in who they *think* they are or in their highly exalted placement. A person *secure in their flesh* boasts to their own destruction! The prideful leader is deceived and will surely fall. The humble, like Jesus, know how to exert their authority without boasting. The world will recognize their authority in how they carry themselves.

"The wicked flee when no one is pursuing, but the righteous are bold as a lion" (Proverbs 28:1, NAS).

"So that we confidently say, "The Lord is my helper, I will not be afraid. What will man do to me" (Hebrews 13:6, NAS).

One attribute of the fruit of the Spirit is self-discipline (control). As I commented earlier, when you are led by the Holy Spirit, not one but all of the attributes therein will come through you. When you are self-disciplined, there is no law that can come against you. He is the Law! Law reveals sin. Where there is no sin, there is no law to condemn you. There is no sin in him who is in you. Let him lead, and you won't have any trouble or problem come against you that he will not personally overcome.

In the general population of the body of Christ, I notice that *timidity* is greatly mistaken for *humility*. There is certainly a fine line between the two. Timidity is fear, and it makes you tuck your tail, run, and hide from the enemy. Humility, however, is recognizing the authority *in you* and walking courageously, knowing that he who is in you is greater than he who is in this world.

Throughout the Word, God commands his anointed to *be* strong and courageous. It is not a suggestion! God is not a wimp, so neither should you be! Humility is confidence in him, not in self. Confidence in self is prideful. You can pray humbly with intense strength, power, courage, and authority because of him. Do not let the enemy plow you over! Take up strength and courage with confidence. This is for those who love him and keep his commands.

You, the child of God, should make the demons tremble as it happened in the garden. The *soldiers* fell back when Christ revealed himself to them. *He* did not fall back. He was confident in his identity in God. He replied, "I AM." God many times in the Old Testament referred to himself as I AM. He exerted his authority and *they* fell. The second time they asked, he humbled himself and allowed them to take him. Just by saying "I AM," they could not stand in his presence! You have him *in* you; therefore, retain such power. You are not to abuse it, as many do.

Temptation is allowed by God. Satan can't come against God's people without his permission. As soon as you learn to train yourself to be disciplined in any area that is weak, you will no longer be tempted. Temptation is something that draws *you* but not everyone. Alcohol is not a temptation to me, but it is to some. Overspending is to me, but not necessarily to someone else. A true temptation is anything that draws *you* to sin, not what may draw someone else.

The Bible states that you are to prepare your mind for action. You must choose how you conduct yourself. You must make an executive decision that you will be led by he who is in you, who is self-control. Stop being a mess. Stop giving in to every whim that leaves you in a constant condition of defeat. *You* stop! Part of dying to yourself is what leads you to be established in self-discipline. When you die to yourself, there is no longer a self to make decisions that are bad. Your *self* is now controlled by the one with whom you are merged.

Being self-controlled includes *not* being led by your emotions. There is a whole lot of emotionalism within the body of Christ. In the more charismatic denominations, people often are *slain in the Spirit*, crying in the Spirit, and speaking in tongues. I am in total agreement that these are real moves of God. However, there must be balance, which is a part of discipline. I hear so often and have witnessed firsthand much of this, to the point of it simply being a

sideshow or a circus act. Don't for one moment think I am quench-
ing the Holy Spirit; on the contrary. What I see is that when many
are speaking in tongues, crying uncontrollably, or being slain, there
is a spirit of confusion and chaos; neither of which are from God.
God is a God of order, discipline, and self-control.

God's people are to be an orderly, disciplined people. I know
of people who speak in tongues just to irritate those who don't
believe. How does that honor God? It is meant only for evil one-
upmanship. You need to be very, very careful not to do anything *for
God* without love. As a reminder, Paul says in 1 Corinthians 13 that
without love, no matter what gift you have, it is for nothing without
being coupled with love.

When you are led by your emotions, you leave yourself wide
open for Satan to have a foothold. It is altogether possible to speak
in tongues through emotions, but they are tongues of Satan or the
flesh, not God. Many a church has crumbled because *plants* have
been sent to churches to speak in curses through tongues. In doing
it this way, they can speak curses right in the midst of the congregations and leaders! What's worse is that everyone gets in agreement
because they do not follow the instructions of the Father, which is
that there must be interpretation.

This is partly why so many denominations have done away with
tongues completely. Plus, if many people are speaking in tongues at
once, it is madness. No one is edified, and God is not glorified in
the chaos. It turns people *away* from God instead of *toward* God.
Since he is all-knowing, he would not direct that many to speak in
tongues because he already knows the outcome. Be *conscientious of
him* and how he is leading, instead of attempting in your natural
man to simply carry out *acts of his gifts* such as speaking in tongues,
prophesying, or anything seemingly good for the sake of appearance. Wrong motives equal not of God.

Do you see why there is such imbalance within the denomina-
tional churches? It is from a lack of discipline, balance, and understanding of how to die to the flesh. As I have stated many times,

most people want *godliness* without knowing God himself. This is why everything is such a disaster. People want to *look* holy instead of *be* holy.

> If I come to you speaking in tongues, what will I profit you unless I speak to you either by way of revelation or of knowledge or of prophesy or of teaching...unless you utter by the tongue speech that is clear, how will it be known what is spoken? For you will be speaking into the air...if then I do not know the meaning of the language, I will be to the one who speaks a barbarian, and the one who speaks will be a barbarian to me. So also you, since you are zealous of spiritual gifts, seek to abound for the edification of the church. Therefore let one who speaks in a tongue pray that he may interpret...if you bless in the spirit only how will the one who fills the place of the ungifted say the "Amen" at your giving of thanks, since he does not know what you are saying? For you are giving thanks well enough, but the other person is not edified. I thank God, I speak in tongues more than you all; however, in the church I desire to speak five words with my mind so that I may instruct others also, rather than ten thousand words in a tongue.

> 1 Corinthians 14:6, 9–12, 16 (NAS)

Below (Titus 1) is listed the conduct of an overseer. It really applies to you, me, and every believer. We are all to be an overseer on some level. I heard it said once that everyone teaches; everyone is an example. You either teach by your words or actions something of God or of Satan. Your example is one of godliness or ungodliness. You choose. There is always someone watching. There is always someone taking mental notes. If you carry the label *Christian,* you are guaranteed to have spectators.

> For the overseer must be above reproach as God's steward, not self-willed, not quick-tempered, not addicted to wine, not pugnacious, not fond of sordid gain, but hospitable, loving what is good, sensible, just, devout, self-controlled,

holding fast to the faithful Word which is in accordance with
the teaching, so that he will be able both to exhort in sound
doctrine and to refute those who contradict.

Titus 1:7–9 (NAS)

Be temperate (self-disciplined), dignified, sensible, sound in
faith, in love, in perseverance … to be sensible, pure, workers at home, kind … so that the Word of God will not be
dishonored. Likewise urge the young men to be sensible;
in all things show yourself to be an example of good deeds,
with purity in doctrine, dignified, sound in speech which is
beyond reproach, so that the opponent will be put to shame,
having nothing bad to say about us.

Titus 2:2, 5, 6, 12 (NAS)

I reiterate that you really need to understand the meaning of *let*. Just
as the word *be* has an understood *you* in front of it, *let* does likewise.
Let means that you *allow* something. These two small words are
commands from God, not suggestions. This is also self-discipline.
You *let* Christ rule in your heart or you don't. You *let* yourself conduct yourself in a manner worthy of Christ or you don't. You *choose*
to lose control or not. You *choose* to be easily offended or you don't.
You *choose* to cry all the time or you don't. *You* have to reprogram
yourself through his Word. Once you begin to declare daily that
you die to yourself, that choice begins a reprogramming process.
Your thinking will begin to get lined up with God's.

These next texts cover the *letting* of your conduct as one led
by the Holy Spirit. *Let* your answers be grounded in the gospel so
that you are not double-minded. *Allow* peace to rule in your heart.
Choose to die to yourself. The list goes on. Pray for wisdom that is
pure, peaceable, easily entreated, without hypocrisy, full of mercy,
and grace.

"But let your statement be 'Yes, yes' or 'No, no'; anything beyond
these is of evil" (Matthew 5:37, NAS).

> Be angry, and yet do not sin; do not let the sun go down on your anger ... him who steels must steal no longer; but rather let him labor, performing with his own hands what is good so that he will have something to share with one who has need. Let no corrupt communication proceed out of your mouth, but that which is good to the use of edifying, that it may minister grace unto the hearers ... let all bitterness and wrath and anger and clamor and slander be put away from you, along with all malice.
>
> Ephesians 4:26, 28, 29, 31 (NAS)

Let, let, let! Allow yourself to be disciplined. For instance: Say you are someone who cries all the time. Better yet, you are someone who only cries when you talk about the greatness and goodness of God. You say, "But I can't help crying when I talk about him. I just love him so!" Crying irrationally, at the drop of a hat, without warning or at any inappropriate time is a lack of discipline. Again, to say that you can't help it, means you are either spinning out of control or you like the attention you receive when it happens.

I know. I used to be this very person. I would attempt to teach Sunday school and cry aloud while proclaiming the goodness of God. All that did was draw attention to myself. I did not do it on purpose; I simply did not know how to die to my emotions, be led by the Holy Spirit, or to command my will to die. I had no concept of discipline. Jesus never cried while ministering to others. You lose credibility in your God-given authority when you do. Jesus wept privately or with his closest family. When you are teaching, preaching, ministering, prophesying, or operating in a level of authority, you should never cry, unless it is genuinely the Holy Spirit weeping through you. You lose credibility because you appear out of control. Authority in itself is discipline in every area.

This may be revelation to you, but you do not have to give into every emotion you have! In fact, with the Holy Spirit leading, you become self-disciplined and *never* give in to your emotions. I get angry with people. My fleshly nature is to tell people off. Confrontation comes *naturally* easy to me. You need to become *supernatural* like God. Are you a person who loses your temper? You need to train yourself to die to the reaction of the desire. It is not your personality that needs to change, but your conduct within your personality. Many say, "Well, this is just how I am. I'm German," or "I was raised this way," or "I'm Irish, of course I'm a drinker," or "I'm white, of course I'm prejudiced," or "I'm fat, of course I overeat," and so the list goes on without end.

Whatever you *don't* control *does* control you. I choose not to quench the Holy Spirit; therefore, he controls me. You can choose to control him by allowing your will to override his. Pray for the mind that is in Christ to be also in you and renew your mind. The next time an old habit tries to control you, command your body to get lined up with the Word of God. You have authority over your own person!

Recently, I had an issue with a family member. I wanted to verbally retaliate! With what had been said to me, the world would agree that I had every right. My flesh would have loved that! But I had to forgive that person and then remind myself that to give back what was given to me would be unbecoming of the gospel of Christ. Also, I would feed the power of the enemy and lose ground spiritually and authoritatively. I had to speak to Satan/demons and tell him/them that I refuse to fight flesh and blood (which is exactly what he wanted me to do). The Word says that you are not to fight flesh and blood, but powers, principalities, and forces of darkness. That kind of warring I do in prayer. If I were undisciplined as I used to be, I would have done as my fleshly will desired. I would have been breaking down the person that I am to build up. I, like Christ, have not been assigned to tear down but to build up!

I want to share a new perspective about your enemies. Mostly, remember that nothing is about *you!* Everything is always about *God.* Your enemies can be one of the greatest blessings to you if you will allow. Let me explain. Your friends exhort, edify, and build you up. Your enemies, on the other hand, tear and break you down.

What does that do to you? It either makes you worse, or it forces you to draw nearer to the throne of grace!

Your enemy should always make you cling closer and closer to God. This is where Romans 8:28 comes in; what Satan means against you for evil, God turns it for your good if you love him. That is what happened with Joseph. There will always be enemies because the enemy (Satan) is still in operation, and he hates you. It is better to learn to grow in Christ *through* the enemy you have because once they are gone a worse one can come in! We sometimes get consumed by praying out the enemy we have but forget to realize that the next giant may be bigger, meaner, and stronger!

You are always going to have evil thoughts throughout your life. Of course, they lessen as you draw nearer unto God, but there will always be someone or something that triggers a bad thought from time to time. That is not sin in itself. This is where you begin to pull down strongholds and imaginations (I Corinthians 10:4–5). Don't go into guilt, shame, and fear because of a bad thought. Take the time to process the thought, determine if it is of God, and then deal with it accordingly. A great gift of God is your thought life. It is to be a channel to process good and evil. It is the mediator between God, Satan, and actions. He allows your thoughts to be private. The enemy does not know if he is getting to you, unless you reveal your thoughts through words or deeds. It is the *action* of an evil thought that becomes sin. Let me add that the word states in Proverbs 23:7 that "as a man thinks, so is he." This means that, if you do not pull down bad thoughts as soon as you recognize them, you will be overtaken by them and become them.

When I deal with my relative mentioned a few paragraphs back, I don't instantly have victory over it, though I get it more and more quickly as I am provoked. I have to process how I feel about what they are saying or doing. That is done through my thinking. I have conversations in my head with them, I tell them off, and give them a *piece of my mind.* Then, I check myself with the Father and allow the Holy Spirit to reveal to me whether it is aligned with his

Word. Of course, it is not! Then I forgive them by choice, ask God to forgive me for judging them, bind away hatred and judgment *from* myself, and bind peace and love *to* myself. This is the *taking control* through self-discipline. *My* will would be to blast them! But instead, I crucify my will and allow his will (humility and obedience to the Word) to overtake me.

If you look at me and think I have it all together with Christ, it's because I finally understand the process of dying to the flesh. It does not mean I don't think wrong thoughts. It does mean I *continue to learn* to take every thought captive before I allow an action. When I do slip (and I do occasionally), I repent immediately and allow his forgiveness to cover me. I do not allow myself to spend a moment in self-pity. God does not have time for that in my life or yours!

Remember, the enemy, though he means things against you for evil, God intends it to push you nearer to himself. If there is no trial or obstacle, there is no temptation, so there is no need or use for victory. Your enemy that is a thorn in your side (like Paul's) will keep you humble and refine self-control—and that is a good thing! No matter how far I rise in my walk with Christ, I always have that person, group of people, or thing to keep me humble; to keep me practicing what I preach. In that, this person is a tool *for* Christ instead of *against*, hallelujah!

"Therefore, having these promises, beloved, let us cleanse ourselves from all defilement of flesh and spirit, perfecting holiness in the fear of the Lord" (2 Corinthians 7:1, NAS).

■ ■ ■ ■ ■

Prayer

Dear heavenly Father, I pray, Almighty God, that you will enable me to die to myself, that I may become disciplined like you in every aspect of my life. Illuminate the eyes of my understanding, that I can see as you see; open my ears to hear as you hear; let the mind that is in Christ be also in me. I bind away from myself by the authority of Christ Jesus a spirit of selfishness, worthlessness, emotionalism, independence, disobedience, and pride. I bind to myself selfless-ness, the worth of the blood of Christ Jesus, the Holy Spirit, and humility. I claim that I will begin today a walk worthy of the gospel of Christ. I will no longer be led by my mind, will, or emotions, but rather the Holy Spirit who is within me. Quicken my spirit to life that your Spirit be fully able to commune with mine allowing me to be self-disciplined in all my ways. I bind away from myself spirits of fear, death, lies, shame, and condemnation. I bind to myself truth, faith, life, and confidence in he who lives through me. I praise you, Father, that there is now no condemnation in Christ against me since I choose to live by the Spirit of the living God instead of my flesh. Thank you for your life breath and the Holy Spirit whom you freely offer. I receive you! Amen.

Joy and Gladness: How to Attain and MAINTAIN

Strength and power in Christ come from your confidence being completely placed in him. With this, you can then walk in absolute power, authority, joy, peace, patience, boldness, courage, humility, love, and contentment in every circumstance. The world pushes confidence, but it is always in the flesh and the things of this world. God pushes confidence, but in him and in your identity that comes only from him. The world's confidence comes from stature, money, looks, education, etc.—anything other than God and the blood of Christ. It is false and leads you to a life of sure destruction. It is not confidence at all, but rather insecurity. The world's *confidence* makes people greedy, hateful, lustful, and always ready to fight and kill for what they want or want to keep. They must always be more powerful, richer, more beautiful, more successful, more, more, more—never content with anything. They are eating, yet never satisfied. They are always fearful that, no matter how much they attain, they will lose it. Hollywood is the perfect example.

Paul is one of the greatest examples of an imitator of Christ that I can see. Although the Word states that he was a "defender of the gospel" (Philippians 1:16–17), this does not mean he went around arguing with others about his religious beliefs. He was humble at all times and was genuinely concerned for the well-being of God's people. He walked in love, compassion, and patience. This could only be as he was keenly aware of his identity in Christ—his confidence in the faithfulness of God's holy Word. Real identity in Christ is knowing not just that you are blood-bought, but that in being blood-bought, all promises are real, true, and trustworthy until death. Paul *defended* the Word when the character of God was displayed through him.

Everyone quotes Philippians 1:11, stating that Paul learned to be content in all circumstances. Most miss the fact that he could only be this way in *knowing* that God is faithful to his own. He was one of God's; therefore, he would never be without God. It says he *learned* to be content. He could not learn if there were no trials and tests to stretch him in this area. Also, the first part of that verse says, *"Not that I speak from want."* Not only did he need nothing, he wanted for nothing! In becoming confident in his Savior's faithfulness in all situations, all needs and wants were dissolved. Faith destroys lack. Faith through confidence in him allows you to call forth the things that are not as though they were until they are!

Because Paul's heart and spirit were set on God and the ministry of Christ Jesus, true love was poured into him. This supernatural love then poured out of him into people who were ungrateful and worldly. Understanding humility, he wrote to them letters that were bold and courageous, yet in the natural he was quiet and mild-mannered. In 2 Corinthians 10:10–11, he even addressed the people saying, "For they say, 'His letters are weighty and strong, but his personal presence is unimpressive and his speech contemptible.' Let such a person consider this, that what we are in word by letters when absent, such persons we are also in deed when present."

Many came against him, insinuating that he was not in person who he was in his writing. He was in fact bold, but only when necessary. He did not toss about his authority and power at random.

It is the love of Christ that allowed him to humble himself to such a degree that others thought him weak. That same humility allowed him to repeat the word over and over. He was so grounded in the love of the Rock of Salvation that his patience did not wear thin. Remember Philippians 3:1, which reads, "To write the same things again is no trouble to me, and it is a safeguard for you"? I tend, in my natural condition, to grow weary to tell a person the same things twice, much less three or four or a thousand times! This immeasurable patience was huge in his successful walk with God. Though he did tire, it was never to the point of giving up and viewing ministry as a waste of time. He kept his eye on Christ and his holy Word instead of the weaknesses of the people.

He understood weakness because he realized that he himself was weak. In this understanding, he stayed humble on all occasions. He understood that repetition was a safeguard for the people. By walking in close relationship with God, he was able to maintain joy and patience and was able to rejoice in all circumstances. The whole book of Philippians is about the love, patience, hope, and joy in Christ. He says repeatedly "hope, love, be confident, I am convinced." His whole walk centered on his confidence in the one *in* him. Look at a few examples and see the pattern:

> For I am *confident* of this very thing…I want you to *know*…to be *sure*…for I *know*…according to my earnest *expectation* and *hope*…*convinced* of this…I *hope* in the Lord Jesus…*trust* in the Lord…be *anxious for nothing.*
>
> Philippians 1:6, 12, 15, 19, 20, 25; 2:19, 23, 24; 4:6 (NAS)

These references are all about knowing him and having full assurance of what God was going to do in every situation without fear that he may not come through. With such hope and faith, fear was forced away from him; joy abounded because he was confident in the fact that the love of Christ would ultimately do the work. He spoke words, yet it was the love factor that was the real minister. James 1:20, as I have already referenced, reads, "for the anger of man does not achieve the righteousness of God." What Paul does not cover about patience, James does. Impatience does not bring about godly righteousness. Joy in the Lord automatically ushers patience.

Here are some snippets of Paul's words in Philippians. I want you to pay close attention to the love behind all words, whether he says the word love or not. Paul knew the secret of the power of *love!* He truly loved people, despite their shortcomings. He knew how to love them genuinely, without allowing them to control him. He was always humble toward them, yet knew when to speak boldly.

> I have you in my heart ... how I long for you all with the affection of Christ Jesus ... I pray that your love may abound still more and more in real knowledge and all discernment ... who will genuinely be concerned for your welfare ... longing for you all ... to write the same things again is no trouble to me ... my beloved brethren whom I long to see, my joy and crown ... not that I seek the gift itself, but I seek for the profit which increases *to your account.*
>
> Philippians 1:7, 8, 9; 2:20, 26; 3:1; 4:1, 17 (NAS)

Paul's objective was always that God be glorified, and that the people were able to grow in Christ. When the people sent him a gift, he was glad simply because it would go to *their* spiritual account, not for his own selfish gain. Because of his selflessness, he maintained joy and persuaded others to rejoice in all things. It was this very joy that strengthened him in his endeavors. Take a look:

> Whether in pretense or in truth, Christ is proclaimed; and in this I rejoice ... and joy in the faith ... make my joy complete ... I rejoice and share my joy with you all ... receive him then in the Lord with all joy ... rejoice in the Lord ... rejoice in the Lord always; again I will say, rejoice! ... but I rejoice in the Lord greatly ...
>
> Philippians 1:18, 25; 2:2, 17, 9; 3:1, 4:4, 10 (NAS)

Paul did not allow adversity of life and ministry or the shortcomings of others to rob him of his joy. He understood the very nature and heart of God. As he was forgiven much, so he was able to see through the eye of forgiveness himself. God not only spared Paul's life when he tormented his people, but he went further and anointed Paul to confound the godly and the ungodly! How could anyone forgiven so much ever turn and complain against someone else?

"Do not speak against one another, brethren. He who speaks against a brother or judges his brother, speaks against the law and judges the law; but if you judge the law, you are not a doer of the law but a judge of it. There is only one Lawgiver and Judge, the One who is able to save and to destroy; but who are you who judge your neighbor" (James 2:11–12, NAS).

When you really begin to understand how God operates in love at all times, you too will be able to administer the Word without judgment or impatience. Begin to see yourself as lowly and forgiven. It is when you view yourself more highly than you ought that you begin to judge others and grow weary and impatient. I heard a quote at prison, "I'm no one's judge since I haven't a heaven or hell to place them."

Here is the bottom line. Jesus, Paul, John the Baptist, Jonah, Moses, Abraham and all the others who have gone on before you delivering the message of Christ were simply called to walk in and reveal love and truth to the people. Their job was *not* to force them to get it! Some will receive, and some will not. Our concern should not be the *outcome,* but rather the act of obedience in love. This way, your level of joy will not so easily fluctuate. Your joy will be grounded completely in the Instructor instead the instruction and someone else's reception of it.

What I mean is that often times, when a person is obedient in speaking a word from the Lord and a person *receives,* we rejoice as if we ourselves have accomplished something. Our zeal is through the roof! On the other hand, when a person is obedient to speak a word from God and a person *rejects* the word, the level of joy plummets to sub-zero. We seem to take it personally as though they have rejected us, when in fact, they have rejected God. Our level of joy should not be moved either way. Happiness is emotional and it comes and goes due to circumstances. Joy, however, should be based on the faith of who God is and not on what is seen with the eyes.

Jesus and those who imitated him walked in pure, joyous love, which kept them balanced. They repeated the word as many times as necessary so that the people would be safeguarded. When you get angry when others don't receive the word of God from you, it is pride in *you* that brings up the irritation. It is you saying that they should do as *you* say, and if they don't, they aren't as good as *you.* Maintain humility, and your only goal will be to deliver the Word, whether they receive or not. Keep your eye on being obedient to glorifying Christ. True love does not puff itself. True love is always humble and courteous.

"Why should any living mortal, or any man, offer complaint in view of his sins" (Lamentations 3:39, NAS).

"Do all things without grumbling and complaining" (Philippians 2:14, NAS).

It is imperative to all believers to not grumble or complain in any circumstance. Yet, without fail, the vast majority of God's people have not figured out that this rule applies to them. I love this verse in Lamentations stating that no human being has any cause for complaints in view of your own unrighteousness and sinful state. We are to do all things *without complaint!*

This means that, in situations large or small, you are not to murmur or complain but rather seek the face of God for understanding. Many Christians often take this *no complaining rule* to mean that this applies in large problems like sickness or money issues. It does apply to these circumstances. However, it also applies to the simple things in life that do not go your way, like bad traffic, bad bosses, bad employees, or a lack of accessibility to things you want or think you need. If in fact things are not going your way, first look at yourself and see what you have done wrong. If you are at fault, repent, allow God to forgive you, forgive yourself, rise up, and do what is right in the sight of God. If, on the other hand, you are not at fault, and you stand pure before the Savior, look at what Satan is trying to do to destroy you, your job, availability to the word, money, or anything else. Always, always, always look into the spirit realm and ask God to reveal to you what is really going on beyond the earthly realm. Satan may be trying to steal your joy, gladness, word, relationships, and so on.

Instead of complaining about things or people who aren't doing right by you and God, go to war in the prayer closet! All things can be handled through prayer and supplication. Understand that Satan *does* want to destroy you, your walk, and your testimony. Satan has come to steal, kill, and destroy as the Word clearly states. That includes you. You need to know how to pray in the things God wants prayed. If you stand around in self-righteousness, complaining about all that is wrong, you are feeding the desires of the enemy's kingdom set against you and the body of Christ. Learn how to decree and declare victory over your situation. Learn how Jesus handled situations. He took everything to God in prayer. He did not stand around murmuring about what was not going his way, or that he was rejected by people. He did not complain when he had to suffer, though he desired not to suffer. He was always focused on what God was revealing to him in the heavenly realm. He did not once deal with things in the natural. I suggest reading the four Gospels and see exactly how Jesus conducted himself in every situation and circumstance. Read the Gospels until you get it in your heart and head and begin to walk and talk like him! It was Jesus' true joy because of who he was in God that sustained him. He saw the big picture of others being rescued through his sacrifice.

Before you open your mouth to complain, seek God to show you what you need to see and learn. Ask for revelation knowledge to be downloaded to you and find out how to pray and war. You cannot effectively complain about a circumstance or person and genuinely be praying over it/them at the same time. It is a high-minded person that stands around complaining about other Christians or non-Christians that don't do things their way. Keep your brothers and sisters in Christ covered by the blood of the Lamb!

> ...and in the morning you will see the glory of the Lord, for he hears your grumblings against the Lord; and what are we,

that you grumble against us?" Moses said, "This will happen when the Lord gives you meat to eat in the evening, and bread to the full in the morning; for the Lord hears your grumblings which you grumble against him. And what are we? Your grumblings are not against us but against the Lord." Then Moses said to Aaron, "Say to all the congregation of the sons of Israel, 'Come near before the Lord, for he has heard your grumblings.'" It came about as Aaron spoke to the whole congregation of the sons of Israel, that they looked toward the wilderness, and behold, the glory of the Lord appeared in the cloud. And the Lord spoke to Moses saying, "I have heard the grumblings of he sons of Israel; speak to them, saying, 'At twilight you shall eat meat, and in the morning you shall be filled with bread; and you shall know that I am the Lord your God."

Exodus 16:7–12 (NAS)

"Because you did not serve the Lord your God with joy and a glad heart for the abundance of all things; therefore you shall serve your enemies whom the Lord will send against you, in hunger, in thirst, in nakedness, and in the lack of all things; and he will put an iron yoke on your neck until he has destroyed you" (Deuteronomy 28:47–48, NAS).

You probably know well the story of the Israelites; how God personally rescued them from the bondage of the Egyptians and brought them to the land of plenty. For forty years, he graciously fed them with supernatural manna from heaven. One minute they would bless him, the next they would curse him. God hates grumbling from an ungrateful heart! You too should despise grumbling and complaining. You should hate what he hates and love what he loves.

When a Christian has a heart set on the will and the mind of Jesus Christ at all times, they will never be found mumbling aloud, under their breath, or in their hearts. A person set on Christ is a person with joy and gladness in their hearts and lips in any circumstance and in every situation.

In the parable in Matthew 20:11, there is a landowner that hired several workers throughout the day. He offered the same pay to each set of workers. The ones who worked the longest hours were angry that he paid each the same wage. Why were they angry? Jealousy. Instead of being grateful that they were paid an honest days wage previously agreed, they looked at the others out of an ungracious heart, even though they got exactly what they were guaranteed.

Have you ever done that? Have you ever felt slighted that someone got the same reward as you even though they did not do as much? God calls this ungrateful. You should keep your eye on the Father and not on what everyone around you has.

> Therefore the Jews were grumbling about him, because he said, "I am the bread that came down out of heaven"...Jesus answered them saying, "Do not grumble among yourselves"...But Jesus, conscious that *his disciples* grumbled at this, said to them, "Does this cause you to stumble?"
>
> John 6:41, 43, 61 (NAS)

The Pharisees and Scribes had a self-righteous attitude toward Jesus because he spent time with *unsavory* people (Luke 5:30, 15:2, 19:7). They snubbed their spiritually prideful noses at him because he did not do things the way *they* did. The disciples also grumbled. "Does this cause you to stumble?" Jesus asked. The point is that whatever makes you grumble is what is making you stumble. Grumbling is a result of falling away from God.

Have you (those who are "religious" or even spiritually strong) ever judged another Christian because they don't do what you do or the way you think they should? Are they not growing fast enough for you or maturing as you think they should? You do not have that right. God is patient with *all men* and tells you to do the same. If you judgmentally complain that someone else is not like you, you are in sin, and God hates it. Why would you jeopardize your walk with God simply because you could not hold your tongue? A grumbler and complainer conducts himself as a Pharisee, scribe, or even a disciple, and their actions are against God Almighty.

"Nor grumble, as some of them did, and were destroyed by the destroyer" (1 Corinthians 10:10, NAS).

"These are grumblers, finding fault, following after their own lusts; they speak arrogantly, flattering people for the sake of gaining an advantage" (Jude 1:16, NAS).

"You have put gladness in my heart, more than when their grain and new wine abound" (Psalm 4:7, NAS).

"Be glad in the Lord and rejoice, you righteous ones; and shout for joy, all you who are upright in heart" (Psalm 32:11, NAS).

"You have loved righteousness and hated wickedness; therefore God, your God, has anointed you with the oil of joy above your fellows" (Psalm 45:7, NAS).

Clearly grumbling is of Satan and it paves a path to destruction! The lack of joy and gladness in any situation brings you into the submission and slavery of your enemy. Satan is the enemy, and whomever or whatever he is operating through in your life.

When you are filled with Holy Spirit, and you allow him to lead in all things, then gladness, rejoicing, songs of praise to him, and the anointing of joy will supernaturally naturally flood and flow through your lips. This means that *supernaturally* it will become *natural* for joy to rise up even in the face of adversity. When you give him total command and charge of your being you will know that he is in love with you and wants the best for you. Because of his unfailing love for his own, he will pour upon you his blessings when you praise your way through a situation instead of murmuring.

Ecclesiastes 9:7 reads, "Go then, eat your bread in happiness and drink your wine with a cheerful heart; for God has already approved your works." If your walk with Christ is upright, holy, and pure, God says that he has approved your works. If he has approved your works, you have nothing to worry about when the trials of this life surround you. You can have absolute confidence in him, that he is your Protector. In knowing this, the joy of the Lord cannot help but pour through you in the hard times. Knowing this, worry (which brings about impatience, murmuring, and complaining) will be far removed from your heart and lips. Out of the overflow of the heart, man speaks. If the joy is truly in your heart, your lips and actions will prove it. An ungrateful heart can only be hidden for a season. It will be revealed.

"Though the fig tree should not blossom and there be no fruit on the vines, though the yield of the olive should fail and the fields produce no food, though the flock should be cut off from the fold and there be no cattle in the stalls, yet I will exult in the Lord, I will rejoice in the God of my salvation" (Habakkuk 3:17–18, NAS).

"Consider it all joy, my brothers, when you encounter various trials" (James 1:2, NAS).

This makes it apparent that no matter what the circumstance is—in feast or in famine, in peace or at war—you are to exult in the Lord. Nowhere in the Word, from Genesis to Revelation, does God ever recommend murmuring or complaining! Never does he suggest that complaining or negative speech is acceptable in certain instances. "His master said to him, 'Well done, good and faithful servant. You were faithful with a few things, I will put you in charge of many things; enter into the joy of your master," reads Matthew 25:21. When you are faithful over small situations, he will expand your territory. For instance, if you have people around you that absolutely get on your last nerve, and you are a faithful steward over your lips and actions by not grumbling or complaining, the Lord will be faithful to not only bring you through it, but will increase your ministry. You cannot have more territory to minister if you cannot deal with one or two people that irritate you or come against you.

Make my joy complete by being of the same mind, maintaining the same love, united in spirit, intent on one purpose ... but even if I am being poured out as a drink offering upon the sacrifice and service of your faith, I rejoice and share my joy with you all. you too, I urge you, rejoice in the same way and share your joy with me ... receive him then in the Lord with all joy, and hold men like him in high regard.

Philippians 2:2, 17, 18, 29 (NAS)

When you walk in faith in Christ, there will be continual, perpetual joy! Joy comes from Holy Spirit, not your feelings, circumstances, or emotions. Joy is a growing process. You have to learn to walk like Christ, just as you have to learn to walk as babies in the natural. You must choose to *condition yourself* over time not to be given over to what your emotions dictate. Your feelings, when not under the authority of Holy Spirit, will eventually lead you to grumble. The Holy Spirit will always lead you to rejoice!

"None of these things move me," it states in Acts. Nothing in this condemned world should *move you* to do anything, to say anything, or to think anything lest it be a move of Holy Spirit! *Do not* be moved by your will or emotions! Your emotions will tell you to cry, rebel; as well as take vengeance, gossip, slander, project anger, greed, and malice against someone who has hurt you. Do not give in to it! Be moved only *by* the Holy Spirit.

Set your focus on God and ask him to put a watch over your mouth. God hates gossip! Do you revel in speaking evil of others and then justify it self-righteously? Gossip is lawlessness in God's eye. You should hate it so much that you will not gossip or entertain others when they do so. This is one of the hardest lessons for all people in Christ.

"…and though you have not seen him, you love him, and though you do not see him now, but believe in him, you greatly rejoice with joy inexpressible and full of glory" (1 Peter 1:8, NAS).

Now to him who is able to keep you from stumbling, and to make you stand in the presence of his glory blameless with great joy" (Jude 24, NAS).

■ ■ ■ ■ ■

Prayer

O Father, hallowed be thy name. How precious is your everlasting love, joy and patience. Show me, Jesus, how to walk a life of humility, obedience, and patience as Jesus Christ himself walked this earth. Bind to me love, joy, peace, patience, kindness, goodness, faithfulness, gentleness, and self-control. May joy rule in my heart and life. I pray that I will keep my eyes on you, your Word, and your work at all times without veering to the right or to the left so that your joy may be made complete in me. Show me your ways, O Lord, that I may be a poured-out drink offering unto you, emptied of self and filled with the Holy Spirit. Allow me and reveal to me how to be an effective doer and not a forgetful hearer of the Word. Constantly remind me that happiness is based on emotion, but true joy comes from you who are within; it is not based on outward circumstances. You are my all in all, O Holy One of Zion.

Lies, Fear & Betrayal: Overcoming Human
REACTION

> But there is nothing covered up that will not be revealed, and
> hidden that will not be known. Accordingly, whatever you
> have said in the dark will be heard in the light, and what you
> have whispered in the inner rooms will be proclaimed upon
> the housetops. I say to you, my friends, do not be afraid of
> those who kill the body and after that have no more that they
> can do. But I will warn you whom to fear; fear the One who
> after he has killed, has authority to cast into hell; yes, I tell
> you, fear him!
>
> Luke 12:2–5 (NAS)

I open this chapter by saying that my desire (as I believe it is the
desire of the Lord) is that this word minister to both the liar and
the one betrayed by a lie. I encourage the one currently trapped in
their own web of deception to confess as soon as possible, regardless of the possible consequence. Your penalty will be far less than
what it will be if you delay. The longer you wait, the worse the fate,
especially if you get *caught* as opposed to *willingly relinquishing* the
information that has been concealed. The lie from Satan is that you
can successfully get away with whatever you are hiding. There is
no such thing as a *little white lie!* Lies are neither white (pure) nor

small in their effect. Lies are *always* wrong, and they breed destruction. There is a reason the Lord has so many references to honesty and integrity.

Remember, everything that God has created in purity, Satan has distorted and turns and presents the perversion to *appear* as truth. Everything Satan offers in this world is *fool's gold*. This is where the old saying comes, "Everything that glitters ain't gold!" Satan's version of the truth dictates that hiding, ignoring, or running away are your best and only options. In reality, these become fates worse than death. Honesty is *always* the best policy. No matter how long you may turn a blind eye, how deeply you may cover up, or how far you run, there is no escaping the crooked foundation you have laid with a lie; there is no freedom beyond confession and repentance. Even if you convince everyone you know that you are telling the truth, so that they turn and go so far as to defend you, you cannot be free from the torment of your own heart, mind, and conscience. The lie keeps you in perpetual chains. They grow heavier with every passing moment until you either break, tell the truth, and humbly accept your punishment or your heart becomes as cold as ice, and you are turned over (by God) to a reprobate mind (Romans 1:28).

In reference to the one who has been offended and affected by a lie, the goal is to teach you (the believer) to stop reacting with *human nature* when a lie is revealed, no matter the magnitude of it. Human nature tends to generalize the application of the lie to every part of life instead of localizing it. We immediately assume that if one lie has been told, everything else in a relationship must be a lie, therefore terminating the whole thing. It's like having a wound on your finger; you don't apply medicine to your whole body when only the finger is in need of healing. You apply ointment directly to the wound. You don't kill your body because one portion has been harmed. Worst case scenario: let's say you have a limb needing amputation. The correct reaction is not to commit suicide in hopelessness, but to allow a skilled surgeon to cut off whatever needs to go in order to save and restore healing to the remainder of the body. The Bible states that if the hand offends then cut it off!

No one can *honestly* say that they have never lied. It starts before we can walk or talk. As soon as a baby realizes that crying gets them attention, they cry manipulatively though there is no real need. Once we can talk and barely understand the meaning of words, we distort the truth to get off the hook of spilling milk or breaking something. Not one living soul can say in truth that they have never lied. Likewise, unless you live under a rock or in seclusion, you have been lied to.

What is it about a lie that rips the heart in two, that angers the soul to wrath unspeakable, that destroys a foundation that has been laid for years? What is it that destroys things that had once been built in truth? Lies and their effects are a mystery to me, yet the Word of God is filled with verses on both lies and truth. Truth is the very nature of God. Lies and deceit are the nature of Satan.

This message is neither to offend nor defend the one lying (we all reap what we sow) or the one who has been lied to. Rather, it is one to bring balance, wisdom, and freedom to all involved. Just as we are not to lie, we are equally to be *forgiving* that we may receive forgiveness. Bringing balance into your situation will open the door to unity within the body of Christ, homes, marriages, businesses, and the relationships in your life in general. The sooner we under-stand balance, the sooner we will see ourselves as the ones who have lied to God, but he willingly extended perfect forgiveness when we did not deserve it!

Have you ever been in a relationship for months or years and were sure that things were blissful? One where you had a level of comfort and security that almost made you judgmental toward oth-ers whose were not so great? Then in one fell swoop, a lie that had been laid a long time ago by the one you trust came to the surface! It may be a small, seemingly insignificant fabrication that the one who told it forgot. Maybe it has been an ongoing act of decep-tion in one area of life. Because of this one indiscretion, your entire foundation is shattered! You can't seem to force yourself to believe anything that person says in the future. In fact, you begin to allow your mind to wander to a place where you doubt everything they have ever said. Now, the place that used to be one of comfort and serenity has turned into a swamp of torment. In the natural, this is completely understandable.

However, we need to take into consideration that if you are indeed a born again believer, you are not human and do not have the allowance of acting *human* like the rest of the world. What is *acceptable* to the average man is *unacceptable* to the supernatural child of God! This is where Holy Spirit must be active in your life. Aside from Holy Spirit, who resides within to give life, we are just worthless earthen vessels, no different than any other human to ever walk this earth. I don't know about you, but God Almighty says emphatically that I am *set aside unto him* (2 Corinthians 6:17; Hebrews 7:26; James 1:21; Matthew 20:17; Psalm 4:3), which means I am special and different than my surrounding environment.

My point is that now, being supernatural, we are to think and act like Christ (Colossians 2:2–3). Christ Jesus forgave *before* we repented. Also, Jesus, while walking this earth, allowed the Holy Spirit's discernment to be active in his every word, thought, and deed. When he was dealing with someone truly repentant, he showed mercy and kindness. God is quoted in Romans 9:15 as saying to Moses, "I will have mercy on whom I have mercy, and I will have compassion on whom I have compassion." When with those like the scribes and Pharisees, he operated with wisdom so to allow them become trapped in their own deception. They were attempting to trap him in his words of truth, but because he walked in integrity, his integrity and wisdom protected him. He was no fool, nor was he a doormat for anyone. Because he was obedient to the heart of his Father, the Father allowed him to be "as shrewd as serpents and innocent as doves" (Matthew 10:16, NAS).

There is a grand lie from the enemy that masquerades as truth. It is a mindset where you believe that becoming pure in heart like Christ will leave you vulnerable, naïve, and accessible to every work of evil. In translation, it is that you must become more evil and perverted in order to not be done in by evil. It is a thought pattern rooted in fear of destruction. That fear, however, will lead you straight into the pit of destruction. Christ is portrayed by the world as a nerd, pansy, and worst of all, an idiot! No one wants to be any of those things, so we follow the deceptive, crooked paths of Satan in search of any way possible to keep from being hurt, taken advantage of, or killed.

Sins are hated by everyone, even the ones who consciously do them. For example, those who hate, hate being hated; those who steal, hate being robbed; those who cheat, hate being cheated; those who lie, hate being lied to; and so on. Everyone thinks that he/she is the only one who is supposed to be exempt from repercussions of sin or being treated as they treat others.

I deduce that the hatred of sins being carried out against us (though we execute them toward others) is because of this text in Romans 1:18–19 (NAS) which explains,

"For the wrath of God is revealed from heaven against all ungodliness and unrighteousness of men who suppress the truth in unrighteousness, because *that which is known about God is evident within them; for God made it evident to them. For since the creation of the world his invisible attributes, his eternal power and divine nature, have been clearly seen,* being understood through what has been made, so that they are without excuse."

Notice the italicized words above. *All* of mankind is created in the image of God; therefore, whether we choose to walk with him or not, his invisible attributes are in each of us. This means that whatever he hates, we hate. We hate it being done to us even if we choose unrighteousness and conduct ourselves in ungodliness against others.

This brings me back to the mystery of how ill-affected we are when we are lied to. My thought the other day that began my search for understanding was, "Why can't we just get over it when lied to? Why can't we just let it go, especially when it was from someone we love and know to otherwise be a decent person?" The frustration was with myself that there have been certain things that I have been unable to *fully* let go. Even when I have already completely forgiven that person for their transgression, I have found it difficult to *allow* them to reestablish trust with me when they are in every way attempting to do so.

Please clearly know that I am in no way speaking of a person who is a consummate liar and does so without remorse, repentance, or any desire to change. That is a person whom you need to forgive, bless, and walk away from! Give them over to God and be on your way. Knowing *when* to apply *what* is where the wisdom and discernment should come into effect. This topic is more for the relationships that have potential hope, grounded in Christ Jesus.

I have in the past acted in certain situations as though *I* have never lied and needed to be forgiven; as though *I* have never faltered and needed mercy and compassion. Yet, I have held their wayward deeds bound in my heart of hearts, waiting to pull them out at will as a weapon of defense. Worse, I compare them to wickedness that had been done to me many years ago by someone else. I wrongly treat the new person with disdain and anger because I am comparing the deeds of one truly wicked with the one who loves me but made a mistake because of their own fear and shame. I found myself (after seeking wickedness in my own heart to be revealed) concerned about being humiliated a second time! That is called pride. For that moment in time, I was more concerned about self-preservation of *my* dignity than truth.

This is what I mentioned in the beginning where we *generalize* things instead of applying wisdom, discernment, understanding, and discretion to each and every situation. This is an outcome of the scheming of Satan. He lures one person to lie. Then he stirs emotionalism in another. Bring those two together and you have a perfect mix of nitro and glycerin! Then the destroyer steps back and lets us kill each other without ever having to do another thing. We become our own enemy—forget Satan and his legion of demons! He sets the trap, we take the bait, and the rest is history. Homes, churches, and God-ordained relationships have been ruined in just this order of events.

Lies are set to manipulate us into a place of self-doubt and the doubt of those around us, making a place of absolute fear! They coerce us to a place of insecurity, instability, hardness, harshness, suspicious thinking, anger, meanness, and depression. I used the word *coerce* because we each have a will, and we can always *choose not* to be manipulated and controlled. I cannot stress enough that emotions are established by God to be a tool to aid us to be like Christ; they allow us leeway to purge ourselves of things that have effect in our lives, good or bad. But, like everything else pure, Satan twists them into something unrecognizable. Emotions, when not under the direct influence of Holy Spirit, are used to make us volatile, hostile, unforgiving, angry, hard, harsh, suspicious, mean, depressed, anxious, sad, and fearful. Do you see the parallels? Both lies and emotions have the potential lead to a world of fear. Fear is always bondage.

We all need to take hold of faith in Christ, cling fast to wisdom and understanding, and desire to actually be "shrewd as serpents and innocent as doves." This would be a paradox in the world's eyes. A paradox is a figure of speech in which apparently contradictory terms appear in conjunction. The world does not believe that one can be innocent and wise at the same time. Innocence in its truest form has been so maligned that what it really is has been covered by a lie. All physical lies (those formulated by man) stem from the massive root of hell and its author. Because of this, the blatant lie of one leads inadvertently to the lie of many due to our minds wandering away from the facts and into an *illusion* of truth.

We grow up on old wives tales such as, "If a person can't look you in the eye, you know they're lying." Right off the bat, a lie from the pit of hell lays a foundation in your heart and mind. I know people who could lie and look you straight in the eye, telling it better than one telling the truth. On the other hand, I know people who have confessed something, speaking the truth doing it, but because of shame (a whole other study!) they could not look in the eye the person with whom they are making the confession. Then there's, "Don't tell; no one will be the wiser!" How utterly foolish! It's all steeped in pride to protect our *reputation* that doesn't really exist.

The truth will always set you free, even if you physically get locked up. I would rather a thousand times over have peace in my mind and heart while behind bars, than have all the world at my disposal but not be able to rest for a moment. For what is a man advantaged, if he gain the whole world, and lose himself, or be cast away (Luke 9:25, KJV)? Even within the body of Christ, we witness lies and deceit of all kinds, and we rationalize and justify all of it.

When will we realize that it is better to hear painful truth than to hear a soothing lie? At least with painful truth, you have a *firm foundation of knowledge.* You know what you're dealing with and can move accordingly in the right direction to remedy the problem. With the lie, it appeases you for the moment, but that consolation will be ripped away in your future and rob you of your past, present, *and* future. Lies kill, steal, and destroy (John 10:10) because they are rooted in hell. We as a people of God need to stop yammering about wanting truth, and then when we get it, condemn the one confessing. We are all guilty of making a mess in this world, so no one is completely innocent in any given situation.

For the liar: force yourself as an *act of your will* to trust with faith the absolutes of God. Those who have the authority to sentence you (literally or figuratively) will have much more mercy and compassion on you if you confess as opposed to being *called out* from a lie.

For the one lied to, seek the Father to guide you in discernment *beyond your natural capability* to judge every situation with clarity of mind instead of from the stance of how it *hurt your feelings.* Seek now, before offences come or are revealed, to be a person of God who is self-disciplined, wise, steady, and unshakable in all of your ways so that you are never swayed by the circumstances of life. We need to seek understanding to know the heart of God so that we will know when and where to give mercy and compassion, and when to bring forth a righteous judgment.

Judgment does not mean to be *judgmental*. They seem the same but are completely different. Simply put, being *judgmental* is when you pass a prideful measure against someone based on your human standard. To *judge righteously* is to allow the Holy Spirit to *reveal* truth in every situation, *assess* correctly what action needs to be taken, and *act* accordingly to what will bring holiness, balance, and peace. In judging righteously, you will know through keen discernment and wisdom whom to keep in your life and from whom you should be removed.

There are all types of lies and deception that we bring into our lives. Some are not as easily detectable by the human eye. These are the ones where you cover up your past sins through shame and fear of rejection. Since you have become something completely different, you assume that those who know you post-sin will be shocked, devastated, and/or judgmental against you if they knew your past. Again, this is fear, and fear is not of God.

This is where my *open door* philosophy comes in. I have heard over and over the statement, "Don't tell too much of your business. They'll use it against you. Be careful not to tell too much or they'll hate you and turn against you." This type of thinking is fearful and will keep you in a condition of bondage. This comes from people in leadership in the church who should know better, more so than from the general population. Once again, I get where they're coming from, but I strongly disagree. People will find any reason in the world to hate you when you follow God. It doesn't have to be true; they'll just make up something and spread it around! Anyone who takes a strong, firm stand for God and calls the body to accountability will be railed against just as was Jesus. That is when you allow *him* to both sustain you and contend with the accusers.

I reason that when you are open and above board without concern or fear of who might hear or know, you will not be put to shame. Your enemy will have nothing to *catch you* since you laid it all out up front. You don't have to talk about your past as though bragging, but you also don't have to hide it in fear that someone will deem you unworthy to walk with God or man.

First and foremost, we are all unworthy no matter how pristine our life has been! It is he whose life breath *in us* makes us worthy; nothing of ourselves matters. Secondly, you will be in a growing state of freedom when you are no longer afraid of questions that you may be asked about your past. You won't be afraid of inquiries from peers, leadership, employees, family, friends, or enemies!

Have you ever had someone ask you a question about your life, and you tense up for the thought of answering? It is a terrible feeling! Maybe it is a boss, pastor, parent, teacher, student, or your child as they get old enough to wonder how you have handled life. You become defensive with the thought, "Why do they need to know my business? If I tell the truth, they'll lose respect for me and turn and do the same thing." Fear grows ever stronger. Then you may tend to speak poorly about them to others, saying how nosy they are; this is to divert attention from yourself. You are never obligated, unless under oath, to tell anyone your business. It is we who allow ourselves to be controlled and manipulated into thinking we must answer. Really, though, who cares if they know? Do you have something to hide? If so, we're back to confessing to the right people before you get caught!

I have a muddy past at best. I was married to an adulterer, carouser, liar, cheater, hater, abuser, and many other vile things, and he was the one I met at church who said he wanted to be a pastor on the mission field. After he left me with a note on the coffee table, I was devastated. I didn't want anyone to know how my life had been up to that point. I was ashamed. This is a condition also steeped in pride because my focus was on what people *thought of me* and not on how my whole life in general was not aligned with God to begin (though everyone perceived me as a "good Christian girl"). I became confused and angry, and a completely different person. Later, I married a decent man and, because I was not walking with God, *I* became an adulterer and liar because "as I passed judgment on him, I turned and did the same thing."

Then I made sure (pride) that people were clear that I was

separated from my then-husband before I lay with another, as if that made me any less an adulterer! There are no varying degrees of adultery in the eyes of God. I made sure that I told no lies (because I did not want to be like my first husband—judgment). So, I worked around the truth with a twist here and there. As with any sin, it's all the same to God because it is not pure. He does not measure us against one another, but against the holiness and righteousness of himself, who is forever blameless, spotless.

There are people in my life who have known me more than half my life. They have seen me go from good Christian girl to angry, devastated, dumped, crushed ex-wife, to fornicating, lying, backstabbing, rude adulterer, to imbalanced, indecisive flake who couldn't decide between God and the lures of the world, to someone who is irreversibly in love with the Lord, Savior and Redeemer of all; a person truly transformed by the renewing of my mind, led by Holy Spirit, and repentant as soon as sin is revealed.

These people, unfortunately, like to throw my past in my face and toss it around to anyone who'll listen to them bash me. The wonderful thing about this situation is that I hide nothing. Among my friends, family, and those to whom I minister, there are no secrets. I refuse to be afraid to tell something (that may otherwise be embarrassing) to someone I barely know. I stopped a long time ago being scared of what I used to be. As far as I'm concerned, more importantly as far as my God is concerned, that old person is literally dead and buried! The person they insult, gossip about, and try to torment with the past has no meaning to me because I am not that person. The only bearing the past has on my new life is that it is a reminder of who I do not want to be ever again.

When the Word says to put the past behind you and press on toward the mark of Christ (Philippians 3:14), I do exactly that. Yes, of course, I would rather those people embrace me and love me for who I am today, but praise God, I am no longer led by emotions! Now post-transformation, I choose to utilize the emotions God gave to *push me into a place of mercy* toward my enemy. Because the heart of God and his ways are now my own, that leads me to bless those who curse me.

The past is now what I feed from to ensure holiness. The manure of the dead self has become fertilizer to my new life in Christ Jesus. When I don't give off the presumed lie of being perfect, it shuts the door to the enemy who is trying to lash out against me with memories of who I once was. I keep no shame, and I take no pride. I have no *feelings* or emotions about them whatsoever. It is something that once was and is no more. The more open you are about what you were in your past life without God, the more God is glorified in who you are becoming in him.

Of course, it stands to reason that you need to be balanced in this area. Don't give *testimony* about how bad you used to be and never exalt the transformer of the defiled. Many want to bring attention to the old, woeful self, and that's all they focus on. Again, you don't have to preach a sermon on the past, but when it comes up or is appropriate within a conversation of teaching, be willing to be completely above board; never shrink at the thought of its topic.

It is the open door of truth that is able to build a new foundation and structure, and even rebuild what has been torn down by the deceitfulness of lies. No matter how steeped in a falsehood you may be, take charge over yourself and the spirits of lies, fear, shame, manipulation, dread, death, and torment that have surrounded you. Wrap the peace, stability, and sound mind of Christ Jesus to yourself and speak the truth in love. Approach your situation with humility of heart, ready to tell any truth to uncover any and all lies that have been laid. The truth *will* set you free, even if for a moment in time the momentary result may appear to be bondage.

The real lie is that anything other than truth will somehow free you from the enslaved, poverty-stricken condition you have found yourself, and will somehow bring release. Your honesty will be an open door for Father to come in and heal every area of brokenness that laid you in waste, muck, and mire. Again, it will allow him to take everything that Satan has meant against you for evil and turn it for your good as you fall in love with him. For those who are in Christ, there is no condemnation. That is an indisputable truth and cannot be denied!

During the restoration period of your relationship, it is just as vital for the offended to be honest with their thoughts with the offender. For instance, things may be going well, and then suddenly, you (the offended) have a flashback of hurt and start acting peculiar. If you don't humbly share in love what you are thinking and feeling, the other person (offender) may misunderstand your mood swing and take it as though he/she has no chance of reconciliation; they will take the swing personally and condemnation will grow within them. For obvious reasons (guilt of their offense), they will already be struggling with overcoming guilt and shame, and working toward rebuilding what (by their hand) was torn down. You only add to that when you are secretive about what is going through your head and heart.

Honesty and communication will be crucial in this team effort to not only rebuild but to make something new and better. Don't speak words or give off vibes that will further humiliate the offender; they can do that to themselves quite well, I assure you! In my personal situation, I had to make myself refrain from saying purposefully negative things that I knew were not of God, but of the anger of my flesh. Always remember that anger does not bring about godly righteousness (James 1:20). Say something positive to assure that person that you are not only willing to partner in the reconciliation, but that you also choose to self-check so that you don't allow yourself room for misconduct. Even if you have to say something regarding the issue, say it in a way that they don't feel you are condemning them. Say those words, "I'm not trying to condemn you, I just need to bring out this or that point," and move on. Crazy though it may seem, the offender needs more encouragement than the offended!

Tap into the true loving and forgiving nature of Christ who is not condemning with *you* when you fail and fall. In everything and in all circumstances, there is a test of faith for *you* to see for yourself how connected you are to the heart of God. As I have said already, hard situations bring out the worst or the best in a person, so whatever is in your heart will be revealed. God will show you how you are culpable in the scenario. View these tests as a blessing from God so to refine you into a better vessel of honor. He wants those things that are hidden within to come out if they are not planted by him. Allow all of the wood, hay, and stubble to be burned so that the flame from them will be Holy Spirit fire within!

■ ■ ■ ■ ■

Prayer

Dear Father, show me how to confess my every lie and sin against you. Teach me to walk upright in integrity, wisdom, and faith in you. Allow me your strength to confess the web of lies I have allowed myself to become ensnared in and to humbly accept the consequences. I desire to be like you, beginning with complete honesty before God and man. Give me the courage to endure whatever lay before me.

Dear Father, teach me to know through keen discernment and wisdom whom to keep in my life and from whom to separate myself. Allow the grace and knowledge to see into the heart of every person in my life, that I may know the intention of their hearts. I seek only your holy, supernatural power to discern right from wrong. Give me your heart, O God. Give me a pure heart of forgiveness for those who have already offended me and for those who have not yet but will. Allow me the ability to forgive and heal those around me.

Chasing a Phantom:
A BEAUTIFUL LIE

Phantom: a form without substance or reality; a mental illusion (*Oxford Illustrated American Dictionary*)

The phantom I am referring to is anything *of the flesh* and not *of the Spirit of God.* It can be wealth, power, sex, fear, anger, greed, or whatever. It is anything that you begin to chase that leads away from God, his righteousness, or the belief in the truth of him. It can be words spoken over you that make you question who you are, who he is, and where you actually stand in the Word of God. It isn't always the obvious things, especially when you are someone who walks very closely to the Lord. Satan has to be trickier and more devious with such people. Be on the alert and sober at all times, for the days are evil.

Have you ever seen a movie where the characters are chasing a shadow, and it's really something they made up in their imagination? Their imagination leads them down a path away from reality. Phantoms from Satan lead God's people away from the reality of his promise, his righteousness, and all that you have been grounded in. The reality of life is not the seen of the earth, but the unseen of the heavenly realm. Our natural minds can only believe in what is seen. This is why we must each pull down imaginations, strongholds, and every high thing that exalts itself above the name of Christ. Anyone at any time can get blindsided by a curveball thrown from left field. We must claim the mind of Christ, believe that he allows us such an honor, and walk out in thinking that is from above. Set your mind on things above, not on the things below.

When I wrote this chapter, I had been dealing with health problems. The Lord has graciously revealed many reasons why this was happening, but that is not my point of reference. I had surgery during all of this. After about a week of recovery, I asked the Lord to please stir within me. I spent time in the Word the next morning and then began my daily chores. As I was ironing, he said, "chasing a phantom." Suddenly, this whole lesson began to materialize. I was thrilled! I sat and began to write. The anointing was all over me. I was telling people about it and getting others excited!

Three days later, I had a follow-up appointment with one of many doctors I had been seeing over the last two or so years. Please note that I had had a variety of inexplicable illnesses leading to this appointment. I had taken an abnormal amount of pain medication over the course of the two years because it took the physicians a while to get to the root. This being said, this particular doctor spoke words over me that literally catapulted me into a place of the flesh! He stated something to the effect of, "You need psychological help because you are addicted to prescription pain medication. You need to find out why you keep making up pain symptoms." He went on to tell me how people become addicted to all sorts of things and that I needed to "take stock" to figure out why I was behaving this way!

I had been blindsided! What I knew I had encountered that moment was an evil spirit coming against me through the physician. By the time I left the office, all I could think about were the words he spoke and if I had actually lost my mind and was in deed as addict! Hours went by and I was still thinking about those words and questioning everything about myself. I wasn't questioning God in the least. But by gearing me in a direction that led me to question who I was *in* Christ, I began to chase a phantom. It was an idea, an illusion, veiling my mind to think only in the natural. They moved me far away from the spiritual truths I know are absolute and who I am as a person.

I knew that I had had a virus on my auto-immune system the last two years or so that was causing the streaming myriad of issues. It took the doctors about a year and a half to discover it because things were coming on me one by one instead of all at once. With the virus, my thyroid went way out of kilter which in turn caused insomnia. I began having constant kidney stones, chest and hand pain, along with severe migraines. Oddly, after he spoke those words, I forgot all about the auto-immune virus and assumed that I was addicted to medications. After all, he was a medical professional, he couldn't possibly be wrong! I was racking my brain trying to figure it all out.

I thought about how a prayer partner and friend had been healed by God many years ago. After her healing, she began to be sick again in the same way. The Lord spoke to her, telling her that they weren't real, that they were indeed phantom pains sent from the enemy to put her back in oppression. She bound them away by the authority of Christ Jesus and they left. Many times this has happened to people. Satan hates when God heals so he tries to fake you out to think you are sick. In doing so, that child of God begins to *chase a phantom,* wasting precious time, energy, and money. When this came upon me, I called her and asked her to pray in agreement that, if these were phantom pains leading me back to medication, they had to leave.

Later, I was talking with another close friend, and as I laid out the picture of what happened, she immediately said, "That sounds like an evil spirit rose against you through that doctor." I knew she was right and remembered that had been my initial impression. We hung up, and I spent a few more hours pondering in the flesh all the doctor had spoken. Even after praying, my mind was here on the earthly level and not in the heavenly. I called her back and admitted that I recognized my fleshly thoughts and that I needed her to pray for me to pull me out of the pit I sadly found myself in. It all happened in an instant!

Throughout all the sickness I had endured, I did not lose faith or heart. My spirit man was strong. I knew the devil could not defeat me or tear down my walk with God. Suddenly, after this short conversation with one medical professional, I was in fact defeated! I felt as though I could not think clearly and began believing I was crazy. I spent the entire day chasing after the wind! I was trying to rationalize something *not* of God. The wisdom of God was *not* what I was operating in. My flesh was fully alive and active, and I allowed it. I wallowed in it a bit. I chose not to let it go. I let it happen through something I *felt,* a common tool of the enemy. Emotionalism (which I have spoken so much about in this book) on any level is a phantom. It leads away from godliness and into a pit of chaos and confusion. By the way, emotionalism is a common tool of Satan found right within the walls of churches all over the world. It is not exclusively for the world.

I see clearly the tactic the enemy tried to use against me. A spirit came against me through a human being, and I allowed it to take hold of my thinking. This is called the wearing down tactic of the enemy, according to the Bible. Satan will wear you down any way he can. He is unrelenting. Through this, I tossed wisdom, knowledge, and understanding of God to the wayside and yoked with a mind of the evil one.

In the end, what the Lord spoke clearly to me was that, yes, it was a spirit that rose against me. It accused me of being an addict, hypochondriac, and hypocrite, but I was none of the above. But he allowed it to test my faith and to retrain me in things of which I had lost sight. My thinking in the area of my personal health had become fleshly, therefore skewing my heavenly thinking. I desperately needed a harsh reminder of how the enemy operates to kill, steal, and destroy.

I am reminded of the prophet Ahijah mentioned in 1 Kings. He was the one that prophesied to Jeroboam that he would be king. When Jeroboam was in wickedness, his young son became ill because of his evil. He disguised his wife to go to Ahijah to get a word from the Lord concerning their child. It states that Ahijah's eyesight was poor because of old age. However, his single vision of the Lord was as keen as ever. The Lord spoke to him, telling him everything in his spirit that he could not see with natural eyes before she ever arrived. He spoke everything to her that God spoke to him without hesitation, though he was unable to physically confirm the Word of the Lord with the natural. Oh, that everyone in the Body of Christ could get that grounded in their spirit man! We are all too busy trying to rationalize the spiritual with the lies of the earthly. God forgive us our wayward, earthly, fleshly thought life!

I want to point out a few of many key people who started out strongly for God, but to God's chagrin, ended poorly. You know the old adage, "It isn't how you start but how you finish." I don't want to get caught in how I started and have nothing to show for it when I stand before God and God's people. I want my end to be greater than my beginning. The only way that will happen will be if I keep my mind—not just daily, but moment to moment—set on him, his ways, and his heart. I must continually draw near unto him, not just fall back today on the fumes of yesterday's obedience and/or anointing. My future (which will become my present and my past) will be strong in him as long as my whole heart is always set on complete obedience to him.

None of us are exempt from the frailty of this life, but if we keep a watchful eye on the kingdom of heaven and his righteousness, he will be gracious to reveal our weaknesses and be our strength through it. He is our perfection, not anything of us. When you stumble—and we all will from time to time—*if* you are in love with him and have a heart set on pleasing him, he *will* turn it for your good. If your heart is not fully set on him, it will be your ruin!

I have been studying the life of King Solomon and have been perplexed at how someone so anointed with the manifold wisdom of God could act so foolishly. I began to realize that, no matter how much wealth, wisdom, understanding, or knowledge one has, even when given directly by the hand of the Most High God, it is worthless unless you have a whole heart for the *Giver* of the gift.

As you probably well know, his father, David, had a whole heart for God, even though he allowed himself to be given over to lust. However, as soon as his sin was addressed by the Lord, he fell on his face before God in absolute repentance. Because his heart was *fully* set on God, he never hesitated to repent and make things right.

Solomon, his child by Bathsheba (the one with whom he had committed adultery), was a man with less than a completely yielded heart for the Lord. He started out well in his youth as king. It was God-ordained for him to become king. As he asked for wisdom to rule justly, the Lord God blessed him, not only with what he asked, but also with a long life. The only *stipulations* for that long life were that he be obedient to the commandments of the Lord and that he would follow him all the days of his life with his *whole* heart. This he did not do. He started very strongly but ended in absolute weakness. He was torn apart by the very gift God had given to him as a blessing.

Solomon was a man highly revered by the entire world. People came from other countries to hear him speak such wisdom with their own ears. The Queen of Sheba even came to test his wisdom and left satisfied. She was quoted as saying that she did not believe that what she had heard was true, but when their time together was finished, she said that she had only heard a portion of his actual greatness. All this being true, how could such a man be given over to seven hundred wives and princesses and three hundred concubines? His insatiable lust for women overcame the supernatural wisdom given from God!

This is the perfect example of what a gentleman God is by allowing his own the choice of his ways or the ways of the world. He is so much a gentleman that when he was reprimanded by God, the Lord said that Solomon would not see the throne taken from him in his day, but it would come about in his son's day. The Lord God honored his sovereign word to *David,* the father of Solomon. Even then God refused to take the entirety of Israel away from Solomon's (David's) people, so to keep his holy Word.

Solomon died in a condition not equivalent to a man blessed abundantly of God. He says repeatedly that he did not know the purpose of anything! "Vanity of vanities," says the preacher (Ecclesiastes 1:2). Also, "All is vanity and striving after wind" (Ecclesiastes 1:14).

> And I set my mind to seek and explore by wisdom concerning all that has been done under heaven. It is a grievous task which God has given to the sons of men to be afflicted with…and I set my mind to know wisdom and to know madness and folly; I realized that this also is striving after wind. Because in much wisdom there is much grief, and increasing knowledge results in increasing pain.
>
> Ecclesiastes 1:13, 17–18 (NAS)

Those are heavy words! I would hate to be so burdened by the weight of God's anointing. I dare say that, in my opinion, Solomon's life would have been long had he been obedient. That was the stipulation to his *long life*. Understand also that long life is not measured necessarily by physical years. Life is not life at all, even when one is breathing on earth, if it is too heavy to bear. Solomon's life was too heavy to handle long before he died. He reigned as king in Jerusalem and all of Israel for forty years. He was a young man when he became king, so by deduction, he was physically young when he died (even by today's measure of life).

By all accounts, Solomon was worn down from chasing a phantom, so to speak. Though he had a partial heart for God, it was not good enough. God calls his people to yield 100 percent and nothing short of that. As I wrote earlier, he started out very strong, but his allegiance to the One True God waned tremendously. He sought after the *idea* that physical pleasure would bring him abundance and satisfaction. He thought that marrying into forbidden countries would protect him, and physically it did for a season. But that was never God's way.

He married Pharaoh's daughter to keep peace between the

nations. That is fine and well when the natural is all you are concerned about. But God had spoken that his people were never to marry outside of their own. This was because the other countries served other gods, so by marrying into them, they mixed their idolatry with the One True God. Such idolatry defiled their camp and the holiness within. Pharaoh even destroyed a whole city, Gezer, to make a doorway to his daughter.

Sadly, such a man gifted in many areas (spiritually, mentally, physically, emotionally, and financially) eventually allowed his emotions to override the abundance of God. Yes, he more than sought after and physically fulfilled his lust for sexual and emotional desire, yet without ever being *filled*. He engaged in activity with over one thousand women! I would say that if it were possible to be sexually sustained, Solomon would have been the man to succeed in this area! But the evidence is abundantly clear that without pleasing God (the giver of all good things) there is no life and no peace of that life.

He chased the phantom of lust with women, emotions, and people pleasing. He engaged with these women and was so overtaken by them that he must have thought that if he caved and took in their gods, all would be well. Obviously, by pleasing them, their home country would be at peace with his. That seemed reasonable to him instead of allowing God to bring true peace.

I am astounded when I read Proverbs with all of its incredible wisdom and knowledge displayed for anyone to read and learn. Then I turn to the next book, written by the same man, and it is packed full of depression and woefulness! Wisdom is meaningless when not driven and sustained by its Creator and Giver. The same can be said for any anointing. No matter how strong the anointing, that person is not exempt from the punishment/penalty of disobedience. Disobedience is the deal breaker in covenant with God. His stipulations are always and in everything to love him, be obedient to all his commands and fear him. Everything else falls in line under these. When you stop at any time from following these rules, all promises will begin to cease. These rules are mandatory!

Nothing gets past God, in case you are wondering. Just as he raised Saul as king knowing he would rise up in pride, he knew all along that Solomon would fail him. God plans every move he makes strategically and all before the foundation of the world. You can bank on that fact!

First Kings 11:14–15 states that *God* raised up an enemy against Solomon. It was someone that God put in place back when David was king. Hadad (of the royal line of Edom and enemy to Solomon) was a young man that fled to Egypt when he was a boy, back when David and his troops defeated and struck down every male of Edom. God allowed this young man to be spared, knowing that one day he would use him to defeat a man who was unworthy of the calling and blessings of God.

Here is the thing: God is always prepared to handle those who become disobedient and arrogant in heart long before he ever allowed their birth into this world.

Here is another case in point. Look at 1 Kings 11. This is where God raised up Jeroboam to be king in place of Solomon's son, Rehoboam. There were many events that took place before and as he became king, as God had spoken. Rehoboam, as God prophesied, became king of Judah in place of Solomon. In verse fifteen, when Rehoboam chose unwisely not to listen to the counsel of the elders, it reads: "…it was a turn of events *from the Lord,* that he might establish his word, which the Lord spoke through Ahijah the Shilonite to Jeroboam the son of Nebat."

Clearly God planned for Jeroboam to become king of Israel. But in 1 Kings 12:26–33, we see the following: Jeroboam said in his heart, 'Now the kingdom will return to the house of David. If this people go up to offer sacrifices in the house of the Lord at Jerusalem, then the heart of this people will return to their lord, even to Rehoboam king of Judah; and they will kill me and return to Rehoboam king of Judah. So the king consulted, and made two golden calves, and he said to them, 'It is too much for you to go up to Jerusalem; behold your gods, O Israel, that brought you up from the land of

Egypt. He set one in Bethel, and the other he put in Dan...now this thing became a sin...then he went up to the altar which he had made in Bethel...which he devised in his own heart..."

Basically Jeroboam removed himself from a place of humility. He took his eyes off of the God that ordained and anointed him, and he set his sights on himself (self is always rooted in pride). Again, pride always leads to a place of fear, which leads to a place of sure destruction! See where it reads, "which he devised in his own heart"? His eyes were on his own desires and ability (or rather inability) which is simply a draw of things of this earthly world. The *fear* of his enemy was a ghost, or rather, something not real, a mental illusion. God's people must have their inner vision set always on the supernatural ability of God and never the inability of human frailty. This fear led him to do great and exceeding wickedness and blasphemy in the sight of God. He even raised up false priests that were not of the Levitical priesthood.

His punishment, among other things, was that his son, Abijah, the only good that would have come from his line, had to die (1 Kings 14:13). We reap what we sow, whether through ourselves or our children. Solomon reaped what his father had sown, the good along with the bad. David's lust for women was greatly intensified in the next generation. He also reaped the promise of God to David that he would keep a remnant for David always and forever. That saved Solomon on many levels.

Rehoboam reaped what his father, Solomon, had sown. Solomon misused the awesome gift of wisdom bestowed by God when he chose not to apply it to his personal life. That was intensified in Rehoboam by making such foolish decisions concerning the nation.

Let's look at another man of God, in 1 Kings Chapter 13. There was a young prophet of God from Judah sent to Jeroboam to warn against his evil ways. Jeroboam, after his warning, asked the young prophet to go and dine at his home. He said, "Come home and refresh yourself." The prophet sternly quoted the words of the Lord: "...if you were to give me half your house I would not go with you, nor would I eat bread or drink water in this place. For so it was commanded me by the word of the Lord, saying, 'you shall eat no bread, nor drink water, nor return by the way which you came'" (1 Kings 13:8–9, NAS).

Notice, at first, how quickly he did exactly as the Lord commanded. Surely he was exhausted, hungry, and thirsty from his long journey to the king. Yet, he denied himself physical gratification in the face of *obvious* sinful, lustful temptation: the lust of a good meal, refreshing drink, rest, and a change of clothing. As it turns out, around verse eleven, it tells us that an old prophet living in Bethel got wind of this anointed young man. He was very drawn to him. Probably he just wanted to be in the presence of one so anointed of Almighty God as he once was. Or, possibly and most likely, he wanted to disprove the young man's prophetic anointing due to his own personal insecurities. This is referred to as a critical, jealous spirit. So, what did he do but allow himself to chase an illusion led by his fleshly desire to meet this young prophet. He had heard that he was not to eat or drink nor return home by the way he had traveled.

He found the young man under an oak. He offered him to come to his home and eat and drink. He offered him the very thing he knew was against the will of the very God he himself served. At first, again, the young man refused by quoting the Word of the Lord. He said, "*No.*"

The old prophet did not relent and deceitfully said, "I also am a prophet like you, and an angel spoke to me by the Word of the Lord, saying, 'Bring him back with you to your house, that he may eat bread and drink water,' but he lied to him." What would make a prophet of God do such a wicked thing as to purpose to make a fellow prophet of God go against God's direct command? It is simply the lust of the wickedness of the desire of the flesh to do whatever it takes to attain whatever you want. It can happen to anyone anywhere in their walk with God. Hence the word to be careful if you think you stand, lest you fall.

Verse nineteen quickly finds the young prophet eating bread

and drinking water at a table of a liar in the country in which the Lord said, "Do not eat bread or drink water"! All the old prophet had to do was say something to the effect of, "Well, God told me to do so." The young prophet, so it would seem, did not bother to check in with the Lord who sent him on the mission. God would never change his plan unless he first told the person he gave the plan in the first place. As far as I can tell, the only time that happened was when someone appealed to God personally asking him specifically to change his course (King Hezekiah).

He took the word of a total stranger claiming to be a *man of God*. The old one spoke with confidence and persuasion. Do you see how easily both men were led by the nose of something deceitful in the sight of God? The old one was led by the desire to be around God's anointed. He forsook wisdom and leaned upon his desire to be around a man led by the God he was getting ready to deliberately disobey! The young one was immature enough to be led by the desire to eat and drink so as to refresh himself.

They both got what they wanted. The anointed went to the old prophet's home to eat, drink, and spend time with him; he received nourishment and rest. Sadly, their natural desires—the phantom—led them both to their demise. As the young prophet traveled home on his donkey, a lion met him on the road and killed him. The lion and the donkey stood beside his dead body on the side of the road. People passed by and saw such a strange sight. Word got back to the old prophet.

He went quickly, gathered the body of the prophet, saddled him on his donkey, and took him back to his hometown to mourn and bury him. The old prophet buried him in his own tomb, saying, "Alas, my brother!" He told his sons to lay his bones beside him when he died. He said, "For the thing shall surely come to pass which he cried by the word of the Lord against the altar in Bethel and against all the houses of the high places which are in the cities of Samaria."

He did and said this because he recognized that absolutely this man he deceived was sent by God. Though he had disobeyed the Lord, the word he spoke was truly from God and would come to pass. I would imagine that the old prophet grieved the rest of his days, knowing that he had a hand in the death of God's anointed.

Obedience is always greater than sacrifice. Each of these people may have felt that they *sacrificed* something that *seemed* to be *right*, when obedience to the Word of God was all that was required. Obedience always leads to success, no matter the suffering of the journey. It is an all-too-common ploy of the enemy to make you think you are doing something good or correct when really you are being led astray from the commandments of God. Forsaking the Word of the Lord, though somehow justifiable in your mind, is always wrong and will lead to your destruction. Illusions of the enemy are allowed in our lives when our mind and eyes are not constantly and purposefully set on the heart of God.

Check within yourself. Ask the Lord to reveal any part of your heart not set on him. Don't be afraid to ask. He wants you to. By asking, that in itself reveals that you desire *him* more than the ways of the world. He already knows what is inside of you—let him expose it to you so you may yield all over to him that you may live a long, prosperous life here on earth!

■ ■ ■ ■ ■

Prayer

O gracious Father, give me the desire to set myself apart wholly to you. Guide me into the paths of righteousness, that I may not cast my foot upon a stone to stumble and fall. Show me, O God, how to reverently fear your holy name. I pray to have clear vision from heaven to know what is a lie and what is truth that I not be lured away by fleshly deceit. Teach me how to seek first the kingdom of heaven and your righteousness so that all other things I need here on earth will be provided without having to ask. Thank you, Father, my Husband, and lover of my soul, for exposing everything that is a phantom in my life. Continue to reveal with your holy light every wicked and fruitless deed of darkness that is attempting to leading me astray. I bind your supernatural strength to overcome the lies. Amen.

Reaching the
Land of Milk &
HONEY

Jesus said to them, I am the bread of life; he who comes to me will not hunger, and he who believes in me will never thirst ... truly, truly, I say to you, he who believes has eternal life. I am the bread of life. Your fathers ate the manna in the wilderness, and they died. This is the bread which comes out of heaven, so that one may eat of it and not die. I am the living bread that came down out of heaven; if anyone eats of this bread, he will live forever; and the bread also which I will give for the life of the world is my flesh.

> Then the Jews began to argue with one another, saying, "How can this man give us his flesh to eat?" So Jesus said to them, "Truly, truly, I say to you, unless you eat the flesh of the Son of Man and drink his blood, you have no life in yourselves. He who eats my flesh and drinks my blood has eternal life, and I will raise him up on the last day. For my flesh is true food, and my blood is true drink. He who eats my flesh and drinks my blood abides *in* me, and I *in* him. As the living Father sent me, and I live because of the Father, so he who eats me, he also will live because of me. This is the bread which came down out of heaven; not as the fathers ate and died; he who eats this bread will live forever."
>
> John 6:35, 47–58 (NAS)

"Then he said to me, "Son of man, eat what you find; eat this scroll, and go, speak to the house of Israel." So I opened my mouth, and he fed me this scroll. he said to me, "Son of man, feed your stomach and fill your body with this scroll which I am giving you." Then I ate it, and it was sweet as honey in my mouth." Then he said to me, "Son of man, go to the house of Israel and speak with my words to them" (Ezekiel 3:1, NAS).

"To eat of his flesh and drink of his blood." This instruction is as hard to comprehend today (if not more so) as it was the day he first spoke. This is because the average Christian still thinks only in the natural, with fleshly thinking. God is the Word. God is a spirit being. Therefore one can only understand spirit with spirit. What is of the flesh is fleshly. What is of the Spirit is spirit. John chapter three, verses five through seven read, "Jesus answered, "Truly, truly, I say to you, unless one is born of water and the Spirit he cannot enter into the kingdom of God. That which is born of the flesh is flesh, and that which is born of the Spirit is spirit."

Jesus is actually saying here that a *believer* must deny himself and allow Christ and *his* will to overtake him. Before Christ died and rose from the grave, only a select few had the privilege of having the Holy Spirit *within.* Since he arose and returned to heaven, he graciously left us with the deposit of what is to come. As a refresher, the Holy Spirit, the Spirit of the Living God, is inserted within the person who receives the word as truth.

Have you ever heard the term, "Whatever you consume, consumes you"? Whatever you eat, you become (bad food, bad health; good food, good health; fatty foods, fat body, and so on). To touch healthy food externally does not make you healthy. It must be taken *into* the body. In the spiritual, you are to *eat* his flesh and *drink* his blood—this is to *consume* and become *merged* with him. This is also why many read the Word but their life never really changes. It is still *external* because their spirit man is not awakened to be able to receive what is of the Spirit. In like manner, what goes in will come out.

If you are not ingesting (consuming, taking into your spirit man) the Word, the Word is not within, so there is nothing to come out of your mouth. Once you begin to eat the Word, your lips will attest to the fact. Ezekiel was instructed by God to "eat the scroll" which was his holy Word. Afterwards, he instructed him to go to the house of Israel and speak with *God's* words. You see, the Word had to be *inside* of his inner man for him to merge as one with God. Then, and only then, could the Word come out of him at the proper time.

So many people read and read and read, but the reading is still on the *outside* of the person. Unless the Word of God is sought after as a hearty meal to satisfy the spirit and soul, it is useless information. The Word of God must be *ingested* before it can be *digested*, before it can come out as fertilizer. If you have a Thanksgiving meal with turkey, gravy, corn, potatoes, stuffing, and all the trimmings, but you merely sit down at the table, look at it for hours and hours, and never eat it, it has no value to your natural man. In fact, it will leave you starving and agitated that you had something so good right in front of you but you did nothing with it.

If you simply read the Word and go through meaningless motions, you will be left empty, agitated, and ready to abandon your faith. The Word of God is from a spirit being; therefore, it must be received by your spirit man, not the natural. The Pharisees were grossed out by the words of Christ about eating his flesh and drinking his blood. The words were detestable to them, and they did not understand. They stumbled over the stumbling block!

"But he answered (Satan) and said, "It is written, 'Man shall not live on bread alone, but on every word that proceeds out of the mouth of God'" (Matthew 4:4, NAS).

"Jesus said, "he who has believed *and* has been baptized shall be saved; but he who has disbelieved shall be condemned" (Mark 16:16, NAS).

This simple fact will always remain. No matter how much physical water you drink or food you eat, you will still physically die. Lest you understand that the Word of God is life, you have no life at all. Seek *first* the kingdom of God and his righteousness, and everything else will follow. Natural food is only of value to you

when spiritual food is considered of the utmost value in your existence. Only through him does anything have any value or worth.

It is a wise person who accepts the Word of God as the only
truth there is. Mark 16:16 reads that the one who believes and has
been baptized spiritually will in turn be saved. It says nothing about
accepting Christ as Savior and then be baptized in the natural in
order to ensure salvation! What it does say is that once you believe
by putting your faith in the Son of the Living God *and* (they go
hand in hand) allow yourself to be immersed (baptized) in his Spirit
only then will you be saved from eternal damnation.

This baptism is the same as being totally consumed by and with
all that he is and desires. This is becoming a disciple (the actual
instruction of Jesus) as opposed to someone who makes a profession externally without transformation. Technically, the meaning in
the word is to be absorbed by God; buried with him completely and
alive only as his life is *in* and *through* you.

Justification and Redemption: Necessity of Proper Application

Justify: 1. show the justice or rightness of; 2. demonstrate the correctness of; 3. adduce adequate grounds for; 4. be such as to justify
vindicate; 5. just, right

Redeem: 1. buy back; 2. make a single payment to discharge; 3.
deliver from sin and damnation; 4. save from blame

"Much more then, having now been justified by his blood, we
shall be saved from the wrath of God through him" (Romans 5:9,
NAS).

"Knowing that you were not redeemed with perishable
things...but with precious blood, as of a lamb unblemished and
spotless, the blood of Christ" (1 Peter 1:18–19, NAS).

> Therefore, brothers, since we have confidence to enter the
> holy place by the blood of Jesus...let us draw near with a
> sincere heart in full assurance of faith, having our hearts

sprinkled clean from an evil conscience and our bodies washed with pure water.

Hebrews 10:19–22 (NAS)

Through the gift of his shed blood, a people who were far-off now can draw near (Ephesians 2:13), praise the Lord! It is through his pure blood *in* you that you are able to draw near to the perfect, pure, and holy God. The price of your sin is paid in full! You are as good as having fulfilled the Law if you allow yourself total immersion in the blood.

Look at it this way. You are not saved *by* the blood, as if to simply be *beside* it as you would stand *beside* a pool of clean water on a hot, steamy day looking upon it from afar. To simply gaze at a pool is not refreshing. You may be extremely uncomfortable in the sweltering heat, yet you rationalize how your clothes would be ruined if you jumped in, or how foolish someone may think you are if you did. Only jumping into it head first brings refreshment. It is startling at first, but then there is a wonderful refreshment you could only have dreamed of!

You are saved *through* the blood. First, you must realize and accept through faith that the life you live outside of Christ is death. It is futile. Becoming one with the Trinity is a passing *through* death (what we are born into) into life. Once you have accepted this realization, then you can allow the blood to bring new life, a kind you have never known. Try to visualize it something like this. It is basically like having swam through the water that ran from his side by diving in head first. It purifies your inner man. Then, Holy Spirit is inserted. Lastly, the pure blood seals him in permanently. It is only through the choice of dying to your flesh (sinful desires) that you are allowed to pass through the water and blood. It is how you receive the Spirit of the Living God.

Jesus Christ *justified* and *redeemed* every human being that ever has, does, or will live. It is for everyone. However, both are rendered useless to those who do not apply the gift of redemption and justification. The thing with God and the birth, death, burial, and resurrection of his precious Son is that, though he completed it *all* on the cross by rising from the dead, it must be *applied*. Acceptance of him brings a guarantee that you will not go to hell when you physically die.

On the other hand, we still have to live here on earth in this mortal body until he sees fit to take us from earth to heaven (whether by death or rapture). There has been much debate over the years as to whether there are still generational curses, or whether things such as witchcraft and curses from Free Masonry can be passed to the next generation. Christians say that there are no more curses of any kind and that we fellow Christians who believe that there are, diminish and nullify the power of the blood he shed at Calvary. The Christians who say there are no more curses say that it is blasphemy when people like me say that there are.

I must disagree, not to be argumentative, but to lend my perspective. The Word is clear that we are each to work out our salvation with fear and trembling. It is my most earnest desire to bring Christians into deeper levels of freedom. My purpose is always and only to shed his light into every area of darkness. I do not condemn or come against my brothers and sisters in Christ who do not agree. This brings me to *application*. If you have a wound and you have ointment in a bottle sitting on your shelf that will completely cure it, it is of no effect unless you pick it up and *apply* it to the infected area. The ointment was paid in full when you passed money from your wallet to the cashier. You even got a receipt as verification that there is no further payment for the balm.

So it is with the blood. Through the pure blood Christ shed on the cross, he fully bought back from Satan the curse cast upon man. Just as you must apply his blood (redemption and justification already supplied in full) to yourself to initially become *born again*, after salvation (confession, repentance, and acceptance) the blood must be *applied* to the specific areas that are scraped, dismembered, or dead. If your arm, leg, and neck are broken from an accident, when you go to the doctor for healing, he wouldn't wrap just the leg and assume that it is wrapped enough to protect and heal your arm and neck. Each area of brokenness must be cared for individually, though the *wrapping* that brings the healing is the same.

Let's look at a few other areas where blood must be applied. The Word is clear that Jesus Christ, in full, gave forgiveness of sins to the *entire world,* yet we know that the majority of the world (no matter the generation) will die and go to hell, because they refuse and reject the sacrificial gift of the pure blood. 1 John 2:2 reads, "and he himself is the propitiation for our sins, and not for ours only, but also for those of the whole world." Also, 2 Corinthians 5:19 states, "...that God was in Christ reconciling the world to himself..." Propitiation is the atoning sacrifice (appeasement) for our sins. It was given for *every* single human that has, does, or ever will live.

With the reasoning of the mindset mentioned above from other Christians, one must also say that to *confess your sins* to receive salvation is to say the payment already given for the world is blasphemy. To seek the Lord through the privilege of his blood for anything hidden within to receive freedom in more abundance would also be to call the blood insufficient, since he gave us complete freedom at the cross.

You cannot aptly say that, in some areas, the blood need not be *applied* because it is complete, but in others it is necessary. This is a contradiction in every way. Everything Jesus Christ did is in full, as already mentioned. However, the fullness of all must be applied where needed. He is Wisdom; therefore, if this way of thinking is correct, since his Holy Spirit lives within the believer, wisdom should not have to be applied. For that matter, you can include freedom, knowledge, understanding, stewardship, aims, goals, purposes, revelation, or even the Holy Spirit himself. Paul told Timothy, a man led by the Holy Spirit, to *fan the flame of Holy Spirit* within.

As it is in the natural (since God created the natural as a representation of the spiritual), the provision is in the spiritual. Otherwise, everyone could accept Christ as their Savior and all would be perfect because he is perfect. In fact, no one would have to accept salvation because it was extended to the entire world. How convenient that would be! Everyone would have it.

To say that it diminishes his blood to have to break curses of any kind, you would have to also say that to pray for healing and breaking spirits of infirmity from the believer is just as diminishing. After all, if this way of thinking were correct, as soon as a person accepts Christ, all problems such as poverty, sickness, foolishness, perversion, and lack of self-control should disappear. I reiterate, just as you must *apply* the healing already provided ("by his stripes we are healed"), you must also *apply* the blood to curses (generational, spoken, witchcraft, cultural) so that healing in that area may begin. Otherwise, the body of Christ will be continuously bruised, battered, blemished, and cursed because we *accept* his blood but have no idea what to do with it. He will not come back for an impure, broken, blemished, unholy bride!

Communion: Internal Before External

Anoint = apply oil or ointment to; smear, rub; baptism.

> …Father, are *in* me and I *in* you, that they also may be *in* Us…I *in* them and you *in* me, that they may be perfected *in* unity, so that the world may know that you sent me, and loved them, even as you have loved me…so that the love with which you loved me may be *in* them, and I *in* them.
>
> John 17:21–26 (NAS)

"Peter said to them, "Repent, and each of you be baptized *in* the name of Jesus Christ for the forgiveness of your sins; and you will receive the gift of the Holy Spirit." (Acts 2:38–39, NAS).

These Scriptures reveal that once the blood of Christ was shed and his flesh broken, salvation is made available to all who will *receive*. Once received, you are *in* him. To be hidden *in* him, there is open access to commune *with* him internally. With this, (as discussed in the first chapter) any *external* communion or worship will be an *outward* display of what is *internal*. Remember, you must ask the Lord to open your *spirit* man so that you can freely commune with the *Spirit* of God.

Notice how many times you read the Word *in* just in these few Scripture references. John 14 reads that he will be *with* you and *in* you. The *with* comes with *in*. Before Christ, in the Old Testament, he would be *with* people, but *in* was not a requirement because it had not been made available. Since *in* is now available, it is not a suggestion, but a requirement in order for him to be *with*.

All the references of *Helper, Spirit of Truth, Comforter,* "You in me and I in you" and things of the like all are about the Holy Spirit who is to be *deposited within* the believer. It is he from whom we draw strength and the one who gives us the *right of passage* into the very throne room of grace. It is *his* perfection within that grants you access to draw near to Father. Salvation is not available to the one who does not receive Holy Spirit *within* themselves. Granted, there are those who have him but do not utilize or acknowledge him, and that is a sad person at best. He does not work with *you* but with himself *in you*.

Gone are the days that you need an intercessor to allow you to come before his holy throne! He is the Intercessor! He tore away the veil that stood between you and God. To take communion in a physical church setting is merely to *represent* what has happened inside you. You received *into* your body a blood transfusion the day you confessed him as Lord and welcomed him into your being. You can't get any closer to someone than being merged as one! You become as his flesh and his blood!

Change of Origin

Then the word of the Lord came to me, saying, "Son of man, make known to Jerusalem her abominations and say, 'Thus says the Lord God to Jerusalem, "your origin and your birth are from the land of the Canaanite, your father was an Amorite and your mother a Hittite. As for your birth, on the day you were born your navel cord was not cut, nor were you washed with water for cleansing; you were not rubbed with salt or even wrapped in cloths. No eye looked with pity on you to do any of these things for you, to have compassion on you. Rather you were thrown out into the open field, for you were abhorred on the day you were born. When I passed by you and saw you squirming in your blood, I said to you while you were in your blood, 'Live!' Yes, I said to you while you were in your blood, 'Live!'

Ezekiel 16:1–6 (NAS)

"... through which the world has been crucified to me, and I to the world" (Galatians 6:14, NAS).

Therefore we have been buried with him (death of our fleshly nature) through baptism into death (depiction of drowning the ways of the world with your flesh), so that as Christ was raised from the dead through the glory of the Father, so we too might walk in newness of life (once raised up from the water, the old flesh and the lusts of the world should stay under the water in death, thereby allowing the new life, a whole new birth, to come into existence). For if we have become united (to become the same as, merged as one) with him in the likeness of his death, certainly we shall also be in the likeness of his resurrection, knowing this, that our old self was crucified with him, in order that our body of sin might be done away with, so that we would no longer be slaves to sin; for he who has died is freed from sin (once the flesh nature is sacrificed to Christ, put to death, we are freed from the sin that condemned us). Now if we have died with Christ, we believe that we shall also live with him, knowing that Christ, having been raised from the dead, is never to die again; death no longer is master over him (since death is no longer master over him and he is in us, it is no longer master over the believer). For the death that he died, he died to sin

once for all; but the life that he lives, he lives to God. Even
so, consider yourselves to be dead to sin, but alive to God in
Christ Jesus.

Romans 6:4–11 (NAS)

As I have stated many times before, true salvation is transformation into a new, heavenly creature that continues, while on earth, to
reside in an earthly vessel. Yes, we must continue to work out our
own salvation with fear and trembling, so it is a continual process
of drawing near unto him and becoming more like him with every
passing day. Begin to see yourself as he is—supernatural. To *be* like
him, we must *think* like him in order to begin to *act* like him.

This is why it is altogether possible and crucial to get your
thinking lined up with God's. His is higher than that of your human
man. Since he is now *in* you, you have access to his thinking. Colossians 3:1–2 reads as follows: "Therefore *if* you have been raised up
with Christ, keep seeking the things above, where Christ is, seated
at the right hand of God. Set your mind on the things above, not
on the things that are of the earth. For you have died and your life
is hidden *with* Christ *in* God."

You are one with the most high God. This makes you supernatural as he! No longer are you to think as the world thinks. Liken
it unto going on vacation somewhere, and the longer you stay, the
longer you miss your home. You can't seem to stop thinking about
it and things of it. The earth is not your home; heaven is. It is where
you are *from* since God is your life, and that is where he is *from*. He,
your new life is of heaven; therefore, you too are of heaven, though
your physical body has not yet been there or seen it. The longer you
walk with him here, the more you will/should think of home and
think as your homeland thinking is. Get your thinking set in the
high place, and your actions and reactions will change drastically!

The New Covenant

"And when he had taken some bread and given thanks, he broke it and gave it to them, saying, 'This is my body which is given for you; do this in remembrance of me.' And in the same way he took the cup after they had eaten, saying, 'This cup which is poured out for you is the new covenant in My blood'" (Luke 22:19–20, NAS).

> Whoever eats the bread or drinks the cup of the Lord in an unworthy manner, shall be guilty of the body and the blood of the Lord. But a man must examine himself, and in so doing he is to eat of the bread and drink of the cup. For he who eats and drinks, eats and drinks judgment to himself if he does not judge the body rightly. For this reason many among you are weak and sick, and a number sleep. But when we are judged, we are disciplined by the Lord so that we will not be condemned along with the world.
>
> 1 Corinthians 11:26–31 (NAS)

The text above reads to "judge the body rightly" before taking holy communion. This is individually as well as with groups such as a family, a church body, or a prayer group. Regardless, each individual must examine himself. This translates that, if you attempt to receive holy communion (the physical representation) without first judging what is in your own heart and repent through purity of faith in the very blood and flesh of Christ (spiritual intimacy), you bring the judgment of God upon yourself. We must all stop trying to attain that which is of the Spirit through condemned flesh.

What I mean is that many people (Christian or not) go through the ritual of communion at a church weekly, monthly, or on holidays as though the mere participation will help them somehow get closer to God. In actuality, when people do it this way, they bring sickness and all types of curses upon themselves as the Scripture clearly states. It is because the *act of communion* was not an outward display of the intimacy with God within. What is the definition of communion anyway except simply to have *fellowship* and to *share in something common?*

Faith in the Son of the living God is the only way to please Father. Many try to attain *godliness* through acts of the flesh. Many *do good things* outside of the goodness and direction of God. To examine yourself is to examine your heart. Where is it set? Is it on Christ above all, or on other people or things and, somewhere down the list, God? As a collective body, are you set on unity in him, or do you (as a leader of any kind) allow discord to rule among you? You can be an authority over one or millions; either way, how do you conduct yourself in the quietude and in the presence of those looking to you as their spiritual mentor? Is your heart set completely on the desire of Christ?

The Scripture reads that the light shined into the darkness, and it did not comprehend. Darkness is the fleshly nature of man. When a person refuses to die to the flesh, the flesh will override your spirit man. When this happens, you allow yourself to stay in darkness and the Light is not allowed to rule. Your acts of *goodness* will soon fade because they were not of the Spirit. They are as wood, hay, and stubble and will be burned in the presence of the Lord as worthless.

When Jesus spoke of the eating and drinking, it was too much for the natural man to comprehend. Most people want a *form of godliness,* yet they *deny the power of God.* When the rubber meets the road, most choose *pretend godliness* and cling to their own selfish desires. In this, they disconnect themselves from the blessings and covenant of God. These are the same people who turn and curse God when things go poorly.

"My son, eat honey, for it is good, Yes, the honey from the comb is sweet to your taste; know that wisdom is thus for your soul; if you find it, then there will be a future, and your hope will not be cut off" (Proverbs 24:13–14, NAS).

"I commanded your forefathers in the day that I brought them out of the land of Egypt, from the iron furnace saying, 'Listen to my voice, and do according to all which I command you; so you shall be my people, and I will be your God, in order to confirm the oath which I swore to your forefathers, to give them a land flowing with milk and honey, as it is this day" (Jeremiah 11:4–5, NAS).

All these Scriptures talk about milk and honey. Even before the coming of our Savior, we are instructed as to the goodness of both. Milk strengthens a young child to adulthood, and honey is the sweet savor of all that is good. The Word of God is as sweet honey to the lips and heart of the righteous. The darkness despises the milk and honey, but the covenant of God through his Son makes what darkness cannot comprehend: sweet to the taste and the belly!

I find it precious to read how Samson tore the lion with nothing but his bare hands. It reveals supernatural strength that only our God can provide through faith. Through the overcoming of the enemy and death, God developed sweet savory honey from its carcass. He could not share such a thing with his parents because of a religious mindset of the customs of the day. Through anointing of God, he will not only provide you defeat of your strong enemy, but will make the enemy serve as a dining table for all that is good!

When Ezekiel ate of the scroll, it was sweet as honey in his mouth. Before Christ, everything was literal. Today, we can *eat* the Word spiritually. We must eat it with our spirit man, or rather, our heart. The only way to speak the Word, his pure and holy Word, is to take in all that he provides. Like I said earlier, he works with himself who is in you. The more of him you consume, the more of him will come out. He wants you to devour the Word as the best meal you will ever eat, that he may take it and utilize it *through you,* the earthen vessel to speak to others.

Most try to take the Word and apply it externally. Doing this, the Word comes out as harsh and without meaning. The land of milk and honey is the life spent here with Jesus Christ inwardly. Yes, there is a day when we the believers will join him in heaven, but we can have the abundance of milk and honey right here if we will only first seek the kingdom of heaven and his righteousness!

■ ■ ■ ■ ■

Prayer

Father, I pray in the holy and precious name of your dear Son, Jesus Christ, to be so immersed with you that the world cannot tell me apart from you. Show me daily how to truly eat of your flesh and drink of your blood. I desire with all that is in me to be unto you as a poured-out drink offering, holy and acceptable. Reveal to me the error of my ways that I may confess and repent with all humility that breaking may come. Break me and make me into the vessel of honor you so richly desire me to be. I love you, my Father, Husband, and Kinsman Redeemer! O Spirit of the Living God, dwell deeply within me that I may go to the four corners of the world and speak your words from my mouth that disciples may be made of many nations! Reveal to me how to leave the old behind and to press on toward the holy mark of Christ my Savior!

Evidence of a True
BELIEVER

"For God so loved the world that he gave his only begotten Son, that whosoever believes in him shall not perish, but have eternal life" (John 3:16, NAS).

> For this is the message which you have heard from the beginning, that we should love one another; not as Cain, who was of the evil one and slew his brother. And for what reason did he slay him? Because his deeds were evil, and his brother's were righteous. Do not be surprised, brethren, if the world hates you. We know that we have passed from death unto life, because we love the brethren. He who does not love abides in death. Everyone who hates his brother is a murderer; and you know that no murderer has eternal life abiding in him. We know love by this, that he laid down his life for us; and we ought to lay down our lives for the brethren. But whoever has the world's goods, and sees his brother in need and closes his heart against him, how does the love of God abide in him? Little children, let us not love with word or with tongue, but in deed and truth.
>
> 1 John 3:11–18 (NAS)

"When pride comes, then comes dishonor, but with the humble is wisdom ... with his mouth the godless man destroys his neighbor, but through knowledge the righteous will be delivered ... he who despises his neighbor lacks sense, but a man of understanding keeps silent" (Proverbs 11:2, 9, 12, NAS).

I find it interesting that John 3:16 describes God's love toward mankind by laying down his life. In I John chapter 3, it mentions the same and then adds that the one who does not do the same for his fellow brethren does not know him. If you do not love your brother and sisters in Christ or your enemies, you are of the evil one, and you do not know the Father or the Son. With the mindset of Christ, you will be willing at all times to lay down your life for your brethren. This too is dying to the flesh. Without the inward transformation into the love of Christ, your flesh will only allow you to exhibit a fleshly love. Such love is false and conditional.

The Word states that anyone who hates his neighbor is a fool and there is no understanding of the Word and truth of God in you. Learn how to be quiet. You are not obligated to say everything you think and feel. On the contrary, you are obligated by God to use discretion, considering the needs of others over yourself. Remember self-discipline?

"The Spirit of the Lord is upon me, because he anointed me to preach the gospel to the poor; he has anointed me to preach the gospel to the poor; he has sent me to heal the brokenhearted, to preach deliverance to the captives, and recovery of sight to the blind, to set at liberty them that are bruised, to preach the acceptable year of the Lord" (Luke 4:18–19, NAS).

Although I have touched on love already, I thought it necessary to have a specific chapter about it. You are to do as he did with the heart of love; loving his enemy as he loved himself. *You* were his enemy before you were ever thought of, yet he died for you. The Word of God is not to be used as a tool to murder others! It is as Jesus said, "to heal the brokenhearted," not inflict more pain and suffering. Anyone who does such a thing is still operating under the wickedness of Satan and there is no light in them.

One of them, a lawyer, asked him a question, testing him, "Teacher, which is the great commandment in the Law?"

> And he said to him, "'You shall love the Lord your God with all your heart, and with all your soul, and with all your mind.' This is the great and foremost commandment. The second is like it, 'You shall love your neighbor as yourself.' On these two commandments depend the whole Law and the Prophets."
>
> Matthew 22:36–40 (NAS)

As I have mentioned, without an understanding of God's unfailing love in your mind, heart, and spirit, you cannot function as the Lord intends. Love is the key to everything else in the kingdom of God. If you operate in any gift of the Spirit and you have no love, the gifts are useless. I'll go a step further and say that if you are not operating in or working toward pure love, you are not a child of God. Go back and look at 1 John 3. It states that if you do not love, you live in death, and you are a murderer. I heard Creflo Dollar say that, to God, love is like a curtain rod. Without it, nothing else can stand. No love, no life.

> A moneylender had two debtors; one owed five hundred denarii, and the other fifty. When they were unable to repay, he graciously forgave them both. So which of them will love him more?" Simon answered and said, "I suppose the one whom he forgave more." And he said to him, "You have judged correctly." Turning toward the woman, he said to Simon, "Do you see this woman? I entered your house; you gave me no water for my feet, but she has wet my feet with her tears and wiped them with her hair. You gave me no kiss; but she, since the time I came in, has not ceased to kiss my feet. You did not anoint my head with oil, but she anointed my feet with perfume. For this reason I say to you, her sins, which are many, have been forgiven, for she loved much; but he who is forgive little, loves little.
>
> Luke 7:40–47 (NAS)

Everyone needs a good dose of understanding of how much they have been forgiven. If you really understood, you would be humbled by the glory, mercy, and compassion of the Lord. Few comprehend that he really did die just for you and your sin nature before you were ever born into it.

My real breaking point was back in February of 2000 when I realized how much I had been forgiven. Until that point, I had condemned my first ex-husband for what a worthless scoundrel he was. But one moment in time, I was humbled to my floor when the Lord began to reveal my darkness within; that my sins were no less black than his. That was humbling, and I praise God that day came so I might be transformed into his likeness!

Stop comparing yourself with those around you and begin to compare yourself to Christ and see how well you fare. The sweetest, kindest, most prim and proper person on the planet would become as ashes and dust compared to the magnificence of Christ, our Lord God Almighty.

An argument started among them as to which of them might be the greatest. But Jesus, knowing what they were thinking in their heart, took a child and stood him by his side, and said to them, "Whoever receives this child in my name receives me, and whoever receives me receives him who sent me; for the one who is least among all of you, this is the one who is great." John answered and said, "Master, we saw someone casting out demons in your name; and we tried to prevent him because he does not follow along with us. But Jesus said to him, "Do not hinder him; for he who is not against you is for you."

When the days were approaching for his ascension, he was determined to go to Jerusalem; and he sent messengers on ahead of him, and they went and entered a village of the Samaritans to make arrangements for him. But they did not receive him, because he was traveling toward Jerusalem. When his disciples James and John saw this, they said, "Lord, do you want us to command fire to come down from heaven and consume them?" But he turned and rebuked (the Lord only rebuked Satan) them, and said, "you do not know what kind of spirit you are of; for the Son of Man did not come to destroy men's lives, but to save them." And they went on to another village.

Luke 9:46–56 (NAS)

"An argument started," the Scripture reads. Right away you know this would not bode well for the disciples. You are commanded to stay away from petty arguments and rivalries. They actually wondered in their conceit who was the best among them. The Lord replied that the least will be the greatest. I like how John then gave a pathetic segue into something else altogether. He did not understand in his spirit that those who have childlike faith, accept, and humble themselves are the ones who will be exalted by God; not the ones who think highly of themselves and put others down according to *their* standards. Humility, not pride, brings the grace of God. So many people are puffed in their so-called spiritual walk. If you are that person, repent of your pride by humbling yourself before Almighty God.

When John changed the subject, he opened another can he could not wrap his brain around. He *snitched* on another person casting out demons in the name of Jesus. He thought he was doing something good, yet Jesus said not to hinder him; he stated that whoever is not against you is for you. The point here is that the disciples wanted everyone to follow them (do it their way or nothing), and if they weren't, they shouldn't be allowed to operate in Jesus' name at all. It sounds extreme, yet this mentality floods the body of Christ—this "my way or the highway" religious thinking. A good example is curses that I covered a few pages back. I may disagree with those who do not have the same perspective as me, but I am not going to argue the case. We should remain sound and united in the fact that our goal to make disciples of many nations is the same.

Remember that this is all before the anointing of Holy Spirit, which took place in Acts chapter two in the upper room. This tells me that people in the body who act like this are *not* Holy Spirit-led. They may have Holy Spirit within, but he is certainly not allowed to move an inch! Most simply look holy instead of striving to attain real holiness. A person truly holy is not as loud as one trying to appear holy.

Okay, now it gets even worse for the great disciples! These men were puffed for walking with Christ, yet walking ignorantly of the very God with whom they walked. They did not understand a Word he spoke! In the next section of these verses, you see his people going ahead to make arrangements in Samaria. The Samaritans rejected Jesus simply because he was on his way to see the Jews. Most know that the Jews hated the Samaritans because they were not purebreds (half-Jewish), and they hated the Jews in return. That is a lesson in itself about not returning hatred for hatred. Bless those who curse you. Return love for hatred, so that the one hating you will turn to love.

After they rejected him, John and James were angry and offered to smite them with fire from heaven to annihilate them. Now there's some true love for you! Isn't it interesting that they couldn't understand anything else, but they understood payback from rage! They did not once offer to minister the love and forgiveness of Christ, but simply to wipe them off the planet! Then Jesus rebuked them. Notice that the word *rebuke* is a common word used for Satan and his demons. Then he said that they did not know from what spirit they were from. He clarified that he came to save, not destroy. How many "believers" operate in hatred and call in *righteous anger?*

The point to all of this is that still today it is apparent that those who think they *know something* of God's Word would rather use it to kill and destroy, like Satan. If that is your nature and you function in it in the name of Jesus, woe to you! It is the Lord's job, and his alone, to convict people of their unrighteousness. It is your job to display in full the unwavering love of the Father. Yes, there are people from whom you must separate yourself, but that does not mean you are to mistreat or slander them in any way. Learn to keep your mouth shut!

> Jesus replied and said, "A man was going down from Jerusalem to Jericho, and fell among robbers, and they stripped him and beat him, and went away leaving him half dead. And by chance a *priest* was going down on that road, and when he saw him, he passed by on the other side. Likewise a *Levite* also, when he came to the place and saw him, passed by on the other side. But a *Samaritan*, who was on a journey, came upon him; and when he saw him, he felt compassion, and came to him and bandaged up his wounds, pouring oil and wine on them; and he put him on his own beast, and brought him to an inn and took care of him. On the next day he took out two denarii and gave them to the innkeeper and said, 'Take care of him; and whatever more you spend, when I return I will repay you.' Which of these three do you think proved to be a neighbor to the man who fell into the robbers' hands?" And he said, "The one who showed mercy toward him." Then Jesus said to him, "Go and do the same."

> Luke 10:30–37 (NAS)

This is a depiction of Jesus Christ. He is the despised one, yet without hesitation, he helped the one who hated him. He paid his bill in full. This is healing the brokenhearted. This is true mercy toward your enemy. You were his enemy, and he died for you anyway, even because of it. The priest and Levite (also a priest) denied the one in need. They had too much piety to get their hands dirty. One even walked on the other side of the road to not have to go near him. These are the ones who believe themselves *righteous*.

Do you do that? Do you snub your spiritual nose at those you don't care for—those who are "dirty"? Are you unforgiving and unkind? Notice that verse thirty-three says that the Samaritan was "on a journey." Could this be a journey representing each person's journey with Christ? In understanding love, he realized that part of the journey is taking time to stop, look, listen, help, and heal.

Now as they were traveling along, he entered a village; and a woman named Martha welcomed him into her home. She had a sister called Mary, who was seated at the Lord's feet, listening to his word. But Martha was distracted with all her preparations; and she came up to him and said, "Lord, do you not care that my sister has left me to do all the serving alone? Then tell her to help me." But the Lord answered and said to her, "Martha, Martha, you are worried and bothered about so many things; but only one thing is necessary, for Mary has chosen the good part, which shall not be taken away from her."

Luke 10:38–42 (NAS)

Are you Martha or Mary? Are you spiritually puffed so to think that you are the only one working for the Savior and then getting mad at Jesus because he doesn't alleviate your work or reprimand the one basking in his glory? Jesus is saying to Martha that it is more important to crawl into the lap of the Savior and spend time with him intimately than to look busy or even be busy. So many do busy work, say it is for God when it is really of their flesh so to look good, and then get angry with God because he is wearing them out. Stop whatever you are doing that is wearing you out and take time to get to know the heavenly Savior. If you do, do, do, and don't bother to know him on an intimate level, your work is in vain.

"A new commandment I give to you, that you love one another, even as I have loved you, that you also love one another. By this all men will know that you are my disciples, if you have love for one another" (John 13:34–35, NAS).

What pleases the Father is his pure love being poured out into a dark and dying world through your body. You are commanded to love him with all of your person and your neighbor as yourself. Do this, and you will please the Almighty. This is *the only way* for others to know and believe! No love, no God, no eternal life! Any action without love is in vain. Seek to grow into a love relationship with him, and it will begin to pour through you.

"Peter said to him, 'Never shall you wash my feet!' Jesus answered him, 'If I do not wash you, you have no part with me,'" states John 13:8. This is simple. Allow him to wash you with the pure water that he shed for you, and you will become a part of him. If you do not, you will not. This is spiritual cleansing that must come to pass. It does not stop after your "profession of faith." First you profess, *then* you grow into relationship.

"What is the outcome then, brethren? When you assemble, each one has a psalm, has a teaching, has a revelation, has a tongue, has an interpretation. Let all things be done for edification" (1 Corinthians 14:26, NAS).

All things, especially the operation of the gifts of the Spirit, must be used to edify the body. Any other reason is of the flesh and it is not of or for God. Woe to the one who misuses any gift for self-gratification and glory.

"In that day you will ask in my name, and I do not say to you that I will request of the Father on your behalf; for the Father himself loves you, because you have loved me and have believed that I came forth from the Father" (John 16:26–27, NAS).

Are your requests being fulfilled? If not, is it because he does not love you, or because you do not love him?

■ ■ ■ ■ ■

Prayer:

O, heavenly Father, hallowed be thy name in all the earth! I seek your face, Almighty God, that you may descend upon me and transform me as Christ himself was transformed on the mountaintop. Make me aware of how much I have been forgiven. Show me, Jesus, how to die to my flesh, that I may operate completely selfless in all things. I lay myself on the altar before you and I ask that you reveal to me your pure love. Teach me how to be unashamed of how you made me, fearfully and wonderfully. Show me how not to be prideful of how I look or what I possess on the outside, for I am saved by your grace like all those before and after me. Teach me how to be a gracious host for your Holy Spirit within. Remind me daily how to walk a walk of love, heavenly love, and not the superficial love that isn't worth more than wood, hay, or stubble. Convey to me, O gracious Lord, how to not only forgive those who have sinned against me, but to repent of my judgment toward them, that I may be forgiven. Father, give me the grace to see the evil I have allowed in my camp. I want my territory clean, unblemished, and spotless before you. Show me which relationships are ungodly and give me the supernatural strength to end them. Bring into my life relationships that are pure and holy. Give me, O gracious merciful God, clean hands and a pure heart before you, before man and before the demons of hell. I pray, O Sovereign Lord, that you, man, and demons will testify that I am a child of the King! Amen and amen. Selah.

Satan Is Dead: He's Only a SHADOW

"For as the woman originates from the man, so also the man has his birth through the woman; and all things originate from God" (1 Corinthians 11:12, NAS).

"Wherefore seeing we also are compassed about with so great a cloud of witnesses, let us lay aside every weight, and the sin which doth so easily beset us, and let us run with patience the race that is set before us (KJV) … for consider him who has endured such hostility by sinners against himself, so that you will not grow weary and lose heart" (Hebrews 12:1, 3, NAS).

"Therefore, since the children share in flesh and blood, he himself likewise also partook of the same, that through death he might *render powerless* him who had the power of death, that is, the devil" (Hebrews 2:14, NAS).

Satan, the enemy of God and man, is dead. He has been declared so by God, the Creator of everything. In this knowledge, one can approach this enemy with a whole new perspective. You no longer need to see him as one you are fighting, but rather as *dead weight;* something cumbersome and heavy.

See in your mind's eye a corpse. It is hard, cold, and difficult to maneuver. I do not know firsthand, but I can imagine that a dead body, because it is stiff and lifeless, is hard to manipulate when attempting to prepare it for burial. If a person suddenly dies and falls on top of you, you are trapped by the weight of one without a will or ability to help you remove them. If a person passes out on top of you, you can at least revive them enough to encourage them to help you shift their body into another position away from you.

So it is with the enemy, Satan. Many quote, "Satan is a defeated foe. I know the end of the book," with great zeal. However, they fail to recognize the meaning, which is that Satan is in fact dead. This is why Satan is such a difficult enemy. He has no ability to be dissuaded, manipulated, encouraged to relent, or to change his course. A live enemy can, however, be encouraged at gunpoint to move out of your way! Satan does not have the means to do so. He therefore must be *pushed* off of you while you *pull away* from him. This pushing off and pulling away is a simultaneous act of your will getting aligned with God's. This is why we need others and must work as one unit. Two can remove a dead body more easily than one. It is all a team effort in this walk with God.

While the true believer (much like Paul, John, Peter, and all those before us) is not exempt from the frailty of life, we do have a great advantage over the unbeliever. Paul writes in Philippians 1:28, "in no way be alarmed by your opponents—which is a sign of destruction for them, but of salvation for you, and that too, from God." This is power! By knowing, understanding, and comprehending in your spirit man that the enemy is in fact already dead to God, you will realize that he is dead to you also. Few ever attain this power.

John 6:28–29 reads, "Therefore they said to him, 'What shall we do, so that we may work the works of God?' Jesus answered and said to them, 'This is the work of God that you believe in him whom he has sent.'" These two simple yet grossly overlooked scriptures say everything about where the power lays to comprehending that the enemy is not alive, but dead. Too many people incorrectly refer to themselves as *believers*. Most, in fact, when it comes right down to the heart of the matter, do not believe at all. They may have enough faith to make a profession of salvation, but that is not the faith that endures; the faith that establishes one in righteousness before God, man, and demons. On the contrary, too many *work* to attain righteousness when the Lord himself said that the *work* is simply *believing*.

Every born again person must work daily on belief, faith, and trust. It is a task that takes many a lifetime to achieve. Belief is the *knowing* that in life or in death, imprisonment, or freedom, in good times and bad, sickness and in health, poverty, or abundance; he is the risen Savior, Christ Jesus, Creator of heaven and earth, the life breath of every living thing, seen and unseen. That is belief, and that is what pleases Father. That is belief that is faith and trust in the One True God. This is faith that when all is being ripped away, you don't say to God, "But God, I…" telling God everything you have accomplished in his name; telling, dictating to him how he should handle your situation. True faith, true belief, is that which endures all hardships, seeing past the circumstance and straight into the face of Almighty God, whom without, you would not exist. Hebrews 5:8 reads that "Jesus learned obedience through suffering." By *learning* obedience, self-discipline over the flesh is developed. Faith and trust are also developed through suffering because there is opportunity for you to see the manifestation of the righteous, magnificent hand of God.

Every believer must pass, at some point, the test of faith. There are many throughout life, but I see that there is generally that one wilderness in life where you must choose him above all else, and it breaks you of your old man forever. And, though other trials may come your way, you have become something completely super-natural that allows your faith in him to keep you humble and an overcomer.

All this being said, let's look at how one must fight a dead foe. Again I say that it is because he is dead that he seems harder to fight than a live enemy that could choose to turn and relent. Satan uses his dead weight to squash God's people. He just sits on top of you in his lifeless condition. He basically pins you to the floor until you starve to death, or you stop breathing from his heaviness which crushes your heart.

First of all, keep in the forefront of your mind that reverent fear, hope, faith, and love are your most important weapons of warfare. Also, we are called to supernatural love that comes only from the God who is love. Thirdly, your faith must be established in him and not in the things you (or any human) can accomplish in this life. You are powerless without 100 percent submission to him. Paul said that the "confidence," which is faith and hope, is a sign of destruction to the enemy. The one who stands confidently in the face of the enemy has already defeated the enemy! It does not mean there aren't hard times; it means you see the end of the hard times before they come.

Psalm 23:4 reads, "Yea, though I walk through the valley of the shadow of death …" Most focus on the word *death*. I say focus on the word *shadow*. Since Satan is dead, the valley you go through is not the valley of *actual* death, but the *shadow* (or impression) of death. What feels like death is not really death to the one who walks in absolute faith that Father will not allow anything to come to the one called out by him. Sometimes the valley *appears* difficult. We have already well-established, the difficult times are arranged by God allowing Satan to do this or that in order to test you to the place of refinement.

This is where one can then claim in total faith, "I will fear no evil." A child no longer fears the boogey man in the closet once they realize that what seemed so ferocious is nothing but the shadow of a thing without life. It is merely a shadow of a hanger or toy. Children of God are like this. The *shadow of death* is a shadow of a creature that is dead. Death through Christ has been abolished by life. Neither the creature, nor its shadow has any power; therefore, there is nothing to fear. Death has neither power nor the ability to move, attack, harm, or kill.

Knowledge of the power and authority of the blood of the Lamb is a key element in overcoming what has already been defeated. Without knowledge, a child is afraid of what isn't real. With light and knowledge that the creature is not alive, the child can lay down its head at night and rest. The light reveals that the image of the shadow is false. Satan's corpse literally covers the face of the earth.

Because of his size, his shadow is large and thick. Have you ever looked at your shadow on the floor? It is disproportioned. It looks larger than your actual physical body. Likewise, Satan's shadow seems bigger than he is, which makes him *appear* all the more scary and powerful.

Knowledge of the blood and its power give the believer rest since he, Christ, is the Rest. It equips the saints with the weapon to push *off* the dead weight of the evil one, pull back *from* the evil one, and be set free from his oppressive deadness. *Fear*, on the other hand, ushers defeat. Fear is Satan's greatest tool against God's people. Since God has provided everything you need for life, to fear the enemy he already died to conquer is sin against the Almighty.

Jeremiah 1:17 reads, "Now, gird up your loins and arise, and speak to them all which I command you. Do not be dismayed before them, or *I will dismay you before them.*" In other words, if God tells you there is nothing to fear, *do not fear!* By fearing your enemy when he said not to, you are saying you have no trust or faith in his word. That is a slap in his face, and he will allow you to be brought down by your enemy because you shame *God*. His Word is true and trustworthy. Since it is, he expects his people to believe it and live a fearless life, trusting that he is your shield and buckler in any situation. He says he will contend with those who contend with his anointed. Let him! Stop trying to fight your enemy with words and weapons of man.

Belief is the tool that makes the *works* of the Father actually *of the Father* and not just something one does to be a *good person*. In fact, there in nothing good except God. I cannot reiterate enough that if your physical works are not through faith in the Son of the

Living God, they are as wood, hay, and stubble, and not acknowledged in his sight. In other words, they are useless. I mention wood,
hay, and stubble throughout the book because they come in many
forms of life.

Obviously, the comparisons I have given are physical ones, but
Satan and his troops are spiritual. Therefore, you must ask the Lord
to open your spiritual eye to see into the spirit realm. I say again
that the body of Christ must stop seeing with a natural, carnal perspective. You need to begin to see obstacles as tools the evil one uses
to destroy you. But, more importantly, obstacles in life, though they
come *through* evil, they are testing tools of God. Satan has no power
except what *God* gives! If Christ has power over death, and Satan
is death, God has all power and authority over Satan. He can't do
anything unless God gives him permission. Recognize that Satan is
a puppet, and God is the Master of the puppet! The first Scripture
reference in this chapter is 1 Corinthians 11:12, declaring boldly and
without question that *all* things originate from God. That does not
just mean the tangible, but the intangible. There is nothing that
does not come from God.

The question most have is, "Why would God give him his
power if he already defeated him?" This is a good question, but
there is an even better answer. As I have stated, testing must come
in the life of every believer. No test, no victory. Our sole purpose
on earth is to glorify the Master in all things at all times with our
spirit, soul, and body; every word, thought, and deed. It is a very
easy thing for one to confess with their lips that Jesus Christ is
Lord. But what about when the rubber meets the road—when the
oppression of life comes your way, what then?

Just as God tested the Israelites to see where their hearts were,
so does he with believers today. It isn't that he does not know, but he
must test you to reveal to *you* where your heart is. None of us know
until testing comes. When it does, most "believers" complain, shake
their proverbial fist at God and say, "How dare you, God! How
could you let this happen to me? Don't you know who I am?" Yet,

for those who know the word, you know that all of God's disciples, apostles, and prophets endured hardships in obedience. Hardships come to the wicked and righteous alike. It rains on the just and the unjust.

That being said, when it rains, do you *trust* him and are you *confident* enough in your righteousness and integrity to say, "I know my God will never leave me nor forsake me. I know in full assurance that as I am obedient to his commands, he will protect me in life and in death." Is your spiritual vision opened to the point that when it rains you can see past the circumstances surrounding you and see the outcome as for your good and not for your harm? Do you assume you are the righteous? Are you sure which side you stand? Allow the circumstances to bring up whatever is not of God and deal with it accordingly.

> For while we were still helpless, at the right time Christ died for the ungodly. For one will hardly die for a righteous man; though perhaps for the good man someone would dare to die. But God demonstrates his own love toward us, in that while we were yet sinners, Christ died for us.
>
> (Romans 5:6–11 (NAS)

"These things I have spoken to you, so that in me you may have peace. In the world you have tribulation, but take courage; I have overcome the world" (John 16:33, NAS).

The first and most important thing Christ accomplished on the cross is demonstrating physically how pure love is spiritually. Romans chapter five states, "God demonstrates his own love…" This emphasizes *his* love, not the distorted love of the world. It reads, "… though perhaps for the good of man someone would dare to die."

One would hardly *dare* to die for someone good, much less a wicked people such as you and me. No one can honestly say that they have never been given or shown true love. What Christ did on the cross was for you personally, whether you believe it or not, accept it or not, know it or not.

A friend told me that the only difference between the ungodly and herself was that she had been delivered. I reminded her that, in fact, the whole world has been delivered. There is no one that *has not* been delivered. The difference then is not that she has been delivered but that she has *received* deliverance. The Word reads that he died, "for all." There are just few who choose his gift of righteousness. Most would rather wallow in suffering than actually take the initiative to rise above the rubble of life and seek holiness. Few want to be accountable for their own actions.

To state the obvious, one must first decide in his own heart what and in whom they *believe.* Once belief is established, you must decide if you are willing to actually put your *faith* in what you believe. For instance, I believe Satan is an actual being. However, I have zero faith in him or his ability to help, save, or deliver me from bondage. I believe in my husband, that he loves me and will protect me. But I do not put my faith in him; rather, my faith is in God, who works *through* my husband to love and protect me. My core faith is always in God, not the people or things through whom he moves.

Faith in the one whom you profess to believe is the victory! It is *belief* in Jesus Christ as the Son of the living God that allows you to be born of God. It is *faith,* on the other hand, that allows the victory to come in each and every circumstance. Many *believe* in God, yet few have actual *faith* established upon him. Faith ushers victory after victory. Faith is living a life that speaks, "No matter what I see with my natural eyes, I not only believe, but trust that God has already done (in the spirit realm) what he has promised. Through such trust, I call into the earthly realm through faith in him that which I do not yet see that is laid aside for me in the spirit realm."

As a reminder, it was accounted unto Abraham as righteousness (Romans 4:22) that he "called the things that were not as though they were" (Romans 4:17). This is referencing God, who called things into existence that were not. He called a universe and everything in it into existence when there was nothing. Abraham (putting total trust in this very God) himself was, through faith, able to do the same. This could happen only through the intimacy and oneness with God that I keep mentioning. Abraham had the power and authority to call forth the unseen (of God) into the seen (natural) because he was one with the all powerful Triune God. In other words, he decreed and proclaimed the things the Lord decreed and proclaimed that were still suspended in the spirit realm, instead of proclaiming the lies of the enemy his natural eyes could see. He basically called heaven down to earth as all believers are commanded and well-equipped to do.

Allow me to elaborate. God promised that Abraham would be the father of many nations and that he would bear as many descendants as the sands of the shores. Abraham believed this promise that had been spoken years before he bore Isaac. Through faith, though his body was as good as dead naturally, he knew that *supernaturally* God would allow his body to function as a young man and be able to impregnate the naturally dead womb of his aged wife. Note that the lie is the near deadness of their bodies; their naturally inability to bear a child. The truth, as it was suspended in the spirit realm, is that God always fulfills what he promises when we allow ourselves to see beyond the natural of this earth. This kind of faith can only come from intimacy; from the place of being so united with the heart of Almighty God that nothing and no one could convince you otherwise, not even the natural circumstances. To this day, Abraham, though long since gone, is still breeding new life daily! Every time a person chooses Christ over Satan through repentance, he bears new seed. Note the following text:

> *Without becoming weak in faith* he contemplated his own body, now as good as dead since he was about a hundred years old, and the deadness of Sarah's womb; yet, with respect to the promise of God, he did not waver in unbelief but grew strong in faith, giving glory to God and being fully assured that what God had promised, he was able also to perform.
>
> Romans 4:19–21 (NAS)

Noah is another prime example. For 120 years he built the ark and prophesied rain. They didn't even know what rain was. They were used to dew from the earth, not from the sky. Noah refused to believe the lie that there was no rain because it was merely natural. He chose through intimacy to believe that, since God said rain was coming, it was an indisputable fact! He endured great hardship through mockery for 120 years. Most of us can't make it a year walking in faith without seeing some form of evidence. But God came through with his promise just as he said.

This is how you stand in a prophetic Word from God whether given through a prophet or through the prophetic written Word of God. Knowing your promises, you can say to Satan, "I believe that what the Lord said about this situation is true. I will not believe the lie of the things I see with human vision. Satan, you are dead; therefore, you have no power in this situation. Whatever God has spoken concerning this, I will wait patiently for its manifestation. I will not grow weary in waiting, because he who promised is exactly he who will perform. I refuse to speak and claim the lies I see with my natural vision."

This is what Christ did on the cross. He put his Promise, the Holy Spirit, within each person who is a follower of the Son of God. With the Promise inserted within the spirit of man, that person has the God-anointed right to command the promises to come forth in their—your—life! You have the power, authority, and right to declare promises you do not yet see such as deliverance, freedom, righteousness, and abundance. He promised that there is no lack in the storehouse of the righteous. This means you can declare that your checkbook is full; that your mental, physical, emotional, and spiritual storehouse is full of whatever you need. Declare it until it manifests!

You have the authority to make such declarations in your life because Jesus' supernatural resurrection from the grave gave to the righteous seed of Abraham (you and me) the keys to the kingdom of heaven. They were taken away from Satan and handed to Jesus who then gave them to the body of Christ, hallelujah! This is supreme power and authority! Begin to claim the promises spoken through the Bible directly to those children of obedience just like Abraham and Noah.

When Jesus told Peter that upon him he would build his church, he was referring to those who believed and put their faith and trust in him like Peter; those who allow the Holy Spirit within to reveal truth that their physical eyes cannot see. Just before verses eighteen and nineteen, Peter had revelation that Jesus was in fact the Christ, the Son of God. Jesus blesses him because he received this information only through the Holy Spirit and not through man. Because of his obedience of listening to the Holy Spirit and putting his faith in the Holy Spirit who was speaking, this is the type person that the Lord is able to operate *through* before his return for the bride of Christ.

He and this type of believer in this age cannot be overpowered by the gates of hell because of such unshakeable faith in the Word of God! This is the power and authority that Satan does not want you to know you have. He cannot remove you from the palm of the hand of God, but he can lay his cold, dead body upon your outer man and make you *think* you are powerless. He can cast the shadow of his dead being upon you and make you *think* you are oppressed and without power when, in actuality, it is just a *shadow* of death. Fear leaves when knowledge of truth enters.

Since it is impossible for Christ to be held down by death, it is impossible for *you* to be held down by death. Satan is confirmed dead! Begin to live like it, set apart from all the fear and anxiety of the earthly realm. Jesus states that there is peace for those who are *in* him. There are tribulations in the world; however, Christ has overcome the world (Satan, that of the flesh). That means everyday circumstances that come your way. He also said that he came not to bring peace, but a sword.

This is not contradictory in any way. You must understand *all* that he says and not just *part*. He came to bring division between the righteous and the unrighteous. The sword, which is the Word of God, divides the wicked from the pure in heart. With tribulation, division comes because it reveals your heart within. Only *in* him can one have peace, because he is peace. Otherwise, the trials and woes of this world will carry you in the undertow and swallow you. There is no peace except Christ himself. How gracious is our God, who says clearly that he did not come to bring peace, but yet still offers himself to each of us that we may have peace anyway.

> For in him, all the fullness of Deity dwells in bodily form, and in him you have been made complete, and he is the head over all rule and authority; and in him you were also circumcised with a circumcision made without hands, in the removal of the body of the flesh by the circumcision of Christ; having been buried with him in baptism, in which you were also raised up with him through faith in the working of God, who raised him from the dead. When you were dead in your transgression and the uncircumcision of your flesh, he made you alive together with him having forgiven us all our transgressions, having canceled out the certificate of debt consisting of decrees against us, which was hostile to us; and he has taken it out of the way, having nailed it to the cross. When he had disarmed the rulers and authorities, he made a public display of them, having triumphed over them through him.
>
> Colossians 2:9–15 (NAS)

First Corinthians chapter fifteen proclaims, "The *sting* of death is sin, and the *power* of sin is the Law." Jesus Christ fulfilled the Law. If the Law is the power of sin, and the Law is fulfilled for all time, there is no power to sin to those *in* Christ. Victory over death is complete. Its power tool was removed through him taking sin upon himself forever. All sin is paid—past, present, and future. With the tool and the sting removed from mankind, there is victory!

He swallowed death for all time. Imagine yourself swallowing a piece of food. How much larger are you than the small piece of food you consume? Compared to Christ, who *swallowed* death, death is small and insignificant. Death itself has been consumed, digested, and sent out as waste. Satan is allowed to move about the earth only upon the power of Almighty God! He can't do anything to any of God's people without specific permission. That means everything that happens is under the authority of God. Even when someone says that they are "under attack of Satan," it is still God at the helm. We all need to stop giving Satan credit, even if he is the instrument utilized by God to bring about purification in the believer. Testing will always come to reveal what is in the heart of a man. With testing, one can choose to crumble and curse God, or break by casting themselves upon the Rock and letting him change you forever.

Ephesians chapter four mentions that he both descended and ascended. It was so that he would fill all things. If he does fill all, there is nothing void of him except the heart of any man who uses his free will to decline acceptance of Christ. Nothing else is without God. That means all circumstances are filled with God, whether you choose to see him or not.

I love that he "descended into the lower parts of the earth." I did not understand until recently that it was not a problem for Christ to enter into hell. Hell is made of fire and brimstone. It was made by God. God is the all-consuming fire. Why, then, couldn't true fire enter fire? What harm could fire cause fire?

I would like to direct your attention to the statement, "he who ascended far above all the heavens." He did not just go *to* heaven (singular), but *through* the heavens (plural)! He burst through all existence! Any possible extra space there may be is filled with God to the fullest extent. There is nothing he does not fill or does not touch or does not control. Nothing!

Hebrews 2:15 makes a good point. Those who *fear* death are the ones that are slaves all their lives *to* death. Fear, once again, is one of the greatest tactics of Satan and he uses it to his advantage always. Fear will drive a person straight to the thing they fear. This is bondage completely. Yet many see fear as healthy or good. Wrong! It is of the devil. You are to fear no one and nothing, O child of the Living

God, except reverently fearing the Holy One who is pure and all-encompassing. I cannot say this enough!

Take a look at the supreme power he has given you. It reads in Revelation chapter one, "I have the keys of death and of Hades." He has the authority of, not only death but also his (Satan's) residence (earth). God gave the keys to Jesus, who is the head over the body. Jesus gave the keys to the body to have authority over the evil one while living a Christ-filled life here on earth. In Matthew chapters sixteen and eighteen, the body of Christ is informed that what you bind and loose on earth will be bound and loosed in heaven. This means that you, the believer, need to utilize the blood of Christ as the weapon against the evil one.

So many get angry at God for not changing a situation when he has already said to you, "*You* take my blood and use it as your tool against the enemy. *You* bind demonic forces away from you and loose the word into situations. I have given *you* the tool, and the power and authority to use it, yet *you* act like I have abandoned you. Learn how to operate in the power I have provided and know that the enemy will have to bow to the name of my dear Son. He died and arose that *you* may live in freedom on earth in this age and in the one to come, yet *you* lay down like a dog to an abusive master. I've told *you* he is dead, and he is the puppet. I am the Master over all!"

"For Christ also died for sins once for all, the just for the unjust, so that he might bring us to God, having been put to death in the flesh, but made alive in the spirit" (1 Peter 3:18, NAS).

> Being found in appearance as a man, he humbled himself by becoming obedient to the point of death, even death on a cross. For this reason also, God highly exalted him, and bestowed on him the name which is above every name, so that at the name of Jesus every knee will bow, of those who are in heaven and on earth and under the earth, and that every tongue will confess that Jesus Christ is Lord, to the glory of God the Father...
>
> Philippians 2:8–10, 27, 30 (NAS)

No More
FEAR

Many years ago I took a job in an office. I was fresh out of high school. I was raised to always say, "I'm sorry." That is fine and well when warranted, but not one thousand times a day for nothing at all! One day a co-worker stopped me and said something to the effect of, "If you say that one more time, I will slap you!" I knew she meant it! I didn't even realize I said it so many times. I was insecure and unsure of myself at best; therefore, I was afraid that people would naturally not like me and that anything wrong would be my fault. I learned, finally, that *all* people have insecurities. With this revelation, I forced myself not to grovel if someone did not speak to me or call me. When the thought went through my head, *I wonder if they are mad at me.* I made a mental checklist to see if I had done or said anything offensive. If not, I told myself that if they had a problem with me, they would either get over it or confront me so I could apologize.

It took quite some time to get over myself, but I did. Condemnation is one of the number one killers of Christians, and it needs to stop. Condemnation stems from the root of fear, which is the absence of faith. I spoke with a minister a few days ago, and he had made a misstep. He commented that he was (figuratively speaking) "whipping himself with a cat of nine tails, but this time he would leave his shirt on!" I couldn't believe my ears. The body of Christ must get over the idea that self-abasement is of God. It is not. Individuals must learn that when they make a mistake, they need to confess to the Lord (and the person, if required), repent, and allow his forgiveness to take effect in their lives. To beat oneself is to hinder the anointing that needs to flow through you. It is a trick of the enemy.

When you think with the natural mind, you are clearly not holding fast to the head of Christ Jesus (Colossians 2). This means that you are not thinking with his mind, which is supernatural. We need all live by Philippians 2:5 (KJV), "Let this mind be in you, which was also in Christ Jesus."

When pride comes over people who are confident, bold, and strong, it is easily detectable. When this type of pride comes over someone who is insecure and timid, it is much more difficult to detect. It is pride that brings fear, depravation, and doom because the focus is still self. Its focus is, "God, what do you think of me," when the focus should be, "God, how awesome you are!" The focus becomes one's own inability instead of God's ability through you, the believer. When anyone focuses on their ability or lack thereof, you are doomed to fail because no one has any ability except that which he provides. This focus and humanistic thinking ushers condemnation every time.

On the other hand, for the ones I mentioned who are confident and admonished by people, condemnation comes when the ones who uplifted them suddenly stop. You can be successful one moment and not the next. Even if you do not feel as though you became prideful in your success when it is removed or when people simply stop acknowledging it, condemnation comes. "If you do well, will not your countenance be lifted up? And if you do not do well, sin is crouching at the door; and its desire is for you, but you must master it," God tells Cain in Genesis 4:7 (NAS). Since the crouching one is dead, he does not lose patience in his waiting.

Flee: run away; seek safety; run away from; leave abruptly; shun; vanish (Oxford Illustrated Am. Dictionary).

"Turn from these vain things to a living God" (Acts 14:15, NAS).

"To open their eyes ... turn from darkness to light and from the dominion of Satan to God" (Acts 26:18, 20, NAS).

"Flee immorality" (1 Corinthians 6:18, NAS).

The Lord our God clearly comes to the aid of his people. However, that does not mean that every time you are approached by evil of any kind, God is going to send an airplane, boat, car, limo, horse, or some other tangible means of departure. Part of his provision is a book packed full of wisdom. Both testaments of the Bible tell you to *flee* from sin and give examples of those who did. Flee means to run away from temptation. But leaving evil translates to so many as *weakness*. People don't want to *appear* weak. It's like the recovering alcoholic that lies to himself by saying, "I can handle it. I can be in a bar or around my friends who are drinking. It won't affect me." To *not* flee is not strength. It is foolishness and pride.

So many have commented, "I don't know why God doesn't take away the desire of the flesh. Why doesn't he love me or hear and answer my prayer to remove this or that?" The person with this mentality is one who does not know the Word of God. If they do, they do not comprehend the Word with their spirit, but with their fleshly man. I am not being critical or judgmental, but factual. When I thought this way, it was because I did not know the Word. I *thought* I did. I was a person raised in the church and saved at the age of six. I was thought to be a strong Christian. I went around talking about God. I spoke of *personal relationship* to others like I knew what I was talking about. What a joke that turned out to be—to me more than anyone!

The very concept of *dying to the flesh* is choosing *not* to do what your flesh wants. Dying to the flesh is not God removing the temptation, but giving each person the opportunity to tap into Holy Spirit within and allow him to reveal the evil one so that you can *choose* to resist. Jesus Christ fasted forty days in the wilderness where *the Holy Spirit* led him. Look in the Bible at Matthew 4:1–11 and Luke 4:1–13. I prefer to combine both so you get a full picture of what the Lord is revealing. I'm going to try to break it down so that you can see what

Christ did to enable himself to supernaturally overcome the enemy. An absence of fear is the key, or rather, faith in God.

Verse one: (both) Jesus did not go to the wilderness by his flesh, but by the leading of Holy Spirit. That means he *followed* instead of led. He was all God but also all human. He allowed his human man to be *led*—he submitted his flesh to the Spirit of God. No one *wants* to go into the wilderness, yet it is altogether necessary to *learn* obedience and submission.

Verse two: (Luke) Jesus was in the wilderness forty days being tempted by Satan. He ate no food during this period. It reads, "When they had finished, he became hungry." Jesus did not become hungry until *after* the forty days when they were *finished* with the temptations.

Verse three: (both) The tempter tempted Jesus to command the stones to be turned to bread.

Verse four: (both) Jesus quotes Scripture, "Man shall not live by bread alone." In Matthew, Jesus goes on to state, "...but on every word that proceeds out of the mouth of God."

Verses five through nine: (Matthew) Satan continues to tempt him and throws Scripture (truth) at Jesus.

Verses ten and eleven: (Matthew) Jesus, still having eaten no physical food for forty days and being tempted by every temptation known to man, *stood*. He said boldly and without hesitation, "Go, Satan!"

The tempter came forty days, finished his business of tempting, then came again against Jesus in his *weakest* condition. When he tempted him by telling him to "turn the rocks to bread," Jesus aptly replied, "Man shall not live by bread alone, but by the very Word of God." How could someone who had not eaten in over a calendar month still have the ability to withstand the enemy? Obviously it was not by the power of his flesh, but by the power of the Living God.

Most importantly, he allowed his flesh to be completely submitted to the Holy Sovereign. He gave no room for the fleshly
emotions to operate. He *willingly* went to a hard place. Since he
was led by the Spirit of God, fasting food was so that he could
meditate on every instruction the Father gave. There were no hindrances of false fillings.

The word says in many places to *stand*. Ephesians 6:13–14 says,
"Therefore, take up the full armor of God, so that you will be able
to resist in the evil day, and having done everything, to stand firm.
Stand firm therefore, having girded your loins with truth, and having put on the breastplate of righteousness."

Jesus Christ himself in the flesh stood firmly against the enemy
because he secured himself with truth. He did this through closing
in with God and allowing nothing to come between them. This is
the process that allows you to stand against the enemy in any and
every situation. It was the supernatural ability to stand that made
the enemy *flee from* him. It is the *standing* in the truth of the Word
that removes your hindrances, not God removing your hindrances.

Standing means that you have discernment from he who is
within to flee situations; to know when to stand against the enemy
and when to just run! Jesus Christ stood against Satan and ultimately defeated him so that you can have the *power* to *leave* the
presence of the enemy when necessary. Also notice that everyone
who quotes Scripture is not of God, but often of the enemy. Satan is
the ultimate liar because he can speak the Holy Word, verbatim but
with misappropriation. Because Jesus was in tune completely with
the Spirit of God, he knew the difference.

I have heard it said, "If you don't want something, ask God
to take it away." This is true. Even Jesus asked for the cross to be
removed if it be the will of the Father. However, it was not the will
of the Father, but rather it was for Jesus to go to the cross. Paul
asked for the *thorn in his side* to be removed, yet it was not the
Father's will so that he may stay humble. The *asking* of removal
of someone or something is not a problem. The problem is that,

generally speaking, he does not remove but expects you to learn self-discipline through whatever the issue is.

Anyone living in the mortal body is susceptible to pride. He didn't remove it from Satan. He removed the one who would not consign pride to God! If the Lord removed every issue from your life, you would never learn anything. He does not remove it so that you can learn to be disciplined enough to say no. The issue could be pride, smoking, cursing, slander, gossip, self-abasement, irritating people, and so on. The list is endless. Eventually, as you discipline your flesh to obedience, the *issue* will stop being so powerful over you.

Standing in the evil day not only means standing against blatant evil, but disguised evil. Blatant evil tends to be easier to see and to flee. It is the masked evil that draws one in because it *appears* good. Remember when the demon-possessed woman followed Paul, claiming *correctly* that Paul was a servant of the Lord? He finally listened to her long enough; Paul cast out the demon spirit that was mocking him and attempting to wear him down. What she was saying was true. The *intent* of the truth was an evil spirit sent to taunt and devour. Be on your spiritual guard because everything that utters truth is not necessarily of truth! You can only know the difference between good and evil by seeking and understanding the mind and knowledge of God.

Fear Not the Enemy

"But for the cowardly (fearful) and unbelieving and abominable and murderers and immoral persons and sorcerers and idolaters and all liars, their part will be in the lake that burns with fire and brimstone, which is the second death" (Revelation 21:8, NAS).

"Take care, brethren, that there not be in any one of you an evil, unbelieving heart that falls away from the living God" (Hebrews 3:12, NAS).

"For God has not given us a spirit of timidity (fear), bur of power and love and discipline" (2 Timothy 1:7, NAS).

The Lord is my light and my salvation; whom shall I fear? The Lord is the defense of my life; whom shall I dread? When evildoers came upon me to devour my flesh, my adversaries and my enemies, they stumbled and fell. Though a host encamp against me, my heart will not fear; though war arise against me, in spite of this I shall be confident.

Psalm 27:1–3 (NAS)

Starting with the text in Revelation, I found it interesting and odd that he spoke of the fearful and unbelieving in the same category with the abominable, murderers, immoral, sorcerers, idolaters, and liars. Not only did he put them together but first on the list! These are those who will have their part in the lake of fire and brimstone.

Now, concerning mankind, every human being that has, does, or ever will live fits somewhere in these groups. This is why all need to receive the covering of the blood of the spotless Lamb. Here's the thing: once the blood is received, you set your mind and person to stop being abominable, a murderer, immoral, a sorcerer, idolater, and a liar. But how many do you know who receive the blood stop being *fearful*?

No one changes overnight because we are all a work in progress. But please hear and understand what the word is saying. All these other sins are things that are obvious sins and need to be removed from the life of any Christian. Yet I know few who realize that *fear* and *unbelief* also must be exiled from the saint.

Most Christians I have experienced read this word *unbelief* to describe those who deny the Son of God. I know few, if any, that even address the *fear*. I believe it has a much deeper meaning than people want to accept. What about the one who professes Christ, walks a Christian life for many years, yet still lives a life of unbelief to the point that they allow fear to come into any situation. Unbelief and fear are simply doubt that God knows what he is doing, and that he will not and has not forsaken his own.

Tragedy strikes and immediately the average Christian is riddled with fear and anxiety. Doubt begins to set in that God has forgotten them, that God must hate them, or that he is punishing them. Some tragedies are in fact punishment, but some are the testing I referred to earlier. Funny, we read right over what happened to Joseph, David, Paul, and so many others as if they are just good stories. Yet when tragedy strikes in our own home, God must not be doing his job! Here again, this is why it is imperative to see with the supernatural eye of God instead of the natural sight that lies perpetually.

The Lord promises to fight the battles of those who are faithful, obedient, and humble. That does not mean that battles are nonexistent in our lives. We are not free from the hurdles; we just need his vision and his voice to know what is happening on the other side.

He commands his people repeatedly to be strong and courageous, be of good cheer, and "don't fear the wicked, for I am with you." This is true faith and trust. Faith and trust are developed over time spent with Father, not from running around quoting Scriptures you don't understand yourself.

The Lord will always go before the righteous and shame the enemy. There is no need to defend yourself. If you have been wronged, allow him his perfect timing to contend with those who contend with you. You don't need to fight with words and demand that the offender recognize that you are in Christ. That is the thinking of the foolish. Be slow to anger, slow to offense: anger does not bring about godly righteousness. A soft word turns away wrath; the mature in Christ are offended by nothing (Psalm 119:165).

Remember the relative that continually comes against me? I have been loathed by this person for many years, but recently the heat has been turned up a notch or two. In the last six months of this writing, I was verbally accosted by this person, and my husband spent hours speaking with this person, trying to get to the root of the hatred. It was to no avail. I was led to write a letter of love in humility to this person. I stated my point of view and continued to let them know that I still love them and am willing at any time to receive them unto myself. At the end, I blessed this person and their household according to the direction of Holy Spirit.

The letter has been perverted into something it is not. I have a copy and could easily send it to other family members caught in the middle. I was instructed by a well-respected couple to show the letter to others. Though I absolutely respect their opinion, my husband and I agreed that it would only further fuel the ever-growing fire of anger and hatred. The Lord spoke to me and sent me to the Scriptures to confirm that I am to duck out of the way and allow him to step in and deal with this matter supernaturally. I have complete faith and peace that his holy name, whose I carry, will be avenged, but he will do it.

Matthew 5:25 quotes that we are to "agree quickly with our adversary." This is because you cannot reason with the unreasonable. No matter how loudly you speak, what words of eloquence and truth you speak, or how long you talk, the enemy will not be convinced that you are right in the matter. So, isn't it better to not waste breath, energy, or precious time? For those who truly walk a life of integrity before our holy God with him as Master of your heart, you will not be put to shame (Philippians 1:20, NAS).

> For after all, it is only just for God to repay with affliction those who afflict you, and to give relief to you who are afflicted … dealing out retribution to those who do not know God and to those who do not obey the gospel of our Lord Jesus. These will pay the penalty of eternal destruction, away from the presence of the Lord and from the glory of his power.
>
> 2 Thessalonians 1:6–9 (NAS)

Second Timothy 2:23–24 says that God's bondservants are not to be quarrelsome and to refuse foolish and ignorant speculations, knowing that they produce quarrels. We are to be quiet when wronged, kind to all, and able to teach. What teaches better than actions of kindness and humility?

What You Love Determines Your Outcome

Love is the single greatest tool you have against the enemy. It is pure love that defeated the enemy. First Corinthians 13:13 reads that we are each to abide in love, hope, and faith. But the greatest of them all is love. The definition of abide is to *tolerate; endure; remain faithful to; dwell* (Oxford Illustrated American Dictionary). I think all these words are appropriate. You must dwell in and remain faithful to these three. However, love is not always easy. That is why Christ's love, the love that is extended to the unlovely, is the only love that will defeat your enemy in the day of adversity. Anyone can love the loveable. *Supernatural love* is what is required in this life to overcome all. It is supernatural love, and that alone, that allows you to *love* your enemy as you are commanded.

The Master of all is the author of love. Those who kill their fleshly pride and let love move in are those the Father knows by name. They are *his* sheep. Those who hate others, their shepherd is the puppet. The puppet is foolhardy because he is made of wood, hay, and stubble. The puppet is the one cut away from the Living Vine, so is therefore made of *cut off* wood. Wood without connection to the branch becomes hard, brittle, rotten, and easily burned. The Master is the Branch. The branch is life. Whatever is *cut away* from it sees death.

Do Not Rejoice in the Defeat of Enemy

"Say to them, 'As I live!' declares the Lord God, 'I take no pleasure in the death of the wicked, but rather that the wicked turn from his way and live. Turn back, turn back from your evil ways! Why then will you die, O house of Israel'" (Ezekiel 33:11, NAS).

"Do not rejoice when your enemy falls, and do not let your heart be glad when he stumbles; or the Lord will see it and be displeased, and turn his anger away from him" (Proverbs 24:17–18, NAS).

'For I know the plans that I have for you,' declares the Lord, 'plans for welfare and not for calamity to give you a future and a hope. Then you will call upon me and come and pray to me, and I will listen to you. you will seek me and find me when you search for me with all your heart. I will be found by you,' declares the Lord, 'and I will restore your fortunes and will gather you from all the nations and from all the places where I have driven you' declares the Lord, 'and I will bring you back to the place from where I sent you into exile.'"

Jeremiah 29:11–14 (NAS)

One of the truest tests of love is to love your enemy. There are many times when the Lord must destroy a wicked person (or group of people) out of your path. However, that judgment does not belong to you. Not only does it not belong to you, but when the Lord comes against your enemy, you must always maintain a compassionate heart. Compassion does not mean that person must be spared, but you are not to rejoice on any level in their destruction! The Lord himself never rejoices in this and desires that *all* repent of their wicked ways.

Jeremiah chapter twenty-nine is clear that he has a plan for every person. It is for good and never evil. He cries out to people to repent, to call upon him with a heart of humility, and he will turn from his wrath and bless.

■ ■ ■ ■ ■

Prayer

I pray, O Father, that I begin to see past the puppet and see only you. You, heavenly Father, are the One in who all is controlled. I confess that there is nothing that does not originate from you. Light my path as I pass through the shadow of darkness. I bless you that, because of confidence in you, I will fear no evil, for evil has been overcome. Remind me daily that, as I walk according to the Spirit, I have power and authority over this defeated foe. Help me to understand your Word, your will, and your way, that I not stumble in the darkness any longer. Make clear and straight paths for my feet. I thank you, Father, that your understanding and knowledge is bound to me. Show me how to bless those who curse me, for all things are set in motion to eventually bless me. I pray that those around me will not be able to tell the difference between you and I. I desire to merge completely with you that I may think, see, hear, and know as you do, Almighty God! Change the atmosphere around me. Strengthen me to such a degree that I will be stronger in you than those around me are in their sin. Teach me how to change the atmosphere around me from ungodly to godly. Hallelujah and Amen.

"No soldier in active service entangles himself in the affairs of everyday life" (2 Timothy 2:4, NAS).

Outside the City
WALLS

For the bodies of those animals whose blood is brought into the holy place by the high priest as an offering for sin, are burned outside the camp. Therefore, Jesus also, that he might sanctify the people through his own blood, suffered outside the gate. So, let us go out to him outside the camp, bearing his reproach. For here we do not have a lasting city, but we are seeking the city which is to come.

Hebrews 13:11–14 (NAS)

The kingdom of heaven is the city which is to come. Jesus Christ is coming back, and if we are not found outside our comfortable, earthly city and in the place of suffering and humility with Christ, we will miss the city! We get so comfy in our earthly place (that of our homes, jobs, ministry, church buildings, relationships with people, family, or whatever surrounding we are used to) we miss the big kingdom picture. The Scripture above reads that Jesus "suffered outside the gate" and we are to "go out to him outside the camp." I don't know how much more clearly it can be stated. We must realize that we must first be "burned outside the camp" in order to be brought in to the holy place. To be *brought* does not mean you take yourself. It means there is someone higher than you in authority that hand picks those whom are worthy *outside* that are ready to be *taken in*.

The only way to be *brought in* is to *go out* to him, to him who suffered for you. There is suffering that is a natural part of being like Christ, yet no one wants the suffering. We as a people only want the *benefits* of the result of suffering. We want to be revered and highly exalted as *good Christians* and *nice people*. We just don't want to put forth the effort required to accomplish the task. We are not to grow weary in well-doing (2 Thessalonians 3:13). This tells me that weariness comes naturally. It is an effect of work. However, there must be an understanding first that he is the One who is to do the actual work, not you. You in human form must exert *effort*, but the *work* is his.

When each individual desires to become pure as he is pure, we will ask the Lord to allow the Holy Spirit to burn us from the inside out; to burn up all that is unstable and flammable. Fire brings purity in precious metals, and destroys that which is worthless. When this happens, the temptation is not *removed by God*, but really it is *removed by you*. It is by your strong desire to please him above all else. At the risk of repetition, with such earnest desire, the temptation, after time, is no longer so tempting.

It is *suffering* to lust passionately a man/woman that is not your spouse, yet resist. It is *suffering* to resist eating a million calories when you are dieting because you know you must take care of the temple of the most high God. It is *suffering* when you are imprisoned, lonely, and resisting indulging a homosexual relationship. It is *suffering* when you resist stealing when you are broke. It is *suffering* when you are physically sick from spiritual warfare, and you can't just bind it away with instantaneous results. It is *suffering* to proclaim freely, "In life and in death I will serve my Lord. Whether I live or whether I die, I am unto Christ Jesus!"

There are too many scenarios to mention, but you get the point. There is suffering involved in this walk with Christ. He is not a vulture. He does not swoop in and eat up all the poisonous dead weight that has pulled you into sin! It is a *sacrifice* unto him to deny your flesh as Christ himself denied his.

He is a gentleman, and he is gracious. He says to us, the members of one body, that he will give the Comforter (the Holy Spirit; John 14:16, 26) completely. He is the *Comforter* because we need to be comforted. By relinquishing our will to take on his will, we still have fleshly desires, especially in the beginning stages. It does get much easier with time because his desires and heart become our own. But again, it takes suffering of many kinds to get to the place where you desire only what he desires. And even then, we constantly need to maintain cleanliness, just as you do your physical home. It is a *growing in relationship,* just as you would in the human sense. It is a give and take. God has *given* everything needed for life. You give up some of your selfishness; you *take* more of his holiness to replace it. You give even more of yourself; you take from his boundless supply for replenishing, and so on. All of his giving is complete. You must *give* of yourself in order to *receive* his provision.

This brings us back to *going outside the camp* to suffer with Jesus. Most want to attain a relationship with Jesus without any willingness to go outside of the comfortable place. What is even worse is that we seem to want to drag Christ into our mess instead of rising up to where he is. It's kind of like Lot and his wife. She wanted what God had to offer, but she wanted to stay where she was and still get it! She was unwilling to move outside the city full of *fun stuff* in order to be blessed by God. Their suffering was to give up Sodom. Lot saw the greater good of God and gave it up. He would rather have gone into a dry wilderness rather than remain where God was not allowed to rule. She, on the other hand, could not see past her fleshly desires, so she died trying to hold fast to this temporal earthly life. Can you look at your life and desire a dry, barren desert with God over the sinful pleasures and modern conveniences you currently have?

"And they took offense at him. But Jesus said to them, 'A prophet is not without honor except in his hometown and in his own household.'" This is written in Matthew 13:57, where he continues to say that he could do only a few miracles in Bethlehem. This makes it clear that, within our familiar places, we will be of little use. He will take you to places that are completely out of your comfort zone, away from those who *knew you when*. When he moves us out, we act like he is trying to destroy us! But in actuality he is trying to save those who will miss out on what he has ordained *you* to give to them. I definitely see this in my own life. There are only a tiny handful of people from family and friends who have embraced me, the anointing, the ministry, and teaching. I will go further to say that even my own race, and childhood denomination, have rejected me within the church. Nonetheless, I go with God, not man.

The *Lord* stands out when you allow him to take you places you would never thought or attempted to go otherwise.

"Behold, I have made him a witness to the peoples, a leader and commander for the people. Behold, you will call a nation you do not know, and a nation which knows you not will run to you. Because of the Lord your God, even the Holy One of Israel; for he has glorified you" (Isaiah 55:4–5, NAS).

If Isaiah had wanted to be comfortable, whole nations would have missed out on what was brought to them through him. God may call you to go unto people who look, walk, talk, and act completely different from yourself. It is intimidating at first! However, when you choose death of your fleshly desires, he takes over and the Comforter comforts you through his plan.

We are to be God-pleasers, not people pleasers. Humans, Christian or non, are natural born people pleasers. In fact, without Christ running the show in your life, I will venture to guess you too are a people pleaser on some level. Only God can give a heart that beats in tune with his. You have to earnestly ask for and receive it. Without the heartbeat of God in you, you will cower in the face of man and do as they, not as he. You can deny it all you want, but look inside yourself and ask him to show you what is true.

This city referred in Hebrews above is not exclusively speaking of the physical or geographical area which you reside. It is talking about life in general. This earthly existence is temporary. The city of God, the heavenly kingdom, is permanent, forever and ever. Jesus

Christ is everlasting, and all that is of him. There is nothing in this life that is even remotely close to the greatness of God, and all he has to offer. Sadly, we only see what is right in front of us. We only see what makes us happy in the moment, not what is eternal. The tangible things of this life are, in God's eye, already decayed. They are already passed away and gone. When we start to see things from a new vantage point, the heavenly perspective, we will broaden our horizons and realize that this world and its ways are bankrupt.

As Watchman Nee wrote in his book *Love Not the World*, "Why would you want to invest in a bank that is bankrupt?" This earth and all tangible within it is as much destroyed as Sodom and Gomorrah! The Lord has already prophesied about the end of the earth. There is no getting around it. Yet, we hold on and hold on and hold on even more to the things dear to our heart. When, O when, will his bride become holy to the degree that we will loosen the grip of the world from our midst?

We need to let go of the worthless things of earth and hold fast to the anchor of all creation! Where is your heart? What is precious to you? What have you been unwilling to relinquish that is hindering you from moving outside the camp with Christ? After purification has come in your inner man from the suffering from the burning, you will be brought back into the camp by the High Priest. This is to bring forth through you the blood sacrifice for the sins of the people. Your obedience of sacrifice is for yourself, those whom you love, as well as for those whom you have never met!

> And no one takes the honor to himself, but receives it when he is called by God, even as Aaron was. So also Christ did not glorify himself so as to become a high priest, but he who said to him, 'You are my Son, today I have begotten you.' And he says in another place, "You are *a priest forever,* in the order of Melchizedek.
>
> Hebrews 5:4–6 (NAS)

I find it interesting in this text that the Father said to Jesus, "You are my Son. Today I have become your Father." I never caught that until now. Anyone can, through the blood of Jesus, become an heir (a son) to the throne of heaven through repentance. However, there is a specific anointing that must come later from Father in order for God to acknowledge himself as your *Father*. Jesus was already his Son which means God was always his Father. But for some reason, though he acknowledges him *as already being* his Son, he then specifically calls out that moment of time to acknowledge himself as Jesus' Father.

Here is what I see. It reads first, "No one takes this honor upon himself; he must be called by God ..." Jesus did everything in human form that we must do so that he would not usurp the authority and proper process of God. He is showing us that, though we become born again believers at one point, we are not to *self-appoint* honor (as so many Christians do). There must be a specific season in each Christian's life where God the Father reaches down his scepter of holiness and dubs you anointed.

Notice that this happened in Jesus' life just as he was *preparing* to *suffer*. He had spent thirty or so years preparing and learning. So, it is a special time of anointing in your life where you are really ready in your spirit, heart, mind, and body to *suffer* whatever must be to glorify the Father. No new believer is prepared for suffering for Christ; therefore, it is not a requirement. They have to spend time getting to know him so that they will fall in love with him. It is the condition of *being in love with God* that allows one to stand in the times of suffering.

Just as a natural child may become king at a young age, he still must *prepare* to become ready to rule. We are called to rule the earth as kings, priests, and judges. Remember what I said earlier? There are different levels of suffering. There is the kind in the very beginning to gut you of your fleshly ways, and then the kind where you are willing, even unto death, to be obedient for the glory of God.

The immature, physical or spiritual, cannot accomplish this.

They would tuck tail and run at the first sight of trouble! But, in your mature state, you will *know* that all that must come is to bring forth the glorious, permanent kingdom of God. We must desire to become mature so that we can attain this level of obedience. It is imperative that the body of Christ become mature so that we can in fact rule and reign on this earth. There is another earth to come, so we need to recognize *now* on the temporary one how to do it. We *should* long to hear our Lord God say, "Today I am your Father!" Its translation is, "Today, you are ready to take on the real tasks!"

Read the passage that follows in verses seven and eight.

"In the days of his flesh, he offered up both prayers and supplications with loud crying and tears to the One able to save him from death, and he was heard because of his piety (devotion). Although he was a Son, he learned obedience from the things which he suffered" (Hebrews 5:7–8, NAS).

This came right after Father proclaimed that he was Jesus' Father. The New International Version and King James Version of the Bible both read, "Today I have begotten you (Thee)." In other words, this was the moment that Jesus was birthed by God to begin a new thing.

Every believer must be birthed anew to really begin a walk of *suffering* where you are totally ready and willing to suffer any situation that will usher the glory of God. It reads "in the days of his flesh…" This denotes that, though he had every temptation and obstacle of the flesh which you and I have today, he, despite the flesh, did all God called, commanded, and created him to do. Then it reads, "Although he was a Son, he learned obedience from the things he suffered."

His anointing where Father said, "Today I am your Father…" came at a time when God knew that Jesus would *please him though still in his flesh*. He would not just suffer for God, but he had a humble, willing, yielded, and teachable spirit. Suffering, whether for God or not, is all in vain if we do not *learn* from it and constantly change. Jesus, though perfect, learned obedience. We must suffer to come into a new place of obedience. Each and every level of suffering will be different because you change through each process; but it will always be a place of teaching how to be more like Christ—*obedient* no matter the temptation or circumstance.

In your early stage, the obedience will be the overcoming of fleshly temptations. These are the external ones of sex, drugs, anger, unforgiveness, bitterness, hurt—basically all the big things that keep you from holiness and maturity. In the later stages, your obedience will look different. Since you will be past the aforementioned, now you will be focused on *staying* clean and pure before Father. These are the more internal issues. When external sins are gone, then the real tests come to get out and keep out the internal things that no one else can see.

I see the graciousness of the love of God in all of this. One does not get *saved* and go immediately into elaborate suffering. Most are just trying to stop cursing, smoking, hating their neighbor, and losing their temper! These are the things most people can see naturally. Yes, we must suffer by giving up fleshly desires, but the real suffering comes much later. The kind where we say, "O, God, that this cup would pass from me. But whatever Thy will, I will. May it be done on earth as it is in heaven." No one can do this in the beginning! That is why there must be time to build a relationship *with* God *through* Jesus Christ. You must *learn* him and how he operates. Through this, you become clean.

After your relationship is more established, steady, and stable, and your heart is in tune with God's because they beat as one, then you should be ready to endure until the end. This is the *keeping* yourself clean, no matter what happens around you. This is when the Lord shows you the things that no one else ever sees; the things that creep back into your heart and mind. Many run the race, but few finish and fewer finish with excellence and honor!

I would like to add for clarification that neither Jesus nor his disciples suffered every moment of every day. Don't think that God calls you to constant, 24/7 suffering. That is an incorrect mindset due to imbalance. That type of thinking is as bad as those who choose to reject suffering in its proper timing. There are *seasons of suffering* throughout our walk of obedience to teach us deeper levels of intimacy. We need to see the whole picture.

I recently became informed that only 20 percent of the Israelites left Egypt with Moses; the other 80 percent chose not to move at all. They were afraid to come out from among the Egyptians and be separated unto God, so they chose eternal slavery! Just as the Lord never intended the 20 percent to suffer as long as they did in the wilderness; nor does he you.

I pray and hope that this book is a help to you so that you may be transformed into the likeness of Christ. If it has, the world in search of God will surely find him through you!

■ ■ ■ ■ ■

Prayer:

Our Father, who is in heaven, hallowed be your name. Your kingdom come, your will be done, on earth as it is in heaven. Give me this day my daily bread. And forgive me my debts, as I also have forgiven my debtors). And do not lead me into temptation, but deliver and give me the strength to run from evil. For yours is the kingdom and the power and the glory forever. Amen (Matthew 6:9–13). Allow me the privilege of having unity of heart with you. I do desire to be like you in everything I think, say, and do. May I go nowhere you are not; and may I leave every place where you are not in control. Help me supernaturally to remove myself from my comfort zone. Take me to the places of discomfort so you will be able to teach me to grow beyond what I can see with my natural eyes. I thank you Lord that I see as you see, hear as you hear, and think as you think. Change my perspective from the earthly into the heavenly. I love and adore you, O God and King! May I never leave you nor forsake you till the end of eternity!

Bibliography:

John and Paula Sanford–*Bitter Root Judgment*

Watchman Nee–*Love Not the World* and *The Latent Power of the Soul*

Contact Information:

Alexys V. Wolf

The Fiery Sword Ministries

Post Office Box 1922

Lexgton, SC 29071

thefierysword@windstream.net

thefierysword.com